More Praise for

TRUSTED PARTNERS

■

"Trust is the fundamental ground underlying financial markets, with their billions of dollars in daily trading. This book provides a detailed blueprint for the complexity of cultivating, maintaining, and guaranteeing trust between organizations."

—SCOTT GORDON, Chairman, Chicago Mercantile Exchange

"For many decades, Corning has worked with trusted partners to achieve its commercial goals. This book is a clear guide for how to build lasting, and mutually beneficial, business relationships based on trust. It is well worth the read."

—JOHN W. LOOSE, President and COO, Corning Communications, and director, Corning Inc.

"As businesses and nonprofits look ahead, cooperation among us will be essential for achieving our common objectives. *Trusted Partners* serves as an excellent guide for forging these alliances."

—JOHN SAWHILL, President and CEO, The Nature Conservancy

"Jordan Lewis has done it again! His new book is for any business interested in building successful alliances with customers, suppliers, competitors, or any other organization."

—PERTTI JOHANSSON, Senior Vice President, Global Account Management, Motorola, Inc.

"The accelerated pace and importance of alliances on the internet have made the principles of trust more essential than ever to our global economic success. *Trusted Partners* provides timely insights and enlightened practices for forging stronger, more effective business relationships."

—KEITH J. KRACH, President and CEO, Ariba, Inc.

"This book is extremely timely as I attempt to lead our organization toward a global structure. It is refreshing to find subjects such as trust and partnership brought to life with real world examples and clear action steps to make it happen."

—MATTHEW RILEY, Director, Global Accounts, Campbell Soup Company

"In today's competitive business climate, our people need an advantage. Jordan Lewis proves that the advantage is one based on trust."

—ANN NOBLES, Vice President, Managed Care and Health Care Accounts, Eli Lilly and Company

"In this excellent new book, Jordan Lewis provides a practical 'how to' guide for building trusting relationships with customers.

—NOEL CAPON, Professor of Business and Director, Key Account Management Program, Columbia Business School

"Here is thoughtful and practical advice to companies considering mergers, acquisitions, partnerships, joint ventures, or alliances with others. Jordan Lewis's insight into building trust is an effective guide for all of us."

—GAIL L. WARDEN, President and CEO, Henry Ford Health System

"A practical guide to forging successful business partnerships founded on trust."

—HENRI A. TEMEER, Chairman and CEO, Genzyme Corporation

"The core of this book is Jordan Lewis's acute understanding of how trust applies to business relationships. For anyone who is in a partnership, entering one, or just thinking about it, this is a clear, comprehensive, and indispensable handbook."

> —JAMES D. ERICSON, President and CEO, Northwestern
> Mutual Life Insurance Company

"Rich in examples, this book will take healthcare managers by the hand and lead them thoughtfully, step-by-step, through the process of building successful alliances."

> —JEFF GOLDSMITH, President, Health Futures, Inc.

"Goes directly to one of the key aspects of successful alliance management: building trust with your partner, building trust about your partner within your own business, and knowing when you have reached the limits of trust."

> —WILL MITCHELL, Professor of Corporate Strategy & International Business, Chair, Corporate Strategy Department, University of Michigan Business School

"Fills a crucial gap in management practice: How to create and manage trust within and between organizations."

> —JITENDRA V. SINGH, Saul P. Steinberg Professor & Vice Dean, International Academic Affairs, The Wharton School, University of Pennsylvania

"A guidebook for developing close, meaningful, and successful relationships between organizations. By building on research by first-rate scholars, the validity of its thesis is enhanced."

> —LOUIS W. STERN, John D. Gray Distinguished Professor of Marketing, Kellogg Graduate School of Management, Northwestern University

"Jordan Lewis presents an excellent process for building and maintaining trust—a concept so simple yet so difficult to achieve. We'd have traveled a smoother road if his guidance had been available when we launched our joint venture."

> —ROGER BRIDGES, President, Deere-Hitachi Construction
> Machinery Corporation

"This book is about how to get results. It deals clearly and specifically with the essential leadership skill of creating high performance alliances, as well as achieving the full potential of your own organization."

> —MICHAEL DEDOMENICO, President, Praxair Distribution, Inc.

"Though trust is the basis of business partnerships, few of us know how to build it. As a global company with deep European roots, we find the principles of *Trusted Partners* to be widely useful."

> —GIULIO MAZZALUPI, President and CEO, Atlas Copco Group

"As one of the largest groups of companies in Latin America, we find *Trusted Partners* to be a useful guide for all levels of management in creating, repairing, or strengthening trust, the basis for any enterprise."

> —GUSTAVO A. CISNEROS, Chairman and CEO, Cisneros
> Group of Companies

"*Trusted Partners* is on my mind every day regarding team members at Electrolux as well as our business partners."

> —MICHAEL TRESCHOW, President and CEO, AB Electrolux

Other Books by Jordan D. Lewis

The Connected Corporation
Partnerships for Profit

TRUSTED PARTNERS

*How Companies Build
Mutual Trust and Win Together*

■

Jordan D. Lewis

THE FREE PRESS

ƒP

THE FREE PRESS
A Division of Simon & Schuster Inc.
1230 Avenue of the Americas
New York, NY 10020

Designed by MM Design 2000, Inc.

Manufactured in the United States of America

10   9   8   7   6   5   4   3   2   1

Library of Congress Cataloging-in-Publication Data Is Available

ISBN 0–684–83651–3

FOR KATIE AND MATT

CONTENTS

■

PREFACE

■

Trust is at the heart of today's knowledge economy. With trust as a foundation, companies—or groups within a company—can share their know-how to achieve results that exceed the sum of the parts. Unlike formal contracts or rigid hierarchies, trust frees partners to respond together to the unexpected, which is essential for mutual creativity. Trust also fosters enthusiasm, ensuring the best performance from everyone.

Rather than being a matter of blind faith, trust must be constructed, one step at a time. Further, building trust between organizations is all-encompassing. It involves their people, politics, priorities, cultures, and structures.

My own interest in trust goes back more than thirty years to when I was working as a scientist in Sweden. Confined by limited resources, my boss asked me to figure out how our group could leverage cooperation with similar groups in other countries to make the most of our funds. He reasoned that, by sharing with others, we could direct our budget to projects we considered most important. The ensuing experience got me hooked on cooperation and changed the course of my career.

Since then, first as an executive and then as a consultant, I've had the good fortune to manage and advise numerous alliances around the world. Simultaneously, as a researcher, teacher, and author, I have advanced my understanding of what cooperation entails. One key conclusion is that trust is at the core.

The practical demands on me as a manager, and on the countless senior and middle managers I have counseled over the years, have sharpened my thinking. Both have driven me to learn more about the essential ingredients of trust and how to employ them effectively. Scholarly research at leading universities has enriched my views.

By now, I have applied the fruits of this learning at hundreds of organizations, ranging from companies with under $20 million in sales, to most firms on the list of Dow Jones Industrials, and to leading companies in Asia, Canada, Europe, Latin America, and the Middle East. It has been encouraging to learn that the principles of mutual trust seem to work everywhere. Despite this solid knowledge base, it would be naive to assert that I have found the one best way to develop trust. But I do claim that *Trusted Partners* offers a better road map for building trust between organizations than existed before.

Though ample experience, including cases in this book, indicates that trust produces better results than strong-arming another organization, some people regard trust as a concept best left to sociologists. The real game for them is power. Encounters with others are chances to grab a one-sided benefit. Their model of cooperation is the prisoner's dilemma, a notion from game theory, wherein acting in one's own self-interest is rewarded.

Recall that this story describes two accomplices who were arrested following a crime. The crux of the dilemma is that, if neither one squealed on the other, they would be convicted on a minor charge and face a brief jail sentence. On the other hand, if one incriminated the other, the informer would go free.

In the prisoner's dilemma, the benefits of pursuing one's self-interest outweigh what can be gained by acting together. However, in situations where more can be earned by cooperating than by following separate agendas, cooperation is the preferred course. *Trusted Partners* explains how to arrange that.[1]

That trust beats power is taught by history and current events alike, in a wide variety of settings. Consider Napoleon. After 1807, he conquered Europe but could not sustain peace. The main reason was that Napoleon confused power with diplomacy. Each successful battle led to a one-sided treaty that bred resentment, which led, just as surely, to another war. Each time, his enemies were better prepared until, at last, they defeated the once invincible master of the Continent.[2]

In *The Connected Corporation,* I described how companies that wield purchasing power over their suppliers, like modern Napoleons, get hostility in return. They also receive much less value from those suppliers—in terms of inferior costs, quality, technology, cycle time, and more—than do firms that develop trust with them.[3] *Trusted Partners* covers how to build trust in any business setting.

The material in this book is based on my experience and research, including personal interviews and published press accounts. Unless otherwise indicated, quoted material is drawn from my own interviews. In some instances, I have changed names and other identifying characteristics of companies and individuals.

I am indebted to many friends and colleagues, whose wisdom has enriched this book. They include:

Ralph Agee, Paul Bechard, Bruce Bendoff, Don Black, Nicholas Brealey, Doug Carnahan, Al Chase, Vince Coletta, Mike Creighton, Cesar de Larrazabal, Paul Evertse, Carol Franko, Pat Gabella, Ray Giese, Susan Ginsburg, Mike Golden, Ricky Gomez, John Hagaman, Don Hammond, Peter Hancock, John Henrickson, Vaughn Hovey, Gene Howie, Bill Johnsmeyer, Jubran Kanaan, Jim Kelly, Rick Kennedy, Takashi Kitamura, Bob Knapp, Steve Kohlert, Hank Kucheman, Gordon Lankton, Paul LaViolette, Al Lorenz, Luke March, Tom Mark, Larry Miller, Judy Moore, Tom Muccio, Dick Murphy, Lisa Napolitano, Paul O'Day, Frank Palm, Paul Peercy, Lou Peluso, Peter Peschak, Barry Potter, John Reeve, Ed Rivera, Rita Rouse, Leona Schecter, Ted Schmidt, Ron Sforza, Roger Shiffman, John Stedman, John Tara, Jerry Toomer, Jill Totenberg, Al Verecchia, Chuck Walker, Ron Walker, Bob Wallace, Barry Wiegler, and Matthew Willsher.

My thanks also to several individuals who shared their experiences and asked that their names not be used. I'm also indebted to five anonymous reviewers of an early version of the manuscript. Their comments substantially influenced how I developed the final product.

Much credit is due to Lee Smith, a member of *Fortune* magazine's board of editors for twenty years, and now on his own. Lee's careful and caring attention helped bring the manuscript I handed him close to its final form.

My executive assistant, Mimi Hemphill, was with me every step of the way. Always with warmth in her words and seemingly tireless, Mimi arranged for interviews, dug up articles and reports, and kept everything coordinated so I could focus on the writing part.

This book describes how to build trust between organizations, and how interpersonal relationships are a critical element of that. Much of *Trusted Partners* reflects my experience with countless alliances. Much also comes from my own personal alliance with Lynn Lopata Lewis, my wife and best friend. More than anyone else, she has shown me how people can be effective together. But her influence on this book has been far wider. As the manuscript developed, Lynn's probing questions and detailed comments helped me convert my often fuzzy thoughts into what I hope you will find to be clear and logical prose. Without her tolerance of my seemingly endless writing, and her making room for this work in her own busy schedule, there would be no book. After thirty six years with her, I have learned what trust is all about.

TRUST
LEADS TO HIGH
PERFORMANCE

.

CHAPTER 1

BUILD TRUST

■

Two giant rivals in the shipping business—Maersk and SeaLand—launched a great undertaking, one of worldwide creative collaboration. Maersk, a division of Denmark's A.P. Moeller, and SeaLand, a division of the United States' CSX Corporation, concluded that the best way for them to compete in an increasingly difficult global market was to form an alliance.

Although they kept their sales and marketing separate, the firms in 1996 began rationalizing their port facilities and combined their two hundred container ships in networks that span the globe. So smoothly do these links work that a customer who hires Maersk, say, to transport machinery from Seattle to Shanghai, or from Rotterdam to Rio, might never know that for part of the journey the cargo passes through SeaLand terminals, is handled by SeaLand longshoremen, and travels in SeaLand ships.

What the two container companies know is that the alliance has enabled them to extend their geographic reach, drive down their costs, and step up their shipping frequency. And as the firms continue working together, their results keep getting better.[1]

Maersk and SeaLand have forged a successful alliance. That is what *Trusted Partners* is about—how businesses can build successful alliances. The same conditions and procedures are essential whether an alliance is between rivals, as in the case of Maersk and SeaLand, between customer and supplier, or for any combination of firms. They apply as well to alliances between divisions within a company, and to mergers and acquisitions.

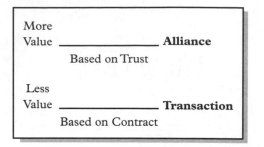

Let's start with an important distinction. There is a night-and-day difference between transactions and alliances. In transactions, contracts spell out everything. Negotiations may be divisive because neither firm cares about the other's well-being. With transactions, information sharing is limited to what is needed to close the deal, because divulging more could yield an advantage to the other side. Transactions also encourage finger pointing rather than creative problem solving.

In an alliance, you can't define every detail. Success depends on creatively joining the ideas and energies of two firms, sometimes more. Though negotiations may be trying, alliances are framed by an understanding that it is in neither firm's interest to hurt the other. Most important of all, alliances depend on trust. No contract can anticipate what two groups must do to be creative together.[2]

I use the term *alliance* to mean cooperation between groups that produces better results than can be gained from a transaction. Because competitive markets keep improving what you can get from transactions, an alliance must stay ahead of the market by making continuing advances.

This definition identifies an alliance by its outcome and implies needed behavior. For superior results you can't simply *call* each other partners. You must actually *function* as partners. Alliances go beyond doing things between firms that become transactions afterward—like licensing, co-locating resources, starting to outsource, or trading a lower price for a longer term. Such tactics may be involved in alliances; alone they produce one-time gains. In an alliance, continued joint creativity leads to regular improvement, outperforming what any single change can do.

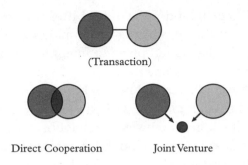

(Transaction)

Direct Cooperation   Joint Venture

Alliances are structured various ways, depending on their purpose. Direct cooperation is the most common form. Joint ventures, where partners create a separate unit they own and control together, are also widely used. Minority investments, a third form, are less common. Regardless, the principles of trust are the same.

Despite the growing popularity of alliances, there are many failures.[3] Consider the arrangement between Northwest Airlines and KLM Royal Dutch Airlines to combine their networks linking Holland and the United States, to build more volume for each carrier. Though the airlines' arrangement is now successful, behind the scenes when it began was what *Fortune* magazine dubbed "an eye-gouging, rabbit-punching slugfest, with accusations flying like dinner plates."

The seeds of this hostility were planted at the start. Soon after taking their own financial stakes in Northwest, co-chairmen Al Checchi and Gary Wilson persuaded KLM to help finance a leveraged buy-out at six times the per share price Checchi and Wilson had paid. Although such premiums are common in U.S. financial circles, they were unusual to KLM's managers, who viewed the arrangement as unfair.

This attitude, plus a growing concern that their partners seemed more like deal makers than airline operators, led the Dutch to try ousting Checchi and Wilson from Northwest and increase their own control. Northwest responded by attempting to limit the stake any shareholder could hold. The upshot: KLM sued

Northwest, Checchi, and Wilson. So bitter was the clash that it jeopardized an alliance producing $200 million a year in operating profits. The feud also halted plans to integrate their cargo operations and reservation systems.

For KLM, the alliance had been a key step in forming a global airline. To realize that goal, the Dutch took several steps. Besides buying more stock in Northwest, they lobbied the U.S. government to relax foreign ownership rules, rejected other European carriers that wanted KLM to drop Northwest in favor of a different linkup, and sought changes in Northwest to support more integration of the two carriers.

For Northwest, though Checchi and Wilson never publicized their longer-term objectives, their leveraged ownership and prior record of skillful financial engineering led KLM to assume they would sell out when their contracts permitted or, as was expected in the industry, when another wave of acquisitions swept through. Further integration with KLM could undermine the financial flexibility needed to sell their stakes.

Seen in this light, both sides were consistent with their separate objectives. Apparently, they never discussed what they knew at the time—the immediate logic of an alliance was overshadowed by basic differences in those objectives. Only after top executives left both companies did repair become possible.[4]

What went wrong with the KLM–Northwest alliance was a lack of trust at the start. Aside from technical or marketing problems, that's what causes alliances to fail. Trust makes successful alliances work. This book shows how to initiate, sustain, and increase trust throughout the life of an alliance.

WHAT IS TRUST BETWEEN ORGANIZATIONS?

Mutual trust is a shared belief that you can depend on each other to achieve a common purpose. In an alliance, where your purpose is to get results that exceed what a transaction can do, mutual trust also means you can depend on each other to adapt as necessary. That involves more than keeping promises, because it entails changes that can't be planned in advance.[5]

An alliance between Canon and Hewlett-Packard in the laser printer business illustrates. In the late 1970s HP was one of a few firms having both computer expertise and a successful peripherals business. At the same time, Canon had developed laser technology for its copier products; laser printing did not yet exist. Frustrated in its own efforts to develop a reliable low-cost printer, HP accepted an invitation from Canon to combine HP's computer skills with Canon's laser know-how.

After some iteration, the firms introduced their first desktop model in 1984. Early sales, forecast to be a few hundred units per month, actually were 3,000 units and soon rose to more than 40,000 per month. Volume grew so fast that the alliance quickly became an important part of each company's business.

Since then, the partners have become major rivals in the bubble jet and ink jet printer business, while their laser printer alliance has blossomed. Today, their collaboration involves many products and more than a thousand people in both firms. Still, they have no contract. Their alliance is too dynamic and involved for that. Rather, it is based entirely on trust.

Trust does not imply easy harmony. Obviously, business is too complex to expect ready agreement on all issues. However, in a trusting relationship conflicts motivate you to probe for deeper understandings and search for constructive solutions. Trust creates good will, which sustains the relationship when one firm does something the other dislikes. Having trust gives you confidence in a relationship and makes it easier to build even more.

"We would not have our results without trust," says Dick Murphy, SeaLand's senior vice president for corporate marketing and chief commercial officer, speaking about his firm's alliance with Maersk. "It is the cornerstone of our relationship."

THE EIGHT CONDITIONS FOR TRUST

As the KLM–Northwest affair suggests, trust exists only under specific circumstances—such as having shared objectives. A logical way to discover these is to start with the definition of trust in an alliance: Each firm can depend on the other to get results that

THE CONDITIONS FOR TRUST

Priority Mutual Need
Personal Relationships
Joint Leaders
Shared Objectives
Safeguards
Commitment
Adaptable Organizations
Continuity

exceed what a transaction could do. That notion leads to a set of eight conditions for trust.

1. Mutual Need Creates the Opportunity

As alliances go, they don't get much better than Hewlett-Packard's and Canon's. For two decades, the firms have enjoyed a thriving relationship. HP has built a world market-leading laser printer business with annual revenues exceeding $2 billion, while Canon has gained handsome earnings supplying components to HP. "While we would be in the same business without Canon," says Doug Carnahan, an HP senior vice president, "we would be behind the pack in the marketplace. With them, we lead the pack."

The laser printer partners illustrate a central feature of alliances: It's not enough for two companies to ally just because they need each other. In an alliance, companies must share valuable resources and adjust their organizations to support joint activities. The management attention needed to do that is not likely to be available unless each firm concludes that the task is important, and that joining forces is the best way to go. In the case of Canon and HP, both firms regard each other as the right choice for meeting important objectives, a condition I'll refer to as a priority mutual need.

Take, for example Nypro, a leading injection molder of plastics and one of the fastest-growing and most profitable. Nypro has ten joint ventures in its core business worldwide, all outstanding performers, plus five in related businesses. Serious conflict with partners is rare. "In forming a JV, we always made sure it is so important to both of us that we would want to work through difficult issues to make it successful," says Gordon Lankton, president.[6]

A priority mutual need is a source of respect, a building block of trust: Each side is bringing unique and significant value to the other and deserves to be heard. If mutual need is not a priority, forget about trust.[7]

One of the first questions I ask companies that seek help with alliances is why they chose each other. The most frequent answers I've received in many years of experience are that it seemed like a good idea or that some executives decided to do a deal. More often than not, that vague starting point has led to failure.

An early step in weighing a possible alliance is to determine whether it will serve an important objective in your firm. Next, determine the best way to achieve that objective. Compare the merits of internal development, alliances, and acquisitions. Before discussions get serious, your firm and a prospective partner should confirm to each other that you are the best candidate for meeting the other's needs.

To get started in the right direction, the units that an alliance will serve must lead partner selection and conclude that the arrangement is their favored choice. Taking that role wins their acceptance and, because they are closest to the action, helps find the best partner. Further, since the alliance will affect their performance, these units must be accountable for its results. Nothing discourages teamwork more than imposing an unwanted partner on people who have a better alternative.

2. Interpersonal Relationships Make the Connection

Alliances live through people—this is how all the parts come together. Deep trust—the essential ingredient for creating the most value and solving the toughest problems—grows as interpersonal relationships strengthen.

Listen to a mid-level manager at HP describe his ties with his counterpart at Canon: "I liked him. We developed a personal relationship. We could always solve the big issues constructively. We became candid with each other because at the heart of many issues were people's attitudes and personalities."

To appreciate the role relationships have in alliances, reflect on your own career. Have you ever been so comfortable with a colleague that you could candidly discuss the politics and personalities in your organization and how things really worked? If you answered yes (which most people do), did these understandings help you do your job more effectively? Did mutual comfort make it easier to tackle tough issues? Again, your reply probably was yes.

Each of us knows that good relationships enhance our performance and that they aren't always possible. But think about this: Inside an organization, if people can't resolve conflicts between them, a higher authority or political process may do so. Even if issues don't get resolved, the firm keeps moving along, carried by its own momentum. These solutions don't exist between separate companies.

3. Joint Leaders Deliver Both Firms

Our experience within companies offers useful lessons for cooperation between them. When top executives work closely together, staffers below know it is safe to cross internal boundaries. By contrast, polarization at the top virtually assures conflicts below, because people respect the turf of those above them. Similarly, an alliance will fail without joint leadership.

For HP and Canon, Doug Carnahan and Takashi Kitamura, now chief executive of Canon's Peripheral Products Operations, led the alliance during its early years of rapid growth. "The two of them could always cut through problems together," says someone who worked with Carnahan at the time. "They got along incredibly well. They really liked each other—it was clear to everyone. In joint meetings they attended there was always a positive feeling that things would work out. The atmosphere was always one of creative problem solving to do what was best for our firms' mutual interest."

Reinforcing this sentiment, corporate presidents Lew Platt and Fujio Mitarai have had a high-quality relationship of mutual trust and confidence that continued even after Platt retired. "This symbol of collaboration at the highest level is important to all of us," says Carnahan.[8]

4. Shared Objectives Guide Performance

Just as mutual need creates an opportunity to cooperate, having a set of mutually agreed-upon objectives guides your performance together. If your objectives are not aligned, expect discord.

Recall what happened to KLM and Northwest Airlines, whose alliance is one of many that have been weakened by conflicting objectives. More than half the underperforming alliances I have seen suffered from hazy or inconsistent objectives.

On the surface, having common objectives seems obvious. But they can be surprisingly hard to develop and the task often gets too little attention when alliances are built. To appreciate this, reflect on what it takes to find common objectives for separate groups within your organization.

Inside companies, people talk about managing by objectives but intuitively know the objectives are not the last word. Think of the last time vague or conflicting objectives caused confusion at your firm. How was the situation resolved? Chances are, someone with authority stepped in to set matters straight. Or behind-the-scenes politics ironed things out.

Again, those remedies aren't available with alliances. Here, your shared objectives must dominate. That's not just because there are no alternatives, but because when people know they will follow the same rules they are likelier to trust one another.

The way to get effective mutual objectives is to develop them from each firm's objectives. Then, if your mutual objectives are met your separate ones will be as well. Your objectives must be clear enough to serve as a practical decision guide at all levels in both companies.

For example, in the Canon/Hewlett-Packard alliance, Canon's goal is to sell more engines to HP, and to remain a global leader in its technology and profit from that; HP wants to build a strong position in the laser printer market. Starting with these separate objectives, the firms derived their shared high-level objective: to grow HP volume.

From that broad objective, the partners developed guidelines for staying on the cutting edge of user satisfaction. They also have rules about wanting to give users more for less and keeping their relationship on a win-win basis. With these rules as a foundation, the partners developed specific objectives and needed actions at the product level—including market introduction time lines, performances, and price points. Their long-term plan goes out at least three years for products, farther for strategic and technology matters.

5. Safeguards Encourage Sharing

Cooperation entails sharing information and making investments with a partner. How far you go depends on your conviction that sensitive data will be protected. Another concern is what will happen to that data, to jointly held assets, and to resources and know-how you developed together, once an alliance ends.

Although nondisclosure agreements are necessary, they don't go far enough. To develop confidence that valued possessions will be handled well, before an alliance begins you must understand each other's firewall policies and practices, agree on who will own joint inventions, and define what will belong to whom after termination.

6. Commitment Creates Enthusiasm

An alliance excels when each of your firms invests its best effort— assigns its finest people, backs them with needed policies and resources, and adjusts its organization. Mutual need creates the potential for this, but does not ensure it. Such dedication can be expected only if each of you believes you are being treated well by the other. That calls for allocating risks and benefits fairly, rather than using win-lose bargaining to get what you want.

"Before we agree to cooperate, we want to be sure we share a strong feeling that each of us wants to help the other succeed," observes Nypro's president Gordon Lankton.

Alliances can run into unexpected events that shift the costs or benefits away from what is fair. Then, to keep trust you have to reset the balance. Doing so is not altruism by whichever partner yields some of its gains. It is enlightened self-interest.

7. Adaptable Organizations Support Alignment

One aspect of Chrysler that made the firm attractive to Daimler-Benz was the remarkable cost savings the American firm had achieved with its suppliers. Among U.S. auto makers, Chrysler was the only one to build true alliances across its supply base. The results showed. Working together, Chrysler and its suppliers made the firm the lowest-cost-per-vehicle auto maker in the United States, possibly in the world. Central to Chrysler's success has been smooth teamwork among its design, engineering, and other functions. Such collaboration is rare at other auto makers, where turf battles and conflicting signals from the various disciplines inhibit suppliers' contributions.[9]

Here is a key to alliances: Organizations that collaborate well on the inside have the skills needed for doing so on the outside. The opposite is equally true. Similarly, companies that really manage by objectives on the inside make better partners because they can more easily link their internal objectives to their alliance objectives.[10]

Some of the most common pitfalls in alliances—poor teamwork, cumbersome processes, and fuzzy objectives—come from within partner firms. It would be a mistake to believe that an organization will change its normal behavior to a more enlightened one for an alliance. Because company cultures evolve slowly, your expectations for an alliance must recognize what each organization can do. IBM and Sears, Roebuck missed this point when they formed Prodigy, the on-line service business.

Alone in a new and promising market, Prodigy was a trailblazer when it began in 1990. Five years later, the service had become a distant third and was fast losing market share. Even though its corporate parents had invested more than $1 billion, Prodigy had yet to see a sustained profit. Both partners bailed out in 1996.[11]

The venture's troubles were predictable. Before Prodigy was created, IBM and Sears had stumbled badly in consumer markets and failed to learn from their mistakes. Lacking useful parent guidance in marketing, Prodigy lost its way. Further, the parents imposed their lumbering styles on the child. To illustrate: After fifteen months of planning, Prodigy introduced prices designed to undercut rival America Online. The speedy AOL matched the cut in six hours.

8. Continuity Sustains Understandings

To maintain superior performance, you and your partner must be confident that your successful collaboration today will continue tomorrow. When those involved in an alliance move on to other jobs, or when new people arrive, you have to keep those attitudes and understandings that were the alliance's underpinnings in the first place. For these reasons, continuity is a condition for mutual trust. Achieving it involves a combination of recruiting, training, career planning, promotion criteria, performance measures, and incentives.

HAVE REALISTIC EXPECTATIONS

How well the conditions for trust are met determines the potential for an alliance. For instance, weak mutual need inhibits internal support; vague objectives invite possibly destructive conflict. To some extent, champions may overcome such problems.

As an example, while Canon is proud of its well-known brand, the laser components it sells to HP do not carry the Canon badge. That has created internal resistance toward the alliance. "I have had to push for the HP relationship," says Takahashi Kitamura. "This has not gotten easier. I have always had difficulties."

At HP, in the alliance's early days many regarded cooperating with others as a heresy. Compounding concerns about a loss of independence was the fact that the new printers could be sold through dealers, whereas HP previously had relied on its own sales force. "The laser printer relationship did not naturally propagate here," notes John Stedman, an early champion. "It really took a lot of work." Backing by Carnahan, Kitamura, and others in both firms, along with the partners' unquestionable success together, have helped.

But championing alone can't explain Canon's and HP's track record. Though early advocates made an obvious difference, they were working in an environment where mutual need was widely recognized in both firms, shared objectives were clear and broadly accepted, and both organizations were able to respond to changing needs.

Don't expect trust between other groups in your firms just because you have been successful together. Those groups may have separate interests, priorities, or styles. An alliance between Ford and ABB to build paint plants was a model of best practice. Yet the auto maker has created rancor at other suppliers and weakened their commitments. The diverse styles at Ford are due to varying norms throughout the company about how to work with suppliers.

The potential for trust between firms is higher the more that both have in common; it is limited by any differences. Despite obvious contrasts, many similarities between Canon and Hewlett-Packard have made their collaboration easier.

Both firms hire individuals who work well in a team environment. Both rely on consensus processes. People in both companies regard their counterparts as easygoing. Unlike employees at most Japanese firms, Canon's are less group-oriented and more individualistic. Compared with most American companies, HP is more group-oriented, while its people are not as outspoken as many Americans. Further, both companies' laser printer units have compatible structures. Another plus: Canon staffers who interact with HP are competent in English, while HP has hired Americans fluent in Japanese, and several others there have learned the language.

Because trust building depends on what happens within as

WHERE THE ISSUES ARE		
	Between Firms	**Within Each Firm**
People, Politics, Organizations	Often Overlooked	Often Overlooked
Tangible Items	Usual Focus	Often Overlooked

well as between firms, you will need to pay attention to personalities and politics, as well as tangible matters covered in transactions—like products and terms. Think about it this way: The most important contract you will have with a partner will be unwritten and unsigned, but very much understood. The essence will be about how people and their organizations behave.

HOW TO BUILD TRUST

Though satisfying the eight conditions for trust is necessary, there is still more to do. You and your partner must also engage in *practices* that build trust and that depend on those conditions. For instance, as the book will elaborate, one such practice is constructive problem solving. To succeed at that requires interpersonal relationships to develop needed understandings, a clear shared objective to guide decisions, commitments to ensure people that the outcome will be fair, and adaptive organizations able to support joint decisions.

How to employ each of the conditions and practices is detailed in Chapters 2 through 7, in a step-by-step fashion, beginning when you first contemplate an alliance and then moving

MUTUAL TRUST
↑
PRACTICES THAT EARN TRUST
↑
CONDITIONS FOR TRUST

through negotiation to implementation. Each step adds a condition to be met or a practice to be used, and each step builds on the earlier ones. Following the road map here will help you avoid having to make a leap of faith that trust will be there when an alliance begins.[12]

As your negotiations proceed, meeting more trust conditions and adapting more practices fortifies trust, smooths the transition to implementation, and increases your performance together. By following the sequence explained here, you will be able to assess progress and foresee problems. If any step seems particularly difficult, you can decide whether to invest more effort or say goodbye.

Chapter 2 sets the stage for later chapters by focusing on those conditions and practices that must be addressed early on. It covers ways to build relationships that will contribute to trust, criteria for selecting joint leaders, and what their responsibilities entail. The chapter also describes key practices like building interfirm teams.

Chapter 3 explains how to combine each firm's objectives and how to use the result as a guiding framework to develop an alliance. Also discussed are ways to be creative together and to resolve conflicts constructively. Chapter 4 describes how to align both organizations around your mutual objectives, develop alliance plans that reduce the risk of failure, and adopt policies that support continuity when people move on.

Chapter 5 presents ways to apply the conditions and practices developed earlier to alliances involving more than one business unit from each partner.

Two more steps get you ready to begin an alliance. One is to select the right structure; the other is to establish effective governance. Both are spelled out in Chapter 6. Launch and implementation are the topics of Chapter 7. These last steps toward mutual trust reflect a key aspect of alliances: Even when you are under way, you can't take anything for granted.

Chapter 8 shows how to repair broken trust. After explaining how to diagnose failure, it presents the sequence of steps needed to get back on a healthy course.

How to build trust with difficult customers is the thrust of Chapter 9. Selling alliances to customers is described in Chapter

10. Because rivals have much in common, alliances between them are now popular. Even so, many are plagued by the problems common to all alliances and have the added burden of starting with hostile attitudes. You will learn how to overcome those handicaps in Chapter 11.

In Chapter 12, the conditions and practices for trust are applied to show how to forge alliances between groups within a company, and how to create a culture of cooperation.

Building trust in mergers and acquisitions is explained in Chapter 13, which draws on material from earlier chapters.

"Tools for Trust," the final section of *Trusted Partners*, describes how to measure trust, and offers guidelines, checklists, and other devices to guide alliance development and management. The Appendix presents scholarly underpinnings of the trust conditions described in this book. It also shows how each of the trust practices depends on one or more of the eight trust conditions.

CHAPTER 2

PICK TEAM PLAYERS

■

Alliances are among people, not just companies. To appreciate this point, compare alliances with transactions. In a transaction, your negotiation produces a detailed agreement—a specification, timing, quantity, delivery, payments, how key contingencies will be met, and so on. Once things are in writing, you can hand the document to others who were not involved, and they will know what to do because it has been spelled out.

Now, consider alliances. In crafting an alliance, the central goal is to grow a creative interfirm team—that's how you will produce new value together. Unlike transactions, in alliances you cannot document intangibles like shared understandings of each other's situation and how to manage change, both of which you will need to be effective as partners. Further, such rapport can't be transferred to others easily.

"It's not two companies," observes Al Lorenz, a key early manager in the alliance between Canon and Hewlett-Packard. "It's two groups of people."

PRACTICES THAT EARN TRUST

Interfirm Teams   *Alliance Ethics*
Keep Promises   *Right People*

CONDITIONS FOR TRUST

Mutual Need   *Relationships*   *Joint Leaders*

Your first step in building an alliance is to conclude that each firm is the other's best choice for reaching its own important objectives. As Chapter 1 notes, if mutual need is not viewed as a priority within both companies, trust is impossible. The next step is to develop understandings about each other and the road ahead.

START INVESTING IN RELATIONSHIPS NOW

Interpersonal relationships will be the conduits through which your understandings flow, the context for mutual creativity. Any delay in building these ties will limit everyone's enthusiasm and lower your potential performance together. "We would have avoided some difficult misunderstandings," said an executive involved in the Maersk–SeaLand alliance, "if we had taken more time to develop relationships at the start."

Some of the earliest issues in building alliances have to do with selecting the right people and learning about individuals and politics in each firm. Personal relationships help you discuss these matters candidly, develop constructive understandings, and reach practical conclusions. Further, more problems in alliances are due to weak relationships than to anything else. Says Bruce Bendoff, president of Craftsman Custom Metal Fabricators, a small firm with many customer and supplier alliances: "Whenever something goes wrong I can almost bet money that there's an ego issue behind it."[1]

Quality relationships are so fundamental to alliances that their absence is an early indicator of impending trouble. If people who get involved are awkward with one another, you have four options: coach them on the appropriate style, replace them with others, reduce your expectations, or end the discussions. Consider the following situation, which is typical of many failures.

In an alliance eventually marked more by conflict than by cooperation, Emory University and Egleston Children's Health Care System, both based in Atlanta, created a joint venture to better serve the youngsters of Georgia. When the venture suffered from clashing objectives, rather than discuss the problem constructively, people avoided one another. In a letter that was about as subtle as thunder, Emory executives indicated that legal issues were involved. Egleston responded in kind and, soon after that, its CEO was harshly critical of Emory in public presentations and later to his own trustees.

It was as if the disgruntled partners thought they could resolve the conflict by mudslinging. "Nobody brought their concerns to the table until the situation had deteriorated," said one executive. "It was ugly," added another. What really failed here was relationships. If leaders on both sides had explored their differences, problems related to conflicting objectives might have been repaired.

Sobering though it may be, most people find that genuine bonds with co-workers don't always develop. Since relationships are the soil in which alliances grow, you have to prepare the ground for them to bloom.

In their initial link-up, HP sourced components from Canon on a commercial basis. Once the firms realized what they could gain by combining their skills, discussions took on a new tone. "One implicit purpose of those meetings was to build mutual understanding, so we could feel comfortable sharing more with each other," recalls HP's Don Hammond, who led early collaboration with Canon. "This was never discussed, but we both knew that to be effective together, we had to understand each other to have a relationship based on trust."

Individuals from both companies made specific efforts to develop such bonds. For instance, on an early trip to California Hajimi Mitarai (initially Canon's lead for the alliance) and Hammond drove to a nearby redwood forest. As they walked the trails they talked about growing up in Japan, discussed how Mitarai's father had nourished his son's career, and compared Japanese and American ways of doing things. "These discussions were important for both of us," says Hammond. "You can begin to trust the details on the business side of the relationship when you feel you know the real person." Over the years the two became so friendly that even after Mitarai's death, Hammond kept in close touch with his wife and children.

Many firms wine and dine potential partners but don't get beyond cordial conversations. To develop deep, solid trust, you have to learn about each other's organizational and psychological worlds. What keeps your counterpart awake at night? What are his concerns? Who in the other firm favors the alliance, and who is opposed? How will you get around the barriers together? What is the best way to raise issues with your partner? Can you tell when the time is right and when it is not?

When your discussions with people from another company first turn to business, begin by sharing your views. Talk about the nature of the opportunity, why you might be each other's best choice for pursuing it, what your separate objectives are, and why these are important to your firm. Also cover key people, concerns and constraints, how implementation might work, and items that will need early attention. The task at this initial stage is not to nail down specifics, but to raise mutual awareness and become more comfortable.

> YOU'LL FIND A SUGGESTED NEGO-
> TIATING AGENDA ON PAGE 220

Consider that Nypro, the injection-molding firm with many successful joint ventures, agrees on a new one only after people have built constructive relationships, usually over several months. Consider also that when Ford and ABB decided to form an alliance to build paint plants, the firms took three months to develop the understandings needed to embark on their first major project. Yet no time was lost. The mutual confidence they developed averted many traditional delay-causing conflicts and led to a plant completion record for the industry.

Numerous events inside your company can affect a partner's attitude. For example, you may have made a recent acquisition that is diverting people's attention, or you may need more time to resolve internal differences. Whatever the cause, any delay, conflict, or uncertainty within your firm may frustrate your partner and cause it to suspect low interest or a hidden agenda. Rather than wait until perceptions turn negative, develop a habit of privately sharing your separate realities with each other, starting with your earliest discussions.

It's impossible to know whether relative strangers' descriptions of how their firm works are accurate or just window dressing. Only candid discussions can help you understand what is realistic. Further, it is unwise to assume that another group can change its culture for your sake. Think about the challenge of adjusting your own culture. Recall from Chapter 1 that Prodigy, begun by Sears and IBM, was almost destroyed by inappropriate parent behavior.

You will encourage high performance by introducing, early on, the idea that fairness in outcomes is needed to ensure each firm's commitment. Since this is one of the

FINANCIAL SHARING PRINCIPLES
ARE DESCRIBED ON PAGE 227

conditions for trust, don't just assume it will happen. To start building mutual faith along these lines, agree on the principles you will use to guide later discussions about financial arrangements. One principle, for example, is to share gains in proportion to the value of your contributions.

Also discuss with your prospective partner how you will resolve conflicts together. The best way is to share openly and get to the root of each issue. If one firm does not normally work this way, it's worth knowing that up front.

Learning that you have conflicting views on various matters is a natural part of cooperation. The better you become at joint problem solving, the more you will trust each other and the more fruitful your alliance will be. The key here is better mutual knowledge.

Canon and HP people, for instance, share a specific goal of developing richer understandings. Says HP's Chuck Walter, manufacturing manager in the laser printer business: "We can be tough as nails together. Our knowledge of each other helps us debate more effectively together because we better understand each other. The close personal relationships we enjoy are a springboard to our success and not a barrier to dealing with each other on tough issues."

An early step in discussions should be to identify issues that you will have to resolve before implementation, including deal breakers for either firm. Explore these candidly to be sure everyone appreciates them. Settling easier questions first fosters mutual confidence and helps you address tougher matters more constructively. Besides, some of the most resolute positions soften when people know each other better.

Be sure to surface any concerns due to past events, discuss these, and agree on how to avoid such problems. During an early meeting about a possible alliance between two package delivery companies, as staffers from both firms worked on a list of issues one participant cited trust. Some months earlier, he noted, his company had alerted the other to an opportunity they had agreed to pursue together. Shortly after that, his firm learned the other company had acted on the idea alone.

It was an awkward moment until someone from the offending company apologized. Internal communications had broken down, which was not unusual, he explained, adding that his firm would have to do better on that score in the alliance. To prevent further misunderstandings, those present agreed to keep each other informed, at least privately, of any relevant thinking in their respective firms.

Healthy alliances require a mix of such group meetings and private conversations. The right time for each depends on what you hope to accomplish. Group sessions generally are best for shared learning and consensus building. But they usually are limited to making politically safe statements, which may inhibit candid explorations needed for problem resolution. In successful alliances and within proprietary limits, there is a great deal of one-on-one sharing that people assume will stay private.

For instance, Ron Sforza and Jesper Kjaedegaard, of SeaLand and Maersk, are jointly responsible for planning their firms' worldwide vessel network. "Some of the most productive meetings I have had have been one-on-one with Jesper," says Sforza. "We have helped each other understand the realities within our respective organizations."

To develop mutual understanding, begin divulging slowly. Watch people's reactions and limit what you disclose until your counterparts start opening up as well. By your behavior, show your respect for what they have conveyed. Creating an equally exposed situation based on mutual sharing and regard makes each of you less vulnerable. Once Canon and HP decided to plow new ground together, "we did not disclose very much at the start, but gradually learned we could trust each other and eventually shared a lot," HP's Hammond recalls.

During both negotiations and implementation, your most important conversations must be face to face. Though travel to meetings may seem to involve more time than phone calls, e-mail, or video links, these arm's-length discussions miss the richness of interpersonal contact. When difficult issues are involved, remote conversations tend to create misunderstandings, which then must be resolved. Reinforcing this sentiment, "There still are benefits to physical person-to-person interaction," Bob Muglia, senior vice president of Microsoft's business productivity group, says.[2]

In building an alliance, think about relationships this way: Reach a level of mutual comfort and understanding such that, if trouble surfaces, you can discuss it logically and candidly. An alliance may fall on hard times. Personal relationships should not.

BEGIN JOINT LEADERSHIP

Only with joint leadership can you expect joint followership. With mutual need and emerging relationships as a foundation, the ground is ready to select joint leaders and assemble the alliance. As you contemplate what you hope to create, discuss within your firm and with your prospective partner who should take the lead and what that will entail.[3]

From early negotiation through implementation, you will need consistent joint leadership at policy and operating levels. The more senior pair of leaders oversees alliance formation and will co-chair the governing team. The second pair heads the day-to-day operating team. For more than one operating team, there may be leaders for each.

Because alliances involve ongoing advances, criteria for policy-level leaders include proven records of leading change. To be effective, their positions should be close to the alliance operating level. If far above it, they probably won't be able to take the time alliance building will need, and communications between the levels will be difficult. To illustrate, alliance development at Ford and ABB was headed by Vince Coletta, Ford's executive engineer for plant facilities, and Tom Mark, president of ABB Paint Finishing. The alliance project managers reported directly to them.[4]

One early step for leaders at the policy level is to define a shared vision—a qualitative description of what both firms hope to achieve together. This vision builds on your separate objectives, will guide the development of your mutual objectives, identifies key activities, and defines the scope of your alliance. Other early steps for policy leaders include securing support within their firms and choosing innovative leaders to spearhead the operating team. As alliance building proceeds, additional tasks comprise gaining alignment within their firms and generally paving the political road.

FOR DETAILS ON CHOOSING THE LEADERS, SEE PAGE 224

With policy-level support behind them, operating-level leaders develop mutual objectives, guide team building, and produce the results. For instance, project leaders at Ford–ABB assembled a highly creative joint engineering team that broke records in paint plant safety, cost reduction, and cycle time.

From their first contact, both sets of leaders instill best practice by visibly modeling the style they want to see in others: openly sharing, learning about and respecting their separate interests, addressing issues constructively, and coaching people as necessary on these and other practices that contribute to trust.

Listen to SeaLand's Sforza comment on Dick Murphy and Knud Erik Moller Nielsen, who jointly led the SeaLand–Maersk alliance during the early years: "I have learned from Dick the importance of building interpersonal relationships to further our alliance. I have seen Dick with Erik. I have seen them be totally open with each other on important issues."

Fundamental to joint leadership is a growing confidence that these individuals can count on each other to serve as champions for the alliance in their firms. "I know that when my counterpart is discussing our alliance with his management, he is representing my company's interests," said the co-leader of a health care alliance. "That raises my faith in our mission together."

In meetings, joint leaders focus on getting everyone's best efforts. During initial sessions, this includes checking for each participant's buy-in, watching to see if interpersonal chemistry is growing, and correcting inappropriate behavior through coaching or (if necessary) replacing someone. To encourage progress, co-leaders draw on individuals who may have fresh views, take tough issues off line, promote communications, sort out personality problems, and keep everything aligned around your shared objectives.

When necessary, both leaders must also be ready to lower the temperature of heated exchanges while affirming each side's contribution. That style sustains respect and helps keep creative energies flowing.

One useful measure of joint leadership is whether people at lower levels in both firms get clear and consistent guidance. Another is how well leaders understand one another's context, which includes people and politics in both firms. With this knowledge they can make realistic plans. A third is their success in delivering needed resources from and alignment in their respective firms. A fourth is the enthusiasm they instill in others.

Vince Coletta was highly regarded at Ford for his technical competence and outstanding interpersonal skills. Both he and Tom Mark, of ABB, are people-oriented and enjoy trying new things. Together, their chemistry was inspiring. "Their joint leadership empowered us, and made our jobs easier," says Larry Miller, a Ford purchasing specialist who worked on the alliance. "They gave us the keys to the car."

COMBINE NEGOTIATION AND IMPLEMENTATION

There is only one way to develop an alliance if you expect superior performance: Have the implementers be the negotiators. It is always a mistake to assign these phases to different people. Some firms make it worse by sending in the "black hats" to do the deal, later replacing them by the "white hats" to make it work. Even without a deliberate switch in styles, newcomers bring their own attitudes, understandings are lost, and behavior patterns shift. Consequently, those involved do not know what to expect of one another. Confusion and poor results always follow.

In alliances, negotiations never end. Because they are intended to make regular advances, alliances depend on ongoing change. Cases in point: Ford and ABB revised the paint plant during construction, and plants they have done since then improved on earlier ones; HP and Canon are constantly developing new products together; Maersk and SeaLand continuously redesign their vessel networks for better cost and performance, and keep working on the rationalization of their port facilities.

The operating teams at the core of your alliance must be anchored in those units that represent your firms' need for each other—like Ford's plant facilities group and ABB Paint Finishing. Otherwise, here's what can happen.

Two companies I'll call BestBank and Consumers Group, an insurer, saw an opportunity to offer tailored insurance policies to bank customers. Both assigned alliance development to their respective corporate strategy functions. However, operating groups slated to run the alliance did not participate in the planning and were disinterested. Plans got stuck at the conceptual stage, which gave everyone a chance to reach his own conclusion about how the venture would work. The confusion that followed seriously embarrassed BestBank with its customers and almost ended the alliance.

Planning your negotiation together builds comfort, reduces surprises, and bolsters trust. So, looking ahead to implementation, agree on a negotiating plan, set a tight schedule for the alliance starting date, and stick to it. There is nothing quite like speed to energize a process and cause people to focus their efforts. If they cannot find time for an alliance it may not be a priority—something worth learning before you go very far.

INVEST IN TEAM DEVELOPMENT

Developing alliance teams involves the same principles needed for internal ones—select the right people, give them a sense of urgency and direction, present a challenging assignment, set important patterns, take time to build relationships, and reward progress. However, team building needs more attention in alliances. With unfamiliar people and organizations, those involved must learn how to gauge their counterparts' judgments, adapt to one another's ways, and develop shared norms.[5]

To avoid putting the cart before the horse, designate team

members—particularly for governance roles—only as alliance development proceeds. The alternative is having to ask people to leave once you find that others are more suitable for the task.

In considering candidates for two-company teams, give weight to personal styles. "We want people who can think out of the box and build relationships," says Tom Muccio, who led the Procter & Gamble team that built his firm's alliance with Wal-Mart. "We select people with less than perfect intellects but with excellent interpersonal skills. The greatest brains can't do anything alone here. Everything depends on real teamwork."

Muccio's point about relationship skills deserves emphasis because it is often missed in practice. In countless alliances, I've found key individuals to be so ineffective together that their behavior inhibited and sometimes prevented their firms' cooperation.[6]

> SKILLS FOR ALLIANCES ARE SUMMARIZED ON PAGE 234

"We have clearly seen that putting people with win-win attitudes at important interfaces with Maersk has had a positive impact on our alliance," says SeaLand's Dick Murphy. Some people in both firms had to be moved as the alliance was coming together.

Creative cooperation requires that people accept one another as equally worthy and deserving of being understood. This attitude takes humility, self-confidence, and a sincere interest in others. Also needed are imagination and comfort with change. Having new ideas, which some people are best at on their own, isn't enough. Those who are especially qualified for alliances excel at exploring differences and finding new approaches tailored to the situation. Being smart isn't enough either. Those who do well in alliances are adept at listening well, reading nonverbal cues, and knowing when and how to raise issues constructively.

Leaders of the Ford–ABB alliance, for instance, chose managers for key roles based on function and personality. Coletta suggested Rudy Golla as Ford's project manager. "I understand how Rudy performs," he explained to ABB's Tom Mark. "He has a win-win attitude, communicates well, and excels at constructive problem solving." For similar reasons, Mark proposed Jim Dixon as ABB's project manager. Golla and Dixon then built and led the team that developed a breakthrough design for the new plant.

In looking back, Coletta recalls, "Jim was outstanding. His chemistry with Rudy made it happen and kept things under control." Adds Tom Mark: "Rudy was the centerpiece of our alliance. And without the outstanding relationship between Rudy and Jim, we would not have been successful."

When building a new relationship, it's an old saw that people are more comfortable with each other when they share something in common. Otherwise, major gaps in age, position, or background can inhibit or even prevent constructive bonds. This truism can be a useful guide when filling leadership roles.

In a link between Butler Manufacturing and a large retailer I'll call SuperSave, longstanding, frequently adverse relationships began to improve after Ralph Agee, Butler's senior project engineer, and Jim Harrison (not his real name), SuperSave's staff architect, found ways to innovate together. "Jim was smart and picked up ideas fast," says Agee. "It also helped that both of us were good old Missouri boys from small towns and shared a down-to-earth style. We just seemed to click."

Ultimately, having people with good relationship skills comes down to your firm's policies for recruitment and promotion, and what qualities are valued internally. If alliances are regarded as important to your future, encouraging such abilities is common sense. An added benefit is that having more people with these skills eases cooperation on the inside.

With the right people involved, and guided by effective joint leaders, a successful negotiation should lead you to the same position reached by Ford and ABB: "We created such a great two-company team," says Larry Miller, "that I felt we could go anywhere and do anything. People personally owned the stretch targets and wanted to meet them. We had confidence in each other."

UNDERSTAND YOUR DIFFERENCES

Some of the most stubborn alliance issues stem from disparate structures and behaviors. Because mutual trust depends on effective interfirm connections, raising your differences deserves early attention. SeaLand and Maersk illustrate.

During an initial planning meeting, executives from both firms explored how their companies differed. Key factors included ownership, their parent firms' other businesses, legal requirements, and organizational structures and cultures.

These discussions revealed important contrasts. SeaLand is organized around the world's major shipping lanes, while Maersk is based on the continents. Another difference is that U.S. securities regulations compel SeaLand, a unit of publicly held CSX Corporation, to disclose more than Danish law requires of Maersk, a unit of privately owned A.P. Moeller. Such constraints limit what the firms can share, because going further would cause SeaLand to disclose sensitive Maersk information.

The firms used these insights to guide their negotiations. Those responsible for various activities had to attend multiple meetings, since the firms' structures were so dissimilar. But people had learned enough to develop clear plans. "Willingly discussing our differences helped us build trust with each other," says Murphy. "It increased our shared understandings, and by acknowledging our differences, we could more easily deal with them."

At this early stage in your discussions, do a brief sanity check of what lies ahead. Go into enough detail to be sure that your objectives are compatible and your organizations can perform as required. If SeaLand had wanted to operate 16-knot slow ships and Maersk preferred 25-knot fast ships, they could not have the sequential sailings needed to reach higher shipping frequencies, a key objective. Also discuss how your alliance will affect customers, employees, and other partners.

TURN TO PAGES 236 AND 243 FOR OBJECTIVES AND ORGANIZATIONAL PARAMETERS TO CONSIDER

DEFINE THE STYLE YOU WILL USE

It is always safe and often true to assume that each firm has distinct views about the right way to plan, make decisions, solve prob-

lems, and run meetings. For that reason, I have found it most helpful early in negotiations for joint leaders to formalize desirable
rules of conduct. Typically, these include a pledge that each side
will treat the other fairly, that open and honest communications
are expected and that, within the alliance scope, neither firm will
act in a harmful way toward the other. Of course such declara-
tions, like corporate mission statements, have value only if they are
reinforced.

Also needed is an understanding about how meetings should
work. In some companies, people start with a list of topics to be
covered and discussions range back and forth among them. In others, the conversation does not move to new topics until prior ones
are settled. In some firms people expect to reach decisions in the
conference room. Others prefer to do that later. In many initial alliance meetings, there is a tendency to hold back out of a concern
for things that could go wrong. Unless you agree on the rules,
you're likely to be playing different games.

For example, once top management from Wal-Mart and Procter & Gamble agreed to build an alliance, staffers charged with its
development met to begin framing mutual objectives and discuss
aspects of how their firms worked. Included in that was a team-
building session that reviewed how their firms could operate as a
single interconnected system. Still, no one was sure an alliance
could actually function. P&G worried that Wal-Mart might tighten
prices so much its profits would suffer. Wal-Mart was concerned
that P&G's promotion policies, which had been a problem for the
retailer, would further erode its margins.

The group's second meeting looked at these issues. For two
full days they explored specific opportunities for working together
and problems they might encounter. Lists of both were recorded
on separate flip charts. Encouraged by the potential they saw, people discussed ways to avoid the difficulties. These were written on
a third chart as a set of operating norms. For instance, to address
their concerns about profits, one norm was to improve the profitability of both companies.

Other norms they developed included a shared expectation to
treat mistakes as chances to learn: The first step when errors were

made would be damage control. To facilitate learning, they would keep a "correction-of-errors" file to help them avoid repeating mistakes. "We solved the negatives so we could work on the positives," says P&G's Tom Muccio.

Team members agreed to apply the operating norms by reviewing them every time they met. They also confirmed a shared expectation that anyone could point out when the norms were not being followed. These principles have become widely accepted on both sides of the firms' interface.

The give-and-take in the meeting, plus informal chats over meals and during breaks, gave participants a lot of insight into one another. Wal-Mart is not process-oriented, and its people were at first uneasy with this discussion. By the second day, though, their attitudes had evolved as they grew comfortable with the process and saw the potential benefits. In looking back, participants see the meeting as an important step toward confidence and understanding. Individuals from different firms were forging a leadership team.

USE ALLIANCE ETHICS

Adhere to alliance ethics—a code of conduct on which both firms concur. As you proceed, explicitly agree that there will be no hidden agendas. Otherwise, you risk covert activities that may undermine trust.

For example, while it's okay to have conflicting objectives, it is not acceptable to be deceptive about your objectives. If mutual need is high and relationships are solid, you usually can find creative solutions to any conflict. However, being less than transparent about your objectives undermines people's confidence. Another practice to avoid is keeping deal breakers under wraps until they can be used for leverage. A third pitfall is to hire your partner's people.

There are two ways to ward off unethical behavior; use both. One is to choose partners with a reputation for integrity. The second is to invest enough time in negotiations to learn about a prospective partner and its interests, to avoid surprises.

Without candid conversations it's impossible to be certain if a prospective partner's apparently hidden agenda was intentional, or

FOR DETAILS ON ALLIANCE
ETHICS, SEE PAGE 226
if the offending undisclosed objective is so widely accepted there that people did not think to mention it. The more you probe each other's thinking, the less likely such problems will occur.

SHOW YOUR INTEREST IN THEIR SUCCESS

Anything you can do for a prospective partner that helps it and advances both firms' interests adds to its early confidence in your new relationship. Take the case of a pair of American and Brazilian firms that were planning a new joint venture near São Paulo.[7]

Central to their plans was a substantial investment to be made by the Americans. For the Brazilians, this was the door to their future. Yet shortly before the funds were to be transferred, their finance chief phoned his American counterpart to advise against it. Local tax rules had just changed, making the investment more costly. As much as his firm needed the capital, he said they could not go forward knowing their partner would be hurt. He suggested possible alternatives.

For the Americans this was a watershed. "There is always some uncertainty about a new partner," their president commented, "but our Brazilian friends showed us their heart and we liked what we saw. With their advice we found a way around the problem." A few months later the Brazilians missed a key business deadline; the Americans simply asked what had happened and how they could help.

CHAPTER 3

DEFINE A SINGLE PURPOSE

■

Global One, the alliance of Sprint, Deutsche Telekom, and France Telecom, failed to follow a basic tenet of alliance building—defining mutual objectives—and paid dearly. After agreeing to build an international business, the firms never discussed in depth what that meant. Busy with other matters, management in each firm assigned much of the negotiation to attorneys, who focused on tax, financial, and legal issues.

The upshot: Once Global One was under way, the Americans thought its main purpose was to give them the worldwide network they needed; the Germans believed that fending off domestic rivals should get top attention, while the French gave priority to local projects that would boost France Telecom's image.

Without shared business objectives, the organization that emerged lacked practical guidelines for basic activities such as investment priorities, linking with other telecoms, and network in-

tegration—making a seamless network impossible. Having nothing more than the partners' overall financial desires to steer them, individual unit heads set their own direction, with little bearing on how it affected the whole. "This company was put together with rough bricks," said one executive. Reflecting their inability to agree on objectives, performance has been dismal and a breakup is imminent.[1]

DEVELOP A SINGLE FOCUS FOR ALL DECISIONS

Superior results will come from blending your separate abilities in a way that best meets your mutual purpose. The sole criterion for deciding what goes into an alliance should be whatever creates the most value for both firms—as defined by your mutual objectives. Use these objectives to plan every aspect—from policies, resources, procedures, and job assignments to organizational design and governance.

In developing a gasoline marketing joint venture in Europe, for instance, Mobil and British Petroleum had to decide whether to use one or both of their brands, or possibly to create a new brand. Their chief objective was improved sales, and consumer studies suggested that the BP brand would attract the most business. So they chose that brand for their venture. Mobil accepted lower visibility and replaced its signs and other company symbols at 23,000 gasoline stations. "There was no room for an ego trip," says Jean-Louis Schilansky, a Mobil top executive. "If we kept the Mobil brand, we would ultimately have lost market share to others."

Conditions were different for a lubricant marketing venture BP and Mobil developed at the same time. In this case each firm's brand had its own loyal following. Consumer research showed that keeping just one brand would cause many customers to switch to rivals. The solution in this case: They kept both.[2]

These examples highlight a basic rule for meeting your shared objectives: There is no room for pride or rigidity if you want to excel together. For Mobil and BP, the right answer involved one brand for one venture and both for the other. In some instances, the best way to meet your objectives may lie beyond both firms' boundaries. Consider the case of two paper companies that created a distribution joint venture.

The partners agreed that whoever was tapped to be CEO should have a strong track record in this business. However, when the firms tried to recruit, none of the most qualified prospects applied. Surprisingly, candidates declined because a company car was not part of the benefit package. As it turned out, the problem wasn't the car but what it symbolized.

The firms' reason for a joint venture was to replace their separate and inefficient practices of delivering products to customers through contractors. Lacking experience in the distribution business, they didn't know that having a car is a normal perk. That oversight led CEO prospects to conclude the companies did not understand distribution, making them uneasy about the job. When they explained the problem to me, I suggested they provide a car, thinking this step would demonstrate their willingness to learn. Both firms refused at first: giving cars to executives violated their policies. After prolonged internal debate, they reluctantly concluded that if their objective was to be in the distribution business, they would have to follow market norms. They got the executive; he got the car.

DEFINE YOUR OBJECTIVES

To be useful, your shared objectives must be clear enough to serve as a practical guide for planning and implementing the alliance. Fuzzy objectives create problems.

Let's say you go no further than stating that your mutual intent is to be the best in the market. If you understand this to mean largest market share while your partner is thinking of highest financial return, you might end up working at cross-purposes. As another illustration, it is easy to agree to be cost effective together. But it is harder to concur, say, on specific costs per unit, which you will need to make plans and set priorities. Only by going into detail in defining your objectives can you both be sure you want the same results and agree on how to get them.

In setting your objectives, reach for breadth and depth. The

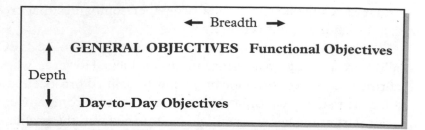

breadth dimension begins with your most general business and financial objectives, and covers all functions to be involved—including, for instance, how your firms will jointly sell to customers or provide service—since you each may have different priorities in those areas. Also agree on specific measurements, rather than make vague statements like wanting to have good service. Best-Bank and Consumers Group, an insurance company, missed this point.

The promising vision of the bank and the insurer seemed about to become reality when an insurance product launched by all the bank's branches attracted many thousands of applications and was celebrated in the press. As part of their offering, the firms had agreed to provide exceptional customer service. Yet the bank, an industry leader in customer satisfaction, and the insurer, having reached high service levels for its industry, never reviewed what they meant by good service. They should have talked about timing.

Within a week of the launch bank customers, used to having their loan applications processed within a day, were complaining that they had not received their insurance policies. After two weeks they were flooding the bank with calls and the press was having a field day.

As the partners later learned, the bank had a one-day response time for loans, while the insurer typically took two weeks to process new policies. Further, thousands of applications were misplaced because no one noticed until too late that bank and insurer computer systems were incompatible. The work had to be done manually, which lengthened the average response time to two months.

Meanwhile, three months were required to reorganize the

insurer's customer service for faster responses and to integrate the firms' operations—tasks that could have been done faster and without a huge backlog before the launch. The bank needed several years to recover from its damaged image.

Besides defining your objectives in breadth, discuss in depth your combined expectations for the operating levels. A useful test of adequacy here is that, at the lowest organization level at which people will work together, your shared objectives are a practical guide for day-to-day decisions. Recall from Chapter 1 how Canon's and Hewlett-Packard's objectives begin with generic guidelines about user satisfaction, and reach down to specific tasks at the product level. To avoid creating a joint bureaucracy, where the firms have clear understandings they do not go into as much detail.

Expect to work through several iterations to define your objectives before you have an adequate and acceptable planning framework. Part of that effort entails getting buy-in within both firms. Each company may have to delegate authority, as well as adjust its recognition and reward systems, to support what you intend to do. As conditions change, objectives development will continue into your alliance. Container shippers Maersk and SeaLand keep sharpening their objectives to stay competitive; Canon and HP revisit theirs as user needs and technologies evolve.

SEE PAGES 235 FOR DETAILS ON DEVELOPING MUTUAL OBJECTIVES

As your objectives come into focus, start identifying key cost and revenue parameters, along with expected benefits, and begin developing a financial model for the alliance. Use the model to help guide your thinking, fleshing it out as your discussions progress.

DISCUSS EACH FIRM'S ACTIVITIES

The only certainty you can have about another company is that it is risky to be certain about anything, unless you have discussed the matter in depth. While it may be obvious that any two firms are different in some respects, the devil, as they say, is in the details. Take the example of Arby's and ZuZu, respectively a fast-food chain and an upscale group of Mexican restaurants.

When the pair agreed to add Mexican meals to Arby's outlets, each assumed the other's methods were similar to its own. Consequently, they didn't identify some key steps needed to make the alliance work. One overlooked item was that Arby's portions came wrapped in paper, while ZuZu's meals were served on china plates. Confused customers who bought Mexican food tossed their empty plates into the trash along with the paper.

Also ignored in their planning was the fact that Arby's low-skilled fast-food crews would not be able to cope with ZuZu's complex dishes. Soon after the alliance began, quality on the ZuZu side fell rapidly. Then, in the perverse way some firms do things when they fail to understand one another, they sued each other.[3]

You can avoid the kind of problem that trashed the Arby's–ZuZu alliance by cross-checking your objectives with each activity to be involved. For instance, if product development is called for, that may require overall objectives for timing, price, and performance, as well as more specific objectives for components and technologies. Together with your partner, decide how to meet each objective.

If your alliance will involve many activities, it can be helpful to lay out the full value delivery process. To illustrate, if your objectives call for a seamless interface with customers, describe every step, from customer selection, promotion, brands to be used, and pricing to sales training, selling, and distribution. Seamless performance calls for tight links between objectives and resources for every task.

DON'T BARGAIN, BE CREATIVE TOGETHER

As you clarify your objectives and the way each firm works, start discussing how you will use these understandings to build your alliance. The best results will come from abandoning any habits you developed for transactions.

When negotiating a transaction the notion is to win the best deal for your side. For that, tactics like posturing, compromising, making trades, sharing information selectively, and using leverage may help you get your way.

At best, such bargaining brings both firms to a middle ground; an alliance is supposed to reach higher ground. Bargaining not only limits information sharing and discourages candor, but can result in one firm getting more and the other less. With little information to combine, no basis for a shared understanding, and a win-lose outcome, there is no chance for creativity and commitment.

What was remarkable about the first paint plant alliance between Ford and ABB was not just their results, which included a 25 percent capital cost reduction on a $300-million facility. That was the natural outcome of a more profound change from traditional negotiations: They chose to abandon bargaining in favor of joint innovation. In their previous—traditional—negotiations each side withheld data, suspecting the other might use it to get better terms. This time, by emphasizing trust, those involved eroded the barriers to sharing what they needed to be creative together.

Intent on doing their firms' combined best, Ford's Vince Coletta and ABB's Tom Mark assembled a joint engineering team and charged members with blending their know-how to find an optimal solution to their safety, cost, cycle time, and other objectives. Ford people contributed their experience with paint plants, while ABB team members shared their knowledge about technologies and processes. The team produced a design markedly different from anything that had been done before. It had a smaller footprint, a multistory rather than a one-story structure, a revised system layout, and a far cleaner internal environment—which made a big quality difference in finished cars.

Mutual creativity is a shared mind-set. As you get better at it, problems take on a different tone. By learning to be creative together, you increase the chances of constructively sorting through your differences, which encourages you to go further. The earlier you adopt this style, the sooner it will start working for you.

In your planning, avoid the common mistake of exchanging written proposals. This practice is akin to limiting your marketing and development people to trading memos about a new product rather than brainstorming together. Dealing at arm's length, a habit that comes from transactions, inhibits team building and creativity. It promotes a discussion of positions rather than an exploration of opportunities.

Start together with a clean sheet of paper. If you developed a plan before your discussions began, consider sharing it to help your partner understand how you think. But don't defend your own plan. Instead, use it as a source of ideas and assumptions to be explored. Only a desire to learn from one another and a face-to-face search for new solutions can build the insights needed for trust and superior results.

The Ford–ABB alliance illustrates. To foster team creativity, Ford people bypassed the company's tradition of dictating how things would be done. Both partners moved team members to a shared facility. Progress meetings alternated between Ford and ABB locations. To bolster cooperation, Coletta and Mark sought wide participation. Individuals from both firms, including those at lower levels, made presentations before the steering committee.

With a clear stretch target to aim for, strong joint leadership, team members chosen for relationship and technical skills, agreed norms for cooperation, and performance evaluations keyed to project metrics, everyone on the team became aligned. The wide participation and information sharing enhanced people's understanding, empowered the combined team, and fueled their creativity. Participants bought into the process, convinced that management valued everyone's ideas.

In many alliances, the handoff to lower levels isn't smooth. For Ford and ABB, the leaders' constant emphasis on teamwork and openness eroded natural inhibitions. Coletta's and Mark's obvious good will and shared convictions encouraged collaborative attitudes. "They were watching us," recalls one participant.

RESOLVE CONFLICTS CONSTRUCTIVELY

Conflict is a natural consequence of having distinct views on important matters. It is healthy if you respond by looking for creative solutions; it can be damaging otherwise. Tolerating unresolved issues will undermine your efforts as surely as sand in a gear box.[4]

In Chapter 1 I noted that, for constructive problem solving, each company must see the other as its best choice for meeting an important internal objective. Satisfying that trust condition, together with constructive relationships, helps in the search for useful answers. Your shared objectives guide you to them.

"We have high respect for each other," says an HP engineer about relationships with Canon. "We do not just accept each other's views—there is a lot of dialogue. Sometimes we really get into it with each other, but we are always guided by what is best for our shared objective. We all have ideas and will have a lot of debate getting to this point. But by continually exploring together we end up with a new product that both companies will sign up for."

The best way to resolve a problem is first to increase the number of possible solutions. Probe to learn each other's views, and expand your mutual understanding of the context; then look for creative approaches. Build on each other's logic. When you don't agree, discuss your assumptions to learn whether you are looking at the situation the same way. This open, exploratory style is the hallmark of people who value constructive relationships. Others don't make good partners.

Take the case of two credit card firms that could not agree on which segments of a new market to go after. To sort through their differences, negotiating team members used their mutual objectives to brainstorm novel ways to look at the market, which uncovered new opportunities. Jointly run focus groups with prospective consumers added to their insights and led to unique products and a successful launch.

Another example of creative problem solving was a pair of energy companies that could not agree on the value of one firm's contribution to a joint venture. Rather than end their discussions or split the difference—both unattractive options—they explored out-of-the-box approaches. In the end, they agreed to value the firm's assets at a lower level and to pay it a royalty on revenues that exceeded what the lower valuation was expected to produce.

When you differ about possible solutions, focus on the issue, not on individuals. Every alliance benefits from productive debate. However, successful alliance practitioners avoid arguments in which tempers get out of hand or that escalate into heated discussions of fault and blame. Confrontations like these discourage participation and may do lasting damage.

Sometimes, for example, a laser printer developed by Canon and HP does not sell well due to problems within one or both firms. "When this happens," says an engineer, "we look for the underlying cause and do whatever is needed to correct the situation—such as lowering production costs or improving performances. Such problems could lead to finger pointing but they do not. We all have to be constructive because we need each other."

Creative problem solving strengthens a relationship because it fortifies a belief that you can produce value and survive conflict together. Says a participant in the alliance between Wal-Mart and Procter & Gamble: "We found we could make great progress by openly putting our problems on the table and working through them without hidden agendas." If some individuals cannot work this way you have two options: coach them or replace them.

Agreeing on prices for laser engines that HP buys from Canon is often a tougher nut for the firms to crack than combining their product and technology know-how. HP may want to buy an engine from Canon, say, for $100, while Canon wants to sell it to HP for $200. Neither company discloses its costs or profits to the other and both seek healthy bottom lines from their collaboration. Those circumstances make pricing between the firms a difficult topic. Even so, they approach the issue as partners should.

"Each of us describes our needs and situation to the other," says HP's Al Lorenz. "Our discussions include only enough detail so that both firms end up where they should reasonably be. We avoid negotiating games or tricks. Instead, we compare and discuss our positions, listen to each other's logic and data, and use this to reach a reasonable conclusion."

When you get stuck in conflicting positions, reject any thoughts about forcing a solution. Nothing can be gained from imposing your will on a partner. Pressing the other firm to retreat, or making implied threats, lowers people's enthusiasm and causes them to withhold information and protect their interests.

Also avoid the temptation to resolve tough issues by splitting the difference, yielding for the sake of relations, or using quid pro quo tactics. Each sets a pattern of evading hard topics. If the pattern continues, creativity suffers. People feel compromised and, understandably, may grow bitter as they give in on positions with which they disagree. To avoid this pitfall, set a mutual goal of improving how you jointly resolve conflicts, and treat every difficulty as a chance to do that.

If you hear that others have become divided by a problem, don't take sides. Instead, encourage them to cool down and explore their differences. By favoring either view you reinforce separation. Besides, secondhand information is often biased and is always incomplete. The most dangerous polarization is when collective attitudes become confrontational. When that happens, people reinforce one another's negative perceptions and repair is the most challenging.

The earlier you foresee issues, the easier they will be to solve. To understand what lies ahead, discuss possible scenarios and how you will respond should they unfold. Some of your speculation may be wrong. But exploring together sharpens your sense of what each firm will do and what the limits are, which lowers the potential for later conflict. For instance, Ford and ABB negotiators identified likely future issues, such as trouble in getting government permits, and agreed on how they would proceed if these occurred.

Being creative and adjusting together does not mean you must refrain from taking fixed positions on all matters. Every company has to protect its central interests. Signaling what they are—even when the details cannot be disclosed—gives you credibility about what is important to you. So be frugal about what cannot be changed, and welcome new insights about everything else. Unresolvable disagreements set an alliance's boundaries. For instance, Wal-Mart would like Procter & Gamble to develop private-label items for the retailer to sell. Since this is an absolute nonstarter for P&G, it is outside their combined interest.

DESIGN A CONFLICT MANAGEMENT PROCESS

You can encourage understandings and reduce friction by making escalation of any issue to higher management levels a last resort. When people ask for edicts to settle issues between them, they lose credibility with one another and compromise their performance together.

To quash this problem, agree early on a conflict resolution process. A typical plan, like the one developed by SeaLand and Maersk, specifies that at every level individuals should solve their own problems according to what best serves their mutual objectives. Top management at both firms reinforces this approach by referring escalated issues back to the source and asking people how they tried to settle them. Sometimes, coaching by senior managers helps. To discourage people from burying issues, those at higher levels regularly ask about progress. More issues get escalated in those instances where local objectives remain fuzzy.

Questions that cannot be decided at lower levels go to the alliance steering committee. Since no one in either firm wants that to happen, there is a sense of urgency to resolve them before quarterly committee meetings. John Clancey and Ib Kruse, the carriers' CEOs, are the last resort.

Like SeaLand and Maersk, Canon and HP have found that including top executives as the last step in a conflict management plan helps ensure objectivity. "We try to stay cool," says Takashi Kitamura, Canon's lead executive, about solving tough issues at his level, "but it can be helpful for the presidents to be involved. If a person is 100 percent involved in the alliance, it may be difficult to have a broader perspective and be dispassionate about a problem."

If you have several alliances with one partner, consider creating a high-level function to help with the toughest issues. The person in this position—always a top executive—maintains separate relationships and steps in only if the matter seems to be getting out of hand. These duties are usually part of the executive's other responsibilities.

LIMIT WHAT YOU SHARE

Just as friends do not share everything in their personal lives, trusting relationships can be close and constructive without disclosing company secrets. Trust requires setting limits that respect your separate interests, being clear about what will and will not be revealed.

Canon's and HP's success builds on synergy between Canon's advances in laser engines and HP's product, software, and manufacturing know-how. The firms share only what is needed to coordinate their separate developments. In proprietary areas they discuss the interface between them—what each firm can do—but little about how they do it. They then seek the best way to connect their activities without revealing the know-how behind these. "We share a great deal of information with each other," says Kitamura. "But beyond a certain point we respect each other. We trust what they say they can do and they trust what we say and do not disclose. A lot is discussed but not our deepest secrets. We disclose more after we have applied for patents."

Even if both companies have well-defined practices for guarding sensitive data, you can build more comfort with a partner by limiting access to what you share. In developing their alliance, for instance, Wal-Mart and Procter & Gamble asked everyone on their interfirm team to sign a confidentiality agreement. This became a useful way to initiate new team members and helped them appreciate the value of confidentiality in the alliance, which encouraged more sharing.

FOR MORE ON INFORMATION SHARING, SEE PAGE 240

How much to disclose also depends on what happens to the information when an alliance ends. To avoid later misunderstandings, make this part of wider discussions about termination while you are planning an alliance.

AGREE ON HOW YOU WILL PART

At some point, even after a long and fruitful relationship, new circumstances—such as a change in either firm's ownership or priorities—may lead you to rethink the merits of continuing. Whatever the reason, separation is as legitimate as spinning off a long-held division.

When an alliance loses importance for either firm, quality, cycle times, and other performances suffer as people turn to more pressing matters. To avoid a prolonged and possibly harmful dispute if that time comes, agree at the outset on how you will part.[5]

Don't expect trust will help you work out termination to mutual satisfaction when one of you is heading for the exit. At that point, mutual need has probably evaporated. And even though you may still share good will, each firm will be looking out for itself. A joint venture between ABC, the broadcaster, and Brillstein-Grey Communications, illustrates. The firms did not develop an exit agreement, which became a problem when ABC was later acquired by Walt Disney. Frustrated by Disney's more aggressive style, Brillstein-Grey's management sold most of its stake in the venture to MCA, Disney's rival. With no exit agreement restricting the sale of either parent's interest, Disney's only resort was to get upset.[6]

FOR MORE ON CONTRACTS AND WORKING WITH ATTORNEYS, SEE PAGE 261

It may seem that discussing termination when you are trying to develop faith in each other could invite hard feelings and is the wrong way to begin. Even so, resolving potentially harmful pitfalls at the start—such as performance problems that could threaten continuation—helps build confidence that things will work out and raises trust.

For example, early in their discussions Canon and HP covered what would happen if HP chose to end the alliance. To protect its partner, HP agreed not to cut back its laser engine purchases by more than a certain percentage per month, absent a market collapse.

When your alliance will create an important business for either partner, the departure of one should involve compensation or allow the remaining firm to keep going. General Electric's Aircraft Engines Group and SNECMA, a French jet engine company, make jet engines together. They agreed, when their alliance began, to concur on future customer support before either could withdraw. They also confirmed that the departing partner would transfer a full set of drawings for its part of the engine, so the remaining partner could continue alone.

CHAPTER 4

ALIGN YOUR ORGANIZATIONS

■

Prodigy, once an on-line service alliance of Sears and IBM, came close to failure before they sold out to another company. The problem? Prodigy's parents had handicapped it from the start. They provided weak internal support, assigned top executives whose backgrounds did not fit the venture's objectives, and failed to give it needed authority on critical matters like pricing. An example: When Prodigy wanted to adjust its pricing to respond to America Online, rather than reach its own swift conclusions, it had to wait while Sears and IBM staffers engaged in separate pricing analyses that dragged on for more than a year.[1]

With your mutual objectives defined, the next step in forming an alliance is to get needed parts of each company to work in concert. Your objectives will be the focus of the joint business plan and will guide alignment within each firm—a step Prodigy missed. Start by defining the alliance's boundary.

PRACTICES THAT EARN TRUST

Clear Scope	*Internal Alignment*		*Realistic Plans*
Information	Creativity		Conflicts
Promises	People	Teams	Ethics

CONDITIONS FOR TRUST

Safeguards	*Commitment*	*Organizations*	*Continuity*
Mutual Need	Relationships	Joint Leaders	Objectives

DEFINE THE SCOPE

You and your partner will be most effective together when all aspects of your alliance meet the conditions for trust. For best results, exclude any technologies, functions, products, or markets for which your objectives conflict or other conditions cannot be met.

In planning the SeaLand–Maersk alliance, the American shipper wanted to retain its position of serving the U.S. military in the Pacific, and Maersk wanted to keep its strong role in Southeast Asia. So they accepted those separate objectives as being outside their alliance. Any rationalization of their combined fleets would exclude those areas.

Most airline alliances have been limited to activities like code sharing, common promotions, linking frequent-flier programs, and sharing airport facilities—all being relatively easy to separate when, as often happens in this business, an alliance breaks up.[2] While more significant changes such as combining marketing and baggage handling or rationalizing their aircraft fleets would create more value, they would be hard to reverse.

Alliances in other fast-changing settings also tend to have short life spans because shifting markets negate the rationale for staying together. This is not to imply that alliances must be brief. GE and SNECMA began the jet engine venture noted in Chapter 3 in the early 1970s, and they are still going strong. Canon and Hewlett-Packard started together at about the same time. In both cases, the partners probably could not do better if they were under one roof. Obviously, though, shorter horizons offer less chance to make internal adjustments and work on trust, which limits your potential.

The fact that some alliances are short-lived does not mean that longer is always better, however. Ford and Nissan jointly developed and manufactured their first minivan, which they badged and marketed separately, because their alliance required less investment than if each had entered the market on its own. They agreed from the beginning to break up after three years, which they did.

The vital exception—where a longer partnership is usually better—is alliances between customers and suppliers. Shifting markets are less threatening to these relationships than they are to other kinds. For instance, while changed conditions may cause airlines to rethink the cities they want to serve, they still need the same kinds of goods and services. With customers and suppliers, anticipating a long future together creates more reason to invest in trust, more cooperation, and more value.

EARN EACH OTHER'S COMMITMENTS

Before Maersk and SeaLand created their worldwide alliance, the firms had an agreement to share vessels on routes across the Pacific. In planning that earlier arrangement, SeaLand blocked Maersk out of the Alaska-to-Asia market. Since Maersk would be operating all the ships using the Panama Canal, it retaliated by restricting SeaLand's use of those vessels. Such tactics—more typical of transactions—weakened enthusiasm on both sides and hampered the carriers' rationalization of port facilities, costly fallout for both companies.

"We could have done better if we had said 'let's find the best way to maximize service in each market segment and be sure both firms' needs are met,'" observes one participant. "Instead, we were each trying to prevent the other from gaining any advantage. So we both lost." To their credit, as they moved ahead the firms shifted from a transaction to an alliance mentality.

If you are used to hard bargaining, you'll have to change your style for alliances. The payoff makes doing so worthwhile. For instance, during an early meeting between Ford and ABB about their Oakville, Ontario, paint plant, Ford's Vince Coletta told the assembled group that he wanted ABB to make an attractive profit on the project—which it did. Coletta's message, and his follow-though, motivated ABB to assign its best talent to the job. Similarly, Canon and Hewlett-Packard expect to look out for themselves. However, says an executive, "We are bounded in our discussions by an understanding that we need each other. If either firm says it is having real difficulties with an issue, the other is willing to help. Neither of us can afford to let the other carry an unfair load."

To win each other's commitment, make the entire arrangement attractive to both companies. This means recognizing all significant costs and benefits—including matters that can be expressed in financial terms and others that cannot.

In the originally promising but soon-grounded link between British Airways and USAir, the U.K. carrier invested $400 million in its financially destitute partner. But as welcome as the much-needed investment was, other aspects of the agreement became daily reminders that BA had won the upper hand.

At ticket counters and in advertisements throughout North America, USAir trumpeted its association with BA, while USAir staffers claimed BA gave their firm less visibility in the United Kingdom. Also, vast differences in BA's trans-Atlantic and USAir's domestic service levels "gave them a chance to remind us constantly that they were better than us," says one of the American carrier's managers. And labor problems, which raised its costs, put it behind in dividend payments to BA.

The final straw was that BA not only controlled the trans-Atlantic routes, which are the most profitable, but kept most of the profits. USAir protested that BA, whose large stake in USAir gave it a strong role on that carrier's board, had repeatedly frustrated its efforts to expand service to London.[3]

> DETAILED GUIDELINES FOR SHARING BENEFITS, COSTS, AND RISKS ARE ON PAGE 227

PLAN THE CONNECTIONS

As with any good business plan, one for an alliance begins with your objectives and describes important markets, products, resources, functions, finances, and timing sequences in enough detail so that those who will contribute know what is expected of them. Your plan should also spell out how both firms will actually cooperate.

Say, for example, a shared marketing objective calls for a seamless alliance interface with each customer. To achieve that, salespeople in both firms must be trained together. You and your partner thus have to plan the course content and decide who will do the training. If one firm's training staff can better meet your objectives, and the other's content can be easily transferred, it may make sense to assign the tasks accordingly.

In deciding what each firm will do, bear in mind that all alliance activities will have to be connected—either within or between your firms. The more new links you have to create, the harder the alliance will be to manage. If many activities will be involved, develop a flow chart that ties them all together. Before you assign tasks based on what is best for your stated objectives, consider organizational simplicity. Though often overlooked, streamling should be an objective for most alliances to ease governance, lower costs, and cut cycle times.

For instance, one hallmark of the GE–SNECMA venture is that the firms sought as few interfaces between them as possible. As a consequence, they smoothed coordination, shortened cycle times, and improved efficiency.

Every link between your firms will involve some degree of teamwork—such as making jet engine parts that must work together, or joint marketing research to define sales training requirements. Once you have found where teamwork is needed, the next step is to align each firm to support the teams. This involves providing necessary resources and authority, setting boundaries, and planning incentives to encourage your joint activities. Each team will also need defined links with the others and a clear reporting relationship to the alliance governing body.

If your alliance's activities will differ significantly from each firm's routines, it may be best to use a joint venture structure. (Chapter 6 details how to decide this.) Even then, a JV is easier to manage if the number of interfaces between it and the parent firms is limited.

DELEGATE AUTHORITY TO EACH INTERFACE

To avoid repeating what undermined Prodigy, give each interfirm team the ability to make operating decisions within its scope. Consider a pair of companies with a jointly owned plant in another country. One firm was organized by nation. Its country unit where the JV was located served the same market as the venture. Local management saw the JV as playing a key role in their performance. Having full authority from their parent, they responded quickly to whatever was needed.

However, local managers in the other firm reported to separate functional chiefs at headquarters, where printing decisions were made. At that level, the alliance had low priority and received little attention. Decisions often were delayed—sometimes indefinitely. The obvious solution would have been for headquarters to delegate needed authority locally. That did not happen, because each functional chief held on to his turf.

Such a failure to delegate plagues all too many alliances. Some companies that normally hand authority to lower levels fear that, by doing so when a partner is involved, they risk giving up control. That concern is groundless if you employ the trust conditions and practices detailed in this book.

A central reason for giving the interface control over an alliance's activities is to avoid saddling the alliance with two bureaucracies. An equally strong argument for delegation is that when team members cannot make decisions together, it weakens their mutual credibility. That breakdown, in turn, discourages collaboration and creativity.

Delegation makes alliances workable. Many large companies now have scores of alliances with customers, suppliers, and others. Smaller firms have a proportional share and the numbers are growing rapidly everywhere.[4] Unless the authority for every alliance is close to the operating interface, your links to others will end up in a few top management offices. That just doesn't work.

SET INTERNAL BOUNDARIES

Because conflict with other activities in either firm may harm an alliance, it has to be insulated—something Apple and IBM did not do in Kaleida, an ill-fated joint venture. In this alliance, the computer firms sought to develop software to allow personal computers and video games to use the same multimedia programs.

Inside Apple, one software group created roadblocks to Kaleida because it competed with the group's work. At the same time, Apple and IBM barred Kaleida from acquiring the tools that outside programmers would need to design Kaleida-based products. The parents were developing their own tools, which were not ready when Kaleida needed them. Without these, Kaleida's software wasn't worth much.[5]

There is nothing inherently wrong with internal competition. Better to cannibalize your own products than to let someone else do it. In fact, Canon and HP, respectively, have thriving bubble jet and ink jet printer businesses that are bitter competitors. In each company, the rival groups are clearly separated by distinct objectives, budgets, staff, and organizational structures. With an approach like this, Kaleida would have had a chance.

If you cannot separate cooperation from conflicting activities within your firms, it may be best to create a separate unit. While doing so drives up costs, these must be weighed against delays and underperformance due to internal strife. Ford and Nissan created a separate unit to plan their minivan, for instance, because locating their designers in either firm's design center would have compromised rival programs.

ALIGN PEOPLE'S INCENTIVES WITH YOUR OBJECTIVES

Since most people like to be rewarded for their efforts, aligning each partner's incentive systems with your shared objectives is another essential step toward trust.

That step was not taken at Procter & Gamble for the first decade of its alliance with Wal-Mart. P&G's corporate culture has long had an inward focus, and resisted changes in the firm's recognition and reward system. Consequently, people at the maker of Tide and Pampers often made short-term decisions that followed old patterns and ignored the companies' mutual interests. Corporate myopia was a particularly serious problem in the early days when getting results was critical to encourage the initiative. Short-sightedness has continued to slow progress since then.

Compare P&G with Ford and ABB, where project co-managers Jim Dixon and Rudy Golla adjusted the incentives of all relevant employees to support the paint plant project. Looking back, participants say that linking their incentives to project metrics reinforced the message from their joint leaders that both firms cared enough to reward them for success.

Effective teamwork with a partner does not require that you reinforce performance the same way. But you should motivate people to achieve the same objectives.

At HP, people are formally assessed on results both at business unit and at product and project levels. Although there are no measures on the alliance's performance per se, its importance at each level adequately reflects individuals' contributions. Also, HP's culture encourages an interpersonal style of being constructive, not misleading or burying issues. Canon, as a Japanese firm, has a more group-oriented culture and uses a combination of group and individual performance measures to encourage work toward their shared objectives.

DON'T PROMISE TOO MUCH

When GE and SNECMA began their jet engine venture in the early 1970s, the partners faced major market risks as well as resistance in each firm. To boost the chances for an early win and mitigate fallout, Gerhard Neumann, GE's vice president for aircraft engines, and René Ravaud, SNECMA's president, chose to limit their risks, including those related to implementation.

Rather than make a big investment in a new product—and to avoid large changes in both firms and difficult coordination between them—they started small by modifying an existing GE product. After they won early success, mutual confidence rose and they became bolder together. Today, these two partners make the best-selling commercial jet engine in the world.

Compare the GE–SNECMA alliance with one between Ford and Volkswagen in South America. The jet engine venture began with a single product, and all work was—and still is—done separately in each firm. Keeping their activities apart and coordinating between them has limited the need for integration, which would entail meshing their distinct cultures.

By contrast, the auto makers—whose defunct venture began with several vehicles—required a full merger of both firms' extensive product development, sourcing, quality, manufacturing, financial, and management resources there. To achieve all that meant blending American, Argentine, Brazilian, German, Ford, and VW cultures into a seamless organization that became the continent's largest employer.

This complicated affair called for consistent joint leadership of the heroic kind. Executives who can meet such challenges are a rare breed. Although outstanding people were appointed, they were soon moved to other places their firms considered more important. Discontinuities at the top led to friction in the ranks, inhibiting the venture's performance.[6]

Every day the newspapers carry stories about new alliances. And almost every piece describes a mega-deal that promises to transform some part of an industry. Why are big starts so popular if small is more manageable? Sometimes necessity drives the decision. Maersk and SeaLand faced global rivals and needed a worldwide alliance to compete. More often, both firms' strategic vision outpaces their thinking about implementation, or a desire for headlines overshadows a more reasoned approach.

In a basic sense, alliance building is a political process for each company. There are always skeptics and others who will lose ground to the initiative. Their resistance can be a problem. Still, doubters are useful because they can be converted—or at least quieted—by solid results, so in their way they encourage good performance.

This fact of organizational life bears a message: Whenever possible, set your initial objectives to gain easy and meaningful benefits sooner rather than later. Early wins hearten the believers and help convert the doubting Thomases. If you are tempted to hit a home run the first time at bat, consider just one task needed to build an alliance: realigning both firms' recognition and rewards systems. While that might be done easily and informally when a few people are involved, broad realignment across an organization may not be feasible. P&G's alliance with Wal-Mart suffered when the soap maker could not modify employees' incentives to garner support for the alliance.

Another reason to start on a small scale is that larger alliances involve more people, objectives, activities, and issues. If you have no choice but to begin on a grand scale, be prepared for future difficulties. Maersk and SeaLand faced this problem when they expanded from their regional link across the Pacific to a worldwide alliance. Although substantial trust had grown by then, the firms were unwilling to discuss all of their objectives, which caused early confusion and impeded progress. More candor—and improved performance—came as comfort grew over time.

YOU WILL FIND GUIDELINES FOR REALISTIC PLANNING ON PAGE 246

A third argument for starting small is to avoid giving advance notice to rivals. When you announce an alliance, the results may be months or even years away, giving competitors time to plan a response well before you hit the market. Starting small and avoiding public disclosure permits you to build strength in private.

RECOGNIZE THE PITFALLS OF DISCONTINUITY

"When we go through trials together we get a shared understanding that is much deeper than if someone else described the experience," says an alliance manager about her counterpart in another firm.

She makes a key point. The familiarity you develop with a colleague that helps you both progress comes from struggling with tough issues and finding a way forward together. When either of you moves—which is inevitable—the relationship will be hard to replace. Such discontinuities threaten many alliances and have ended numerous others.

In the ABB–Ford partnership, neither company has found a way to ensure continuity. "If someone new comes in who has not been down this road before there is no assurance of continuity with the style we have developed together," says Paul Bechard, one of the alliance's leaders.

Discontinuity also weakened and then undermined one of the world's earliest and then most prominent computer outsourcing alliances, that between IBM and Kodak. Those involved in the alliance attributed its early success to leaders Harry Beeth and Kathy Hudson, key executives at the partner companies. Beeth rotated away after six months, while Hudson was recruited to another firm. Each move left a gap in understandings that made alliance building more difficult. Shortly before Hudson moved on, Kodak's chairman asked her when the alliance would be at greatest risk. She replied that it would be the most vulnerable when the original leadership team one level below her left. They are gone now, and things haven't been the same.

Tom Muccio, P&G's lead for his firm's alliance with Wal-Mart, says that during the first decade of his tenure, no one paid attention to choosing his successor. Side-stepping the succession issue would have created a serious vacuum had Muccio departed. Further, the few P&G staffers who remained did so out of personal commitment—and despite a toll on their own careers.

Changes at lower levels prevent the firms from doing their best together. The most frequent shifts are by Wal-Mart buyers and P&G account executives who work with them. That interface is where plans become action. When new arrivals share no history, they have to cover old ground and tend to repeat others' mistakes, which slows progress. Also, while newcomers are always welcome, they tend to ignore what already has been done, which is harmful.

Although discontinuity is often seen as a uniquely American problem due to frequent job rotation in U.S. firms, it is a bane on alliances everywhere. Ask people at HP what might happen when Canon's Takashi Kitamura eventually leaves. The sobering answer from one senior executive: "This could be a problem—there is no good alternative."

Why don't companies ensure continuity? One reason could be that people are regarded as fungible in their jobs. More likely answers in some cultures are inattention to relationships or a tradition of working inside organizations where, if something goes wrong, the authority structure presumably can fix it. Whatever the explanation, there are ways to avoid—or at least greatly reduce—the problem.

PLAN FOR CONTINUITY

Your first defense against fallout from discontinuity should be to adopt the other trust conditions and practices discussed earlier. Freshmen in an alliance will be less disruptive if many of their colleagues recognize their need for one another and have excellent relationships, if objectives and organizations are aligned, and if joint leaders and teamwork are working well at policy and operating levels.

However, leadership shifts or frequent changes at lower levels, as the P&G/Wal-Mart alliance illustrates, may reduce performance or even end an alliance.

The best way to prevent that is to keep people at key interface posts far longer than job rotation practices usually permit. A key to the success of the Canon–HP alliance was that Doug Carnahan and Takashi Kitamura were joint leaders over the eight years of its fastest growth. "Our relationship made a difference because I trusted him," says Kitamura. Due to the strength of their bonds, HP asked Carnahan to maintain his contacts after he was reassigned. Like an esteemed mentor, his role was to get involved in specific issues if there was an escalation.

Another plus for the alliance has been that almost all Canon managers who work with HP have participated for more than twenty years. Continuity and the many friendships that developed have helped them through tough times.

The kind of tenure Carnahan and Kitamura enjoyed may compromise individuals' growth opportunities unless you can make interface positions more attractive. One way to do so is to create career ladders at the interface and provide latitude in job grading, salaries, and responsibilities. This practice worked well for some supplier alliances at Motorola until management shifts ended it. But as P&G's experience with Wal-Mart illustrates, the electronics firm is not alone. Efforts at P&G to create career ladders on its side have not yet materialized. Like many companies, P&G rewards breadth of experience, not continuity.

What has helped the soap maker and retailer has been that the operating norms developed in their early team-building efforts have taken hold. Not only are the norms reinforced at high levels, they are introduced at interface meetings attended by newcomers and informally included in performance measures. The process gets people on common ground fast and helps keep holdouts within bounds. But frequent turnover remains a problem, and the norms are not yet widely recognized in both firms.

If continuity is impossible, the next best response is managing transitions proactively. In an alliance between San Miguel, a Philippine food and beverage firm, and Yamamura Glass, of Japan, lead executives Ricky Gomez and Akira Yamaguchi involve others from both firms in multilevel relationships. They regularly bring together middle managers and high-potential junior managers to build connections and understandings and ease transitions when personnel change. Before anyone is appointed to a key alliance position, Gomez and Yamaguchi discuss the candidates to be sure they are both comfortable with the person selected.

At Canon, experiences with HP are thoroughly documented, which helps ensure continuity in the Japanese firm. Further, Canon staffers slated for more responsibility in the alliance are identified beforehand and brought to all relevant meetings with HP to sit in the background and watch, listen, and learn. After seeing how well this worked, HP adopted the same practice. "We want them to know what is going on and how we work together," says HP's Chuck Walter.

Before someone from HP joins a committee, a member from that firm coaches the individual on what the issues are, how they have been handled in the past, and the history of the relationship. The new arrival is also included in social gatherings with Canon away from business meetings to help build interpersonal relationships. HP's newcomers to the alliance travel to Japan specifically to build rapport with their counterparts before coming on board.

Complementing these continuity practices, HP's culture reinforces desirable behavior so people usually enter the alliance on a positive note. The company also phases departures to prevent staff from leaving en masse. Many people have a long history with Canon, which helps stabilize understandings. While some steering committee members rotate off every two years, others have stayed far longer.

Both Canon and HP have implicit policies that discourage people from upsetting their alliance. An executive in another company whose supplier alliances have been high performers for decades observes that "people who do not respect the continuity of supplier relations do not succeed here."

Whatever you do to get continuity, there is one fundamental principle: Expect each individual coming into an alliance to make relationship building an early personal initiative. Some people look at a new job as a chance to apply fresh thinking, which can be useful. But they overlook the fact that ideas flow best when people have first learned how to listen to one another.

THESE AND OTHER WAYS TO BUILD CONTINUITY ARE SUMMARIZED ON PAGE 247

"Soon after I arrived," says the new co-leader of an established alliance between two rivals, "Barry and I had an incredibly deep, multihour discussion. It really helped us understand the environment each of us is in, and the pressure each of us is under. Neither of us revealed anything proprietary. We reviewed the history of the alliance, the commitments our firms had made, and our objectives regarding governance. We talked about trust and integrity, and our firms' perceptions of each other, including our ethics.

"We also confirmed that we were powerful rivals and that nothing in our cooperation would diminish this. Each of us remains strongly committed to taking market share away from the other—today, tomorrow, and forever."

CHAPTER 5

ORCHESTRATE MANY UNITS

■

When a company is made up of closely related businesses, allying them with another firm's similarly related units can produce far more value than connecting just one part from each. The trick is getting the crew members of all those businesses to pull together.

Tom Muccio, head of Customer Business Development, Procter & Gamble Worldwide, learned that painfully in the early days of building his firm's alliance with Wal-Mart. Says Muccio: "I felt like a deep sea diver, and above me the captain was telling people to start the air pump while others were standing on the hose."

The best way to create a multiunit alliance is to start with a single unit from each firm, adding more after a successful launch. That is how Hewlett-Packard and Canon began their laser printer relationship. Initially, the firms linked Canon's one laser development center with HP's sole laser printer division. As volume grew, they added structure, so that today Canon has three laser

PRACTICES THAT EARN TRUST

Clear Scope	Realistic Plans	*Internal Alignment*
Information	Creativity	Conflicts
Promises	People Teams	Ethics

CONDITIONS FOR TRUST

Safeguards	*Commitment*	*Organizations*	*Continuity*
Need	Relationships	Leaders	Objectives

development centers and a cartridge group, while HP has three corresponding laser printer divisions.

Most of this alliance's activities are between center-division pairs, which helps teamwork. Further, Canon's development centers are cost centers, while HP's divisions are profit centers. Those differences help the firms balance short-term and long-term objectives.

In alliances involving several units at the start, the process cannot be as neat or your initial alignment as complete as at Canon–HP. It is unlikely that all units will regard the alliance as a priority, or that joint leadership will emerge simultaneously at each interface. The task is harder still if your organizations have different structures.

Three cases illustrate key issues in such alliances. Two—Wal-Mart/Procter & Gamble and Kodak–IBM—involve customer-supplier pairs. The third—SeaLand–Maersk—is between rivals. Among them are varying degrees of globalization, organizational differences, and corporate and local participation. Each alliance succeeded by any reasonable measure, including the firms' own objectives. How these firms overcame their barriers, where they faltered, and why one alliance ended offer useful lessons for building complex alliances.[1]

BUILD TRUST ACROSS ALL UNITS

What makes a collection of units an alliance is that their combined performance exceeds what they could do if they were linked by transactions alone. To get the most value from the whole, every link must surpass what a transaction between the connected parts could do.

For that, each unit must satisfy the trust conditions and use the trust practices described in earlier chapters. For instance, the participation of every unit must be seen as essential and relationships must work well at all interfaces. Further, joint leaders and common objectives must govern the collective operation of the units. Additionally, all units must be aligned and benefits distributed fairly to encourage each unit's commitment.

In the alliance between Procter & Gamble and Wal-Mart, the firms' overall objectives include more benefits for consumers and better profits for both companies. Because all business units—P&G refers to them as product categories—sell to Wal-Mart, all participate in the alliance. Key activities include continuous stretching in logistics, marketing research, and other areas that cross-cut both firms. If any P&G unit chose to go its own way, the firms' collective performance would be compromised. Attaining those objectives has required the consumer goods maker to realign all of its units. To the extent that has not gone far enough, results have suffered.

In addition to benefiting from cooperation across all units, you can do even better by orchestrating fewer units to serve more focused objectives. To illustrate, P&G and Wal-Mart have gained from joint marketing research that covers all P&G brands, and by linking their information systems to support the entire alliance. At the same time, executives in individual product categories at P&G (like the one for soap and detergents) work with their counterparts at Wal-Mart on objectives that are both specific to their situation and consistent with the firms' overall shared objectives.

GUIDELINES FOR MULTIUNIT ALLIANCES ARE SUMMARIZED ON PAGE 276

AVOID PAINFUL STARTS

"We wanted to change from an adversarial relationship where we threw nuclear bombs at each other to one that was productive for both companies," says Wal-Mart/P&G leader Tom Muccio. Improve it they did.

Over the first decade of their partnership, Wal-Mart's volume with P&G grew more than tenfold, to exceed $4 billion in 1998—a growth rate surpassing those of their separate businesses. Both firms' gross margins also have gained from their relationship, thanks to large savings from combining logistics across their businesses, better shared understandings of and abilities to satisfy consumer needs, and fresher products on the shelf.

Historically, like many consumer goods firms, Procter & Gamble built strong brands and used them in its advertising to win consumer loyalty. Retailers—P&G's direct customers—were regarded simply as warehouses on the way to consumers. That changed when retailers grew and shifted the power balance. One early consequence was rising friction, in this case between P&G and Wal-Mart. Aiming to improve Wal-Mart's margins, Sam Walton, the retailer's founder, proposed the alliance to P&G's top management.

Initial Efforts Sought Early Wins

A fundamental problem before their alliance was that P&G's promotional discounting conflicted with Wal-Mart's everyday low pricing. Further, management in each P&G unit controlled its ties to Wal-Mart. Each had its own promotions, with no corporate-wide coordination. Such fragmentation exacerbated the retailer's problems, causing it to lose money on its P&G business.

Because Wal-Mart's pricing could not accommodate P&G's promotions, the retailer at times featured rival brands, putting a crimp in P&G divisions' sales to Wal-Mart. To meet their volume targets the units focused more on other retailers, which made Wal-Mart unhappy. The reactions and counteractions put the firms in a downward spiral together.

The first job of the two-company team charged with building the alliance was to identify problematic practices and to find solutions. Sam Walton's early vision for the alliance mainly involved logistics. Following that theme—and to switch to a healthier course—the firms improved the logistics for diapers by managing their inventories and delivery as one connected system. They also changed P&G's pricing to give the retailer more price stability.

The team underscored the firms' new commitment by discussing what each company wanted the other to do, and made it happen. Wal-Mart, for instance, wanted to stock its stores to reflect consumer buying patterns in each geographic region; P&G used its regional data to accomplish that.

Nothing came easily. P&G traditionally focused more on promoting its brands than on meeting retailers' needs. Consequently, management in product categories, which control the brands, has been the political heavyweight within the firm. The alliance leaders came from traditional sales, which carried far less weight. Further, when the alliance began, P&G had less than 2 percent of its total volume with Wal-Mart.

The firms' concept was to define a broad interface between them, expecting to use it to jointly manage and improve company-wide tasks including logistics, order replenishment, computer systems, finance, and marketing research. To implement these activities, operating authority should have moved from P&G's product categories to the interfirm team. But the alliance was countercultural for P&G. Interface team members had little authority for the alliance's first two years.

Despite endorsement from corporate management, team leaders struggled to win top-level attention in the product categories. Division middle managers—encouraged by P&G's culture—became a filter between the team and higher management levels, resisting what they did not like by delaying key tasks.

"The longer it took me to get back to Wal-Mart, the more Wal-Mart wondered if I was empowered to make this work," says Muccio. "The filter also caused compromises—we had to satisfy people in the middle to get things done. That reduced the value of what we could do in the alliance. Sometimes Wal-Mart gave up on an initiative when we could not get our organization to respond." By contrast, needed changes at Wal-Mart were easier because decisions involved fewer people and organizational levels.

What probably saved this alliance from early rejection by P&G's corporate immune system was that some of the firm's most entrepreneurial and politically skilled talent was assigned to the interface. For the first two years, they made progress through a combination of lobbying and politicking, leveraging results to get more authority as they needed it.

One initial task was to align the firms' accounting systems to allocate savings to relevant internal units. The benefits from that change, plus unit revenue gains from collaboration, shifted attitudes there. Still, even today, product category management only goes as far as they believe they must to support the alliance. Their business with Wal-Mart is about 10 percent of their volume, offering alternatives for growth that give P&G more control of the outcome.

Developing a Formal Interface

In most alliances involving direct cooperation, the work is done within each firm and coordinated by various teams that meet as necessary. For P&G and Wal-Mart, the intensity of their joint planning, research, and coordination requires a permanent interface group.

Objectives for the interface cover everything that connects the firms: growth of P&G sales to Wal-Mart, faster inventory turns, increased volume in product categories, and improved store segmentation. Strategies for meeting these objectives are developed through ongoing data analysis and local experimentation. The divisions continue to have the lead for activities like product development, marketing, and brand management that create value for consumers.

Because results depend on cooperation between P&G people at the interface and in the divisions, accountability is shared. For interface objectives such as sales growth and inventory turns, the weightings are 60 percent for the team and 40 percent for the divisions. The ratio is reversed where the divisions have the lead.

To do the work and connect into their firms, each P&G division and Wal-Mart business unit is represented on the interface team. Team members also help each company understand the other's practices and priorities, and how the interface works. As necessary, they blow the whistle on fouls. For instance, if someone in Wal-Mart has a pricing issue and tries to pressure relevant P&G executives, or if someone at P&G tries to contravene Wal-Mart's pricing policy, the interface team points out that such actions are unacceptable.

Leading the interface team are a steering committee and subcommittees that work on functional issues like logistics or specific projects. As necessary, they draw on talent from both firms for specific tasks.

Narrower objectives—such as improved pricing and merchandising for paper goods by region and store size—are served by direct contacts between respective P&G and Wal-Mart units. Joint stretch objectives are set for each product category, with priorities determined by Wal-Mart. Many improvement initiatives begin in a single product category or geographic region, and are adopted more widely if they succeed.

Everything is coordinated by the interface team to serve the overall objectives of maximizing total sales and reducing total cost between the companies. To avoid having category managers cut deals that serve their units at others' expense, the interface limits their access to higher levels at Wal-Mart.

Success Brought Improved Alignment

Significant results have given the interface team leverage to win more support. The team now has direct channels to top management, and as necessary bypasses P&G staffers who are being unreasonable. Further, P&G has been reducing the number of staff in the middle to help the alliance, as well as to lower costs and shorten cycle times.

A monthly letter from the interface team to P&G's CEO brings unresolved alliance issues into the open. The team also uses its annual report to both firms' top managements to surface other issues that impede progress. Embarrassing to those who resist needed change, such communications help overcome the roadblocks.

Barriers to Higher Trust and Performance

Despite the impressive results of this alliance and changes made to support it, political and cultural factors inhibit the firms from doing better together. One ongoing problem is that Wal-Mart has not assigned a full-time leader to its side of the interface, leaving the post vacant most of the time. That has hindered priority setting across the alliance and distracted attention from more substantive work to firefighting.

Internal alignment is another difficulty: The firms' recognition and reward systems have not caught up with their shared objectives. At P&G these systems are still focused internally, which leads to conflicts between the alliance and internal priorities. While those at the interface accept these objectives, many others within the firm do not. Even at the interface, traditional P&G incentives reign. For instance, P&G team leaders' attempt to promote a logistics and inventory expert who had made outstanding contributions failed, because he had not met the company's standard promotion criteria.

Another needed alignment is in marketing research for the Wal-Mart account. To deliver P&G's best abilities, its staff at the interface must go through an arduous process. First, they need company approvals for more funds and an okay to spend these on marketing research. Then, they must go to P&G's marketing research function for staffing. Finally, they have to negotiate with that function on how to do the research.

Building on its Wal-Mart experience, Procter & Gamble has pondered creating a number of profit centers, each focused on a major retail customer. Like the firm's interface with Wal-Mart, the centers would cut across all P&G product categories to give every retailer tailor-made solutions. However, implementation would require assigning needed authority to each interface, and would shift the internal balance of power to being more customer-driven. It will not be easy.

WIN LOCAL ACCEPTANCE

Unless your firm has highly centralized authority, many decisions are made by individual units, to respond more quickly to opportunities. However, too much independence can make building a multiunit alliance akin to getting cats to march in a straight line. The job is harder when units are geographically dispersed, because distance and cultural differences from headquarters reinforce local autonomy.

That was the situation when Kodak moved its internal computer operations into an alliance—still a rarity in outsourcing—
with IBM. Kodak objectives included directing the firm's capital
investments more toward its core businesses and away from data
processing, along with improving applications and increasing service levels. The film maker also wanted to establish a common
global technology for its computer operations and make global applications more consistent.

Plans called for seven regional data centers serving six Kodak
business units worldwide. Since most value creation was expected
to be regional, local cooperation would be the heart of the alliance.
The benefits of a global alliance with one supplier, compared with
working with several firms, included more internal consistency
and the ability to more easily transfer lessons between units worldwide. Having a single supplier also would ease Kodak's expected
consolidation of its data centers around the world.

During its heyday, high service levels made the U.S.-based
data center the country's best performer. The alliance also
achieved exceptional results overseas. For IBM, which enjoyed
lower marketing costs and a long-term profit stream, the greatest
benefits were new competitive skills and broader opportunities.
In fact, the alliance was the launchpad for IBM's global outsourcing business.[2]

In one respect alliance building here was easier than at P&G
and Wal-Mart. Once Kodak decided to outsource, its business units
could not continue as before. What made the task difficult was that
Kodak and IBM cultures and management systems emphasized
local autonomy, and each region was unique in many ways. Local
acceptance depended on attitudes toward buyer-supplier relationships, concerns about people leaving Kodak for IBM, local
policies or work rules, local views on the importance of information
technology, the effects on local profit and loss, and more. In
Europe, for example, Kodak employees saw the linkup with IBM as
a transaction rather than an alliance, and cost reduction was more
important than application consistency.

During the alliance's early years, Vaughn Hovey and Frank
Palm, respectively of Kodak and IBM, were joint leaders at the

corporate level. Like Muccio at P&G, they were not given authority to mandate participation within their firms. Even if they had this, local cooperation depended on building trust in each region.

Corporate Leadership Defined the Course

To prepare the stage, senior management at Kodak and IBM blessed the alliance and set the tone. In a meeting attended by representatives from both firms Kay Whitmore, then Kodak's chairman and CEO, told Palm that "if you do not make a decent profit from the alliance you will not get the support of your senior management, and we will not get the service we need."

"That comment was incredibly important to me," Palm recalls, "because many people in Kodak had pressured me to give them an outstanding deal at my expense."

Rather than launch the whole global affair at once, the firms began with Kodak's data processing in the United States, setting up shop near its Rochester, New York, headquarters. Results were then used to attract wider interest. Hovey and Palm traveled together and brought people from both firms around the world to Kodak, to help them understand the merits. Hovey also made regular presentations to Kodak data managers worldwide, sharing monthly progress with them. Selling Kodak and IBM units on the alliance was jointly managed by both firms.

How the seed planted in Rochester also took root in Japan illustrates the way local leadership built on the corporate initiative and nourished the trust that led to success there.

Local Leaders Delivered Their Regions

As the U.S. part of the alliance bore fruit, Hovey's and Palm's joint selling sparked interest in Japan. When Al Chase, director of information systems for Kodak's Asia Pacific Region, learned of the results he began looking for local opportunities. At about the same time, John Henrickson, director of operations for IBM's service business in Japan, concluded that the prospects for an outsourcing business were good. Soon after that, Chase approached Henrickson to discuss a possible alliance.

Both were interested, but hurdles stood in the way. Outsourcing of data processing was new to the Japanese market, and IBM staffers were reluctant to make needed changes. For Kodak Japan, IBM rivals were offering lower prices. At IBM Japan, the business model used with Kodak in the United States was not applicable due to differences in labor rates, facility costs, ownership and leasing of assets, and a host of other factors.

For both groups the interface would be much broader than when Kodak simply bought hardware from IBM. Different skills and people were required, and there were serious questions about how to manage such a wide-ranging relationship and ensure profitability.

Still, the ingredients for trust and success existed. Henrickson saw a potentially large market for IBM Japan, while Chase had a clear need at Kodak. Both believed an alliance would create more value than a commercial relationship. They also had a shared vision of the results, knew solutions had to be crafted to overcome the roadblocks, and understood they had to lead the process together. Their respective bosses, Bob Smith at Kodak and Hideki Kurashige at IBM, also recognized and supported the initiative. To go further, they drew on the experience in Rochester.

After his initial discussion with Chase, Henrickson brought IBM Japan staff to the United States to visit with management in the computer firm's service business, spending several days in Rochester with Palm, Hovey, and others. Discussions focused on how the alliance worked and was managed, relevant processes, necessary changes and how these were made, and the need for training.

Equipped with these understandings, Chase and Henrickson put the Japanese alliance together. "We were very candid with each other," says Henrickson. "I told him that if we stumble along the way, it will not be because we are not committed. We trusted each other as champions and catalysts. Real success depended on a paradigm shift at operating levels in both firms. Throughout the negotiations we kept encouraging people to find creative ways around the barriers." During the final negotiations, Palm sent a key person from Rochester to be sure the Asian part of the alliance fit into what was being done in the United States.

Echoing Kodak chairman Kay Whitmore's early tone, Chase encouraged IBM's commitment. "It will be critical that IBM make a decent profit," he remarked in one meeting. "This is a long-term relationship and Kodak cannot afford to lose their commitment."

Within the Asia-Pacific region, as in other regions, a management committee of local Kodak and IBM people met twice a year. Below that, a regional operating committee met monthly to review progress. "By far the greatest benefit is produced by these committees," says Chase. "They look at issues on a regular basis and identify alternate solutions. This would not be possible in a commercial relationship."

How Commitments Were Won

In P&G's alliance with Wal-Mart the focus is on the U.S. market, and each firm has a single budget for all of its domestic activities. Accordingly, each P&G unit has gained as its U.S. revenues from the retailer grew, and each gets its share of the cost savings. By contrast, although Kodak and IBM had a global alliance, they did not have global budgets, so benefits had to be shared regionally.

Further, converting to the new arrangement with IBM and joining new projects would cost some Kodak business units more than others. If the higher-cost units did not participate they would miss the benefits, capacity use in each region would be lower, and other units in the region could not get full value from the alliance.

To cross this barrier, Hovey kept a small part of the cash flow in a special account. He used the funds to reduce the high transition costs for U.S. units whenever that was in corporate's best interest. Similarly, IBM offered more benefits to individual Kodak units to win their participation in projects, if doing so was best for both firms in the longer run.

Kodak's budget structure largely prevented use of the special funds overseas, which may have discouraged some transitions there. In each region local commitments depended on attitudes like Chase's. Still, Kodak did not have local budgets to help units overcome hurdles in their regions.

Assembling the Global Alliance

For IBM and Kodak, frequent contacts between the regions helped bring them closer together. For instance, during monthly conference calls between the IBM teams in Rochester and Tokyo, sites of the two largest alliance operations, people shared ideas and kept each other updated on progress.

Both firms also sought a global governance framework, but failed. With Rochester representing 70 percent of the alliance's volume, it was hard to attract support from other regions. Further, Kodak's top management was in transition and the alliance did not get the attention that might have made a difference.

In lieu of a global board, the North American regional management committee became a platform for driving the worldwide vision forward. It had high-level representatives from both firms and, while most were from the United States, attendees also came from other regions. Getting regional participation was important, because it avoided creating the impression that this was entirely a corporate affair. To show the flag and help keep the dialogue flowing, Hovey and Palm sometimes went to other regional meetings.

Hovey encouraged global participation by persuading Kodak's business units to join the alliance for two years. After that, if they were not making clear progress against the objectives, they could leave the alliance, but only if they could show that doing so was a better way to meet those objectives. Although participation varied by region, all Kodak business units in Rochester joined the alliance and stayed with it. Among local units that joined, none left.

The alliance met most of its objectives, except for consistency in global applications. That would have required global governance, more compatible priority setting among the regions, and global alliance budgets in Kodak and IBM. Looking ahead, Kodak expects to move from mainframes to servers in its data centers, which could change its relationship with IBM.

WORKING WITH DISCORDANT STRUCTURES

If placed side by side, Maersk and SeaLand would look like a patchwork quilt. Not only are they major rivals, but their structures and operating philosophies are vastly different. One is highly centralized; the other is not. Adding to the difficulty, legal and regulatory factors limit the alliance to five years—a time frame that inhibits their ability to rationalize port facilities (an important cost factor) and to align their organizations in other ways.

These contrasts keep some parts of both firms whose cooperation is needed from making the alliance a priority. The disparities also have hampered the development of trust in parts of the alliance and made implementation there akin to navigating close to a rocky coast at night.

Despite their enormous differences, the two shippers not only have surpassed their ambitious cost-reduction targets but keep bettering them, and have greatly increased their service frequency and geographic coverage. What they have done to build trust—and where the limits have been—offer useful lessons if you are contemplating an alliance with a firm whose structure does not mesh well with your own company's.

The container firms' primary overall objective is to reduce operating costs. A second is to respond to changing demand. The scope of this alliance begins and ends at their container terminals located at ports around the world. Separately and independently each firm markets, prices, and sells its own services, picking up containers from customers and delivering them to nearby terminals, where they are placed on vessels. After a container reaches the distant port, the originating shipper delivers it to the final destination. From the time the container arrives at the first terminal until it is picked up at the second, the alliance handles it.

Like many other global alliances, Maersk–SeaLand has a regional emphasis. For one thing, competition tends to be regional. Also, each region has distinct shipping patterns and regulatory requirements. Accordingly, the land-based parts of the alliance are organized and managed by region, while the firms' worldwide vessel network is managed globally. These arrangements focus on competition in each region, and enable the shippers to adjust their global fleet to meet demand while managing overall fleet costs.

Below the alliance executive committee, a network planning committee and four regional committees oversee their respective activities. Each regional committee consists of two members, who are the partners' top executives for that region. In Maersk's case, regional executives have a dotted-line relationship with the firm's representative on the alliance's executive committee. SeaLand's regional executives, by contrast, have a solid-line reporting relationship, simplifying that firm's decision making.

Compatibility on the Oceans Facilitates Cooperation

Cooperation in the firms' combined vessel network is far better than that for many land-based activities, largely because it has been easier to meet the trust conditions discussed in earlier chapters. Accordingly, much of the gain from the alliance has come from network improvements.

Being separate from the competitive and contrasting land-based operations, people involved in managing the vessel network have a stronger sense of mutual need. Rather than having to cope with structural differences, Ron Sforza and Jesper Kjadegaard, co-leaders of the network committee, share clear responsibilities for network management and have built a solid relationship. The same structural simplicity has made the definition of network objectives straightforward. Since vessels are easily redeployed, adjusting the fleet is effortless compared with improving port operations.

Differences on Land Limit Coherence

Contrasting structures keep the shippers from articulating clear regional objectives and thus limit their alignment on land. SeaLand is organized around shipping lanes across the oceans, while Maersk's structure is based on the major continents. Each company also has unique substructures in various countries and geographic areas.

In many parts of the world, the same individuals in each firm have marketing and operating responsibilities. Due to the five-year term of the alliance and low volume in some places, it has not been feasible to separate those responsibilities by creating new positions. In fact, the alliance has brought Maersk and SeaLand people who wear both hats closer together at many ports. That proximity heightens the sense of conflict and discourages cooperation.

Operating differences pose yet another barrier to cooperation. Although the firms have tried to set objectives and metrics to govern local activities, they have not succeeded in most places. For example, at a terminal in one port SeaLand may use containers with frames and wheels, which are easy to move, while in an adjacent terminal Maersk may use stackable containers without wheels. The reverse situation may exist at another port. SeaLand uses global processes for cost and activity management; Maersk does that on a terminal-by-terminal basis.

One result of contrasting styles and structures is that even when shared regional objectives exist, accountabilities and priorities often are not—and cannot be—aligned. On a given task, one unit in each company frequently must interface with several units of the other. A different arrangement may be necessary for the next task. This discordance stymies the execution of joint activities in each firm.

Progress in the land-based parts of the alliance has been best where the firms' structures are most alike, and where sales and marketing are separated from operations. In regions where differences are pronounced, shared objectives have been elusive and delegation into the Maersk and SeaLand organizations has been difficult. Local teamwork is consequently weak or nonexistent, leaving much of the initiative for planning and executing cost reduction in the hands of the regional committees.

Within its region, each committee sets priorities to lower port costs and brainstorms to find ways to do that. Each committee is effective to the extent that it works as a team. In some places, though, these efforts are hampered by vague objectives, problems between joint leaders, and fuzzy boundaries between cooperation and competition.

Often, ad hoc subcommittees are assembled at regional, country, or port levels to focus on specific tasks like increasing the number of container moves per hour at a port. When structural differences are large, the committees first must identify who should connect with whom and bring them together. Implementation in those areas depends largely on whether each firm's incentives reinforce a particular task. When reinforcement is weak, committee members have to reach into their organizations to get things done or, if necessary, appeal to higher levels.

Every country unit in each firm is expected to meet periodically with its counterpart to find ways to make local activities more cost effective and customer friendly. How well this works depends on structures, personal attitudes, local reinforcement, alignment of the firms' recognition and reward systems, and whether each unit will gain in the process.

Earning Commitments

The companies tried to develop an overall gainsharing formula that would permit each one to benefit from any change, and thereby encourage cost savings. But they could not find a satisfactory arrangement.

Their basic idea was simple: Find a systematic way to create incentives in both firms to direct every activity to the lowest-cost facility. However, this solution would create a capacity problem at the other firm. While that might not matter if the alliance were long term, their short time frame discourages either firm from closing any facility that might be needed if the alliance ended. Each carrier also sees value in having control over a port facility, to better serve its customers. Further, structural differences prevent them from developing worldwide or even regional formulas, and keep them from agreeing on how long cost equalization will take.

Lacking a gainsharing arrangement, cost reduction has not been systematic. If one firm perceives it is getting less value than the other on an initiative, it will not support the initiative unless benefits sharing can be worked out. Even when both firms will gain, structural differences affect how the benefits are distributed.

For instance, each SeaLand division is a profit center, and each profit center has separate cost centers for ship and land activities. At Maersk both the ship and land activities are profit centers. Thus for SeaLand, an alliance initiative involving a ship or land unit in the same division may incur a cost, but still be attractive to the profit center to which it belongs. By contrast, the same initiative may benefit a Maersk ship service and incur more cost in the land-based unit.

These factors make it harder to get agreement between the Maersk units. They have to negotiate, with one Maersk unit paying the other to implement an initiative involving both units.

SeaLand usually does not have to do such rebalancing within its organization because its profit centers have broader geographic scope, and most rationalization occurs within a single division. When a prospective change would involve more than one profit center in each firm, it is extremely hard to adopt, since both sides have to make internal adjustments to get this done. "It is the hardest part of our alliance to manage," says an executive. "It is the lawn mower that goes down the street cutting a strip in every lawn."

Those at lower levels see themselves as winners or losers, depending on how a specific rationalization affects their local situation. Though the firms have not redistributed corporate or regional financial benefits to encourage local participation, that is being considered as competition drives them to find more ways to lower operating costs.

The Global Part

Aside from occasionally moving vessels from one region to another, there is no multiregional cooperation between Maersk and SeaLand, and none is sought. However, the firms are developing worldwide standards for performance improvement and simplification. Having a global template with common cost categories will permit detailed benchmarking between the regions in each category. Developing that requires consistent cost objectives and metrics worldwide. Getting to this stage has been inhibited by regional differences.

Maersk and SeaLand are also developing global stretch objectives. For example, in stevedoring they want each port to improve its performance to thirty-two container moves per hour. The template will spotlight more opportunities to stretch.

CHAPTER 6

REINFORCE TRUST WITH STRUCTURE

■

As both organizations prepare to work together, you must also choose an alliance structure. The arrangement you adopt will include a governing body to guide the alliance. Beyond that, more senior managers set or approve objectives, appoint people to governance positions, help ensure internal support, ratify commitments, and are a last resort for tough decisions.

Avoid the common but mistaken notion that structure alone builds trust. No organizing framework can create mutual need, grow interpersonal relationships, ensure that competent leaders are assigned, or cause objectives to be aligned.

Still, structure will enhance trust if used appropriately. In any organization the purpose of formal structure, if joined by apt behavior,

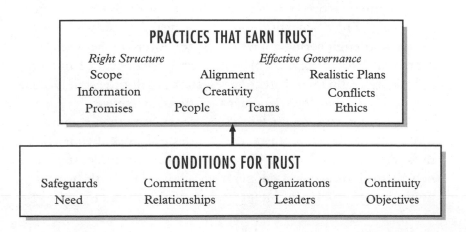

PRACTICES THAT EARN TRUST		
Right Structure		*Effective Governance*
Scope	Alignment	Realistic Plans
Information	Creativity	Conflicts
Promises	People Teams	Ethics

CONDITIONS FOR TRUST			
Safeguards	Commitment	Organizations	Continuity
Need	Relationships	Leaders	Objectives

is to reinforce desired patterns. Structure has the same effect with alliances.

DIRECT COOPERATION

For good reason, direct cooperation is the most common alliance form. Because it does not involve a separate organization, it is the easiest to set up, and permits close operating links and the shortest cycle times between partners. Direct cooperation can support a wide variety of activities, ranging from a brief joint project to large complex alliances like that of Canon/Hewlett-Packard in laser printers and SeaLand–Maersk in container shipping. These factors also make a direct connection the preferable structure for customer-supplier alliances.

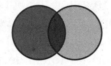

Direct Cooperation

To plan the interface between your firms, consider how you want people to interact. For HP and Canon, most activities are within each firm. Staffers visit one another as needed. In the Ford–ABB paint plant alliance, much of the design work required joint creativity and quick decisions. So during that phase, ABB team members moved out of their offices to be on-site with staffers from Ford. The co-location vastly improved coordination, innovation, and engineering approvals. At the interface between Wal-Mart and Procter & Gamble, there is a great deal of ongoing coordination and joint marketing research. A full-time staff located near Wal-Mart headquarters manages those activities.

Direct cooperation is a less effective structure than a joint venture under certain circumstances. It does not work if your objectives require both firms to invest in the same resource, such as a new plant. Nor is direct cooperation advisable if both firms' activities must be closely integrated, or if the alliance cannot be shielded from conflicts in the partner firms.

Direct cooperation is also the wrong structure for alliances involving significant differentiation from either partner's normal business. Just as you would create a new unit within your firm to support a departure from your current products, markets, or policies, joint ventures do the same in alliances.

FOR MORE DETAIL ON CHOOSING A STRUCTURE, SEE PAGES 250–260

Canadian brewers Labatt and Molson are a classic example. The firms jointly own and operate Brewers Retail Inc., an Ontario business that distributes beer through its own stores and to others. As a chain of retail outlets, BRI engages in activities that differ substantially from those of its parents. A joint venture structure accommodates this.

Another drawback of direct ties is that they can prevent you from capturing all the potential benefits of an alliance, causing underperformance. In computer outsourcing, the usual arrangement is one of direct cooperation. The customer shifts its data operations to the supplier, which uses its expertise to deliver better cost and service than what the customer could do alone. Typically, the supplier may keep any savings beyond agreed cost levels. Since the customer is unaware of the supplier's profits, however, the scheme encourages the supplier to reduce costs for its own sake, at the expense of providing better service.

JOINT VENTURES

Joint ventures can overcome the constraints of direct cooperation, the way structuring BRI as a separate company does for Labatt and Molson. In data processing outsourcing, Ernst & Young and Farmland Industries, a large agricultural cooperative, chose to form a JV rather than cooperate directly and have gained from that.

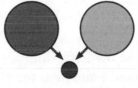

Joint Venture

The venture owns and manages the co-op's information systems, so all data about the operation is available to both partners. Profits from cutting Farmland's computer costs below defined targets are shared, and the partners set priorities for cost and service level improvement together. Since Farmland benefits from any gains beyond the targets, it has an incentive to cooperate with Ernst, which enhances their combined performance.[1]

Because it is a separate organization and may be in a market distinct from those of its parents, a JV may need people, resources, and policies that meet its specific needs—as defined by shared objectives. Also use these objectives to decide on a venture's ownership and governance arrangement.

Choosing People

Central questions in filling senior positions in a joint venture include whether the postings should be temporary or permanent and what particular skills people should have.

At DowElanco, which joined the agricultural products groups of Dow Chemical and Eli Lilly, integration was a key goal. Before

FOR DETAILS ON JV STAFFING, SEE PAGE 258

the JV was formed, the Dow and Lilly components were rivals. Executives on both sides anticipated friction at the start, and believed integration would be difficult. To encourage it, both parents closed career paths back into their firms.

The clear message was that the venture's success depended on people's ability to work with one another, and had nothing to do with their allegiance to Dow or Lilly. Integration was further reinforced by the appointment of a strong human resource executive from Lilly and a CEO from Dow, who, as joint internal leaders, made that a top priority.

Now, consider a pair of ventures created by Corning and Siemens. Both units were built to encase Corning optical fiber in cable, using Siemens know-how. Both were named Siecor, with one located in the United States and the other in Germany.

The American Siecor was born in a highly competitive market, with many customers and heavyweight rivals. By contrast, its German cousin began in a market dominated by the Bundespost, a government agency that at the time had a monopoly in the phone business. Marketing there was generally a matter of taking orders.

For the American venture, the partners chose a CEO with entrepreneurial skills. Parent employees who wanted to join the venture were told they could not return. By tying their careers to the unit's success in its challenging market, this provision helped ensure people's full commitments. The German-based Siecor, by contrast, faced little market uncertainty. Most personnel were there on a temporary basis.

Assigning Resources

The resources you place under the control of a JV should be only those that are unique to its needs. To minimize costs, all else should be drawn from your firms or bought outside.

For DowElanco, manufacturing flexibility was a key objective. Products to be made, plant loadings, timing, and other parameters had to be under the JV's control. Before it was formed, the plants to be involved belonged to Dow, and were tightly integrated into the firm's maintenance, waste management, process improvement, and other procedures. Continuing these ties would be far easier and less costly than recreating all the support apparatus in the venture.

When DowElanco was created, plant ownership was transferred to it. To take advantage of Dow's systems while meeting the JV's needs, it leased the plants back to Dow, which operated them under contract. The plants' performance was controlled by DowElanco, which had an employee on site.

Contrast this with Brewers Retail Inc. BRI owns and operates its outlets—assets that are clearly distinct from those Labatt and Molson use to make and bottle their products.

Setting Policies

A joint venture has to compete in its market for people, customers, and capital. Accordingly, its human resource, pricing, service, financial, and other policies must be tuned to that market. For instance, human resource policies may include different salary levels, incentives, benefits, and educational requirements. Recall from Chapter 3 how the paper companies that created a distribution JV could not get anyone to apply for the CEO position, until they made the benefits—which included a car—attractive to executives in that market.

Choosing a JV Governing Structure

In planning a joint venture, there are three possible governance arrangements. One is full equality, in which the parents decide policy and operating matters together. A second is policy equality, wherein the parents must concur on JV policy items, while one takes the lead in operating matters. Under the third option, one parent has the lead on policy as well as operating questions. Generally speaking, full equality gets the best from both parents, while the lead parent form makes governance easiest.

As a rule, the two forms involving equality in governance require equal ownership (50/50). By contrast, when one parent has a majority stake, that firm takes more risks and gets more benefits. Usually, it is reluctant to share decision making with the less-exposed partner.

The full equality arrangement is essential for joint ventures that depend on both parents for continuing substantial know-how inputs, such as technical or market expertise, at policy and operating levels. With such intangibles, it is impossible to assess whether each parent is making its best effort. And a firm cannot be expected to do that without having a say in how its input is used. Full equality provides the motivation for both parents to give their all.

Full equality will also help produce the best results from a JV that is closely tied to both parents' activities. For instance, the objectives of a venture I'll call Tasty Wares, a retail and distribution business owned by two food companies, include cost reduction in logistics and higher service levels in stores. These activities have to be tightly coordinated with each parent's distribution and marketing activities. Both parents must be equally involved.

You should also use full equality in JVs with rivals, to ward off perceptions of bias or a chance for operating imbalances. This has been the structure of choice for Coca-Cola and Schweppes in a bottling alliance in the United Kingdom, for General Electric and Pratt & Whitney in jet engines, for Labatt and Molson in beer distribution in Canada, and for most other successful ventures between competitors.

Policy equality—the second governance arrangement—encourages both parents' know-how inputs at the policy level and is easier to manage than the full equality form. If you do not expect substantial, ongoing operating-level ties to both parents, and if your firms are not rivals, then policy equality is easier to manage than full equality.

To illustrate, when Nypro, the injection-molding firm, began using joint ventures, its management always wanted a majority role. But, says Barry Potter, who served for fifteen years as president of an early venture with Netstal, a Swiss molding machine maker, "We learned that we get more out of both companies when we are equals on the board."

Nypro and its partners always have different views, and they get their best results when they combine their understandings and expertise. If one partner is in the minority, Nypro found, it feels like a second-class citizen. Because it knows it can be outvoted, it invests less energy in the discussion and may not even raise issues. Behind this attitude at Nypro—and common to all successful 50/50 ventures—are partner cultures that reinforce the needed style. With 50/50, partners must reach a consensus to progress.[2]

When a JV is closer to Nypro's business than to a partner's, Nypro is better suited to manage operations. In such cases, the venture general manager reports to the board chairman, who comes from Nypro. If a JV will draw more on its partner's strengths, Nypro looks to that firm to take the lead. In a venture with Mitsui that serves Japanese business, for instance, Mitsui has the lead because the partners want the venture to mesh easily with Japanese customers. In either case, the full board must reach consensus on all policy matters. The board also develops measures for management, which the chairman uses in performance reviews.

Because equality in governance takes more effort, unless the situation calls for it, a lead parent arrangement is preferable. In such ventures, one partner runs the JV, while the other firm has a voice and veto on designated matters. This option is typical for companies that share the ownership and output of a production facility.

MINORITY INVESTMENTS

In a minority investment, one firm buys a noncontrolling share in the other, which is typically a much smaller company. The main benefits of this structure come from cooperation at the smaller firm's policy level, as well as at operating levels. Ford Motor and Excel Industries illustrate.

Back when Ford wanted to replace its then-boxy cars with ones having curvy contours, making glass with the needed shape was beyond the auto maker's expertise. So Ford sought out Excel, a leading specialist. At the time the glass firm was relatively small. If the project succeeded and Excel did not increase its volume with other customers, Ford could have as much as 80 percent of the firm's output. With that much share of its business, Ford might as well have bought Excel—which was unacceptable to the auto maker. By staying independent, Excel would keep its lower costs and valued entrepreneurial style.

Ford helped Excel develop the needed capacity and meet its growth objective by investing in the smaller firm and taking two seats on its board. In their board role, Ford people shared their

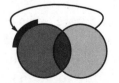

Minority Investment

views on how to grow the business by further penetrating the global auto market, and introduced Excel to Mazda and others. Terms in the firms' agreement prevented the auto maker from having any influence in running Excel. Ford's Taurus, the fruit of that joint effort, quickly became the best-selling car in the United States.

Though it might seem logical to expect, minority equity investments do not increase an alliance's long-term stability. Consider that stability was the rationale for KLM's 21 percent stake in Northwest Airlines, and British Airways' buying 25 percent of USAir (see Chapters 1 and 4). If anything, the investments were like salt in wounds caused by poor relationships compounded by conflicting objectives at KLM and Northwest, and a benefits imbalance in the case of BA and USAir.[3] The fact that KLM and Northwest resolved their differences reflected their need for each other in a difficult market and leadership changes, not KLM's ownership stake.

Consider also that HP–Canon and GE–SNECMA, both successful alliances with no equity involved, still thrive after many years.

In contemplating a minority investment, be sure the other firm is strong and well managed. Since you won't be getting control, there is no chance to turn a weak firm around. In addition, the firm's scope must be focused on your mutual interest. Otherwise, you are unlikely to get much top management attention, which defeats the value of a policy role.

WHAT GOOD GOVERNANCE ENTAILS

Whether you cooperate directly, use a minority investment, or have a joint venture, the governing body guides the effort. To deliver the results, that body must give clear and consistent signals to everyone involved. As you think about what this will take, bear in mind that, within companies, vertical coordination between higher and lower management levels is often a challenge. For alliances, with at least two organizations involved, the task is harder.

Once an alliance is launched, the joint policy-level leaders who shepherded its formation pilot its governance. They head the steering committee together, or serve as chairman and vice chairman of the joint venture board. In each case they set agendas, run meetings, build a consensus, maintain enthusiasm, take tough issues off line, stay on top of matters between meetings, and generally keep the whole apparatus on track.

FOR MORE DETAIL ON ALLIANCE GOVERNANCE, SEE PAGES 253–260

For its own reasons, Wal-Mart has not appointed a peer for Tom Muccio, who heads the Procter & Gamble team in the firms' alliance. One result is that the retailer has no one to drive broad alliance decisions into that company, as Muccio does at his firm. "Without a counterpart, there is no one with whom I can candidly discuss the overall relationship with a shared desire to make it work better," Muccio observes. "Instead, either I have to network inside Wal-Mart, or one of my people does, to get things done. I feel more like a lobbyist than a leader."

Alliance governance involves four tasks: guiding the combined effort, holding people accountable for results, providing support within both firms, and sustaining healthy relationships.

In the HP–Canon alliance, the steering committee sets the course. It defines long-term objectives, aligns product and technology road maps, makes key policy decisions, deals with matters that cut across multiple products, and sets the scope of collaboration. The committee also settles questions like pricing and product definition between the firms, and anticipates other issues or resolves them before they grow.

As with all alliances, relationships are central to the laser printer firms' success together. To stay on top of these, steering committee members monitor teamwork and communications within and between their companies at all levels. Regular discussions about relationships help keep them visible. "This is normal practice for us, because things do not always work as well as they might," says John Stedman, a committee member. When necessary, issues are brought to the attention of the appropriate people for resolution.

Your firm's investment in governance will depend on the size and complexity of each alliance. Craftsman Custom Metal Fabricators, a small (under $50 million) Chicago-area business, works closely with selected customers on fast-cycle jobs. Due to the low volumes involved, a pair of joint leaders serves each alliance as an informal two-person steering committee. By contrast, the larger and more complex Maersk–SeaLand alliance has a hierarchy of guidance levels that include the firms' presidents, a steering committee, a vessel network committee, and three regional committees.

However you organize, each part of an alliance must report to the same governing body. The parents of Tasty Wares ignored this principle and suffered for that. Because Tasty was subject to government regulation, they created a government affairs committee to deal with such matters. But the committee was independent of Tasty's board and had its own ideas about what was best for Tasty. The ensuing clashes weakened the board and contributed to Tasty's decline and near demise.

COMBINE SKILLS, INTEREST, AND AUTHORITY

It was a case of the disheartened abandoned by the distracted. Excited about their opportunity and wanting to show commitment, BestBank and Consumers Group, the bank and insurance partners described in Chapter 2, appointed some of their most senior people to their joint venture board. As this was a small part of each person's responsibilities, their attention was weak and attendance poor. Lacking clear directions the CEO set his own path, skirting issues that might cause parent conflict.

Meanwhile, sensing ambiguity above them, other venture employees turned to their own firms for guidance. My first impression was of a game in which each side was playing by different rules.

When put to the test, this banking-insurance venture's board should have been decisive and clear, but was neither. Because members were three or more levels above the action, the alliance was not a top priority for them—nor could it be without short-changing their other duties. Another cause of their distraction was that, while they had the wide perspective of senior executives, they lacked the detailed know-how the alliance needed.

For a board or steering committee to perform well, members must have the right blend of skills, interest, and authority within their firms. Members should be close enough to the alliance to see it as important to their jobs and to make substantive contributions. At the same time, they must be positioned to make relevant decisions in their firms, while ensuring needed resources, policy support, and coordination.

Recall from Chapter 5 that in Procter & Gamble's alliance with Wal-Mart, the steering committee governs the interface, but not related activities in both firms. Without that authority, the committee cannot make internal changes needed to support the alliance fully.

I have never found it easy for a company to place its most relevant people in alliance governance positions. Almost always, the best candidates are occupied with other matters. Still, you can't expect an alliance to work well without effective governance. If the alliance will serve your priority objectives, it is always worthwhile to manage the politics and get the best people assigned.

In the SeaLand–Maersk alliance, committee members are well-versed in the topics they cover, and the alliance is important to their own performance. Further, members head relevant internal units, which leaves no doubt about the power of the committees. Once a decision is made, execution is assured.

One way to make certain that the governing body will be effective is to assign from each partner high-level managers responsible for relevant activities. However, as BestBank–Consumers illustrates, this approach won't work well if people are too busy to devote necessary time. In these cases, it is best to delegate needed authority to lower-level staff before launch.

For example, in the Ford–ABB alliance, Ford's Vince Coletta and Larry Miller had to first get the okay from senior executives to bypass their firm's normal contracting procedures. After that, there was no reason to include higher-level people on the steering committee. To ensure clear governance in the SeaLand–Maersk alliance, "in many cases individuals had to relinquish some sovereignty," says one executive.

Another approach, used by Nypro, is to establish a clear backup to support the board member. Because each Nypro JV depends on ongoing technology inputs from the injection molder, the board member responsible for ensuring that is supported by the firm's engineering vice president—who does not serve on JV boards. The arrangement ensures that each venture gets Nypro's full support. It also keeps venture management from having to spend time inside Nypro, hat in hand, looking for help.

In assembling the right combination of authority, skills, and interest, you may get staff from different levels in each firm. This blend tests cultures where status is based on position rather than on contribution. For best performance, shun hierarchy. Since people tend to defer to the highest-ranked person present, that individual contributes best by letting the designated leaders run the show. Having a number of management levels does not mean you should select the most senior representatives as co-leaders. That position ought to be filled by whoever is close enough to understand the alliance, is respected by colleagues, and is good at team building.

Nypro staffs its boards largely with middle managers, reflecting its belief that, to be helpful, members must be conversant in the activity. When Nypro has the lead, a corporate officer is chairman during the startup year. After that the whole board, including Nypro's partner, votes on a successor, with the explicit understanding it will be someone from Nypro if it has the lead. The officer remains on the board to show the corporate flag to Nypro's partner, reinforce the injection molder's culture on the board, and ease communications to top management.

By periodically including more senior executives in governance meetings, you help build a political foundation for an alliance. In the Canon–HP relationship, the firms' presidents attend one steering committee meeting annually. Their presence signals the alliance's importance to both firms and ensures it gets priority.

LIMIT MEMBERSHIP

For a board or committee to give clear signals to the operating level, it has to reach a consensus. The more members, the harder it will be for them to agree and the greater the tendency to postpone issues or settle on lowest-common-denominator decisions. For these reasons, small governing bodies are more effective than large ones.

For instance, as the Canon–HP alliance blossomed, so did the steering committee, until there were twelve members. "With so many people it was difficult to have good discussions," says Takashi Kitamura, Canon's leader for the alliance. A reorganization trimmed the number to six.

Nypro management also prefers a six-person board, based on its experience with fifteen joint ventures. The firm reasons that this number gives individuals a larger role. Besides enabling each member to identify more with the alliance, the small size leads to better participation. With eight or more members, people feel they won't be missed if they skip a meeting, have less chance to contribute when they attend, and must work harder to reach agreement.

If you are tempted to include more people to avoid hurt feelings, consider that shrinking the group later by asking someone to leave might cause even more damage. It is better to start with a small, manageable team and invite others' occasional participation as needed.

AGREE ON DECISION MAKING

Imagine you are the captain of a huge oceangoing vessel. You have always been on schedule, have never lost or damaged a cargo, and enjoy a perfect safety record. Yet despite your exceptional skills, you have never taken a ship into a harbor. Instead, you always drop anchor outside and wait for a tiny boat to pull up alongside, wherefrom the harbor pilot emerges, climbs to the bridge, and guides you in.

You willingly defer to the pilot because inside the harbor are narrow channels, shifting currents, and other ships moving about. You follow the pilot's advice; otherwise you may cripple your ship.

Like the ship whose captain turns to an expert in unfamiliar waters, your company has the best chance for success when alliance decisions are assigned to that person or firm with the most relevant skills—rather than on the basis of size or power.

As obvious as this logic seems, practice often follows a different kind of golden rule: Whoever has the most gold rules. While the problem is partly ego, more commonly it is a fear of loss from ceding control. This concern has two sources: discomfort with an unfamiliar partner, and habits formed in companies that emphasize power and authority over teams and relationships.

In a situation I have seen repeated in many places, when a foreign equipment firm and a local partner built a joint venture in Taiwan, the foreigners insisted on having control, arguing that they were providing the technology—the main value-added in the venture. But customers wanted technical solutions tied to their purchases, which called for detailed understandings of their needs. With control firmly in the foreign company's grip, its people chose to ignore much of its local partner's knowledge of customers. Unwilling to share control and unable to integrate their skills, both firms lost money at every turn and, in turn, were lost. It didn't matter that the technology was superior, since it was not well applied. As a final act of ill-fated partnership, they lost the business together.

Rather than wrestle for control over decision making as these two firms did—and to bolster mutual confidence—identify major issues you expect will arise during alliance implementation. Then, before launch, agree on whether you will resolve each one jointly or separately. Following that course averted calamity for Canon and HP.

Early in their relationship, the laser printer partners discussed what to do if either one wanted to develop a product of little interest to the other. They agreed that, in certain areas, each could makes its own decisions. They also concurred that, if either company chose to proceed alone, it had to clone the technology it was getting from its partner or find another source. This prior understanding carried the firms through a difficult time when HP wanted to introduce a color printer, and turned to Konica because Canon was not ready.

Making decisions together does not imply you should have equal weight on all matters. Rather, you must learn to trust each other's judgments.

Canon and HP again illustrate. While they must agree on product development objectives, HP tends to defer to Canon on laser engines, whereas Canon listens to HP on software matters. "We both believe we have good ideas about the other's areas and often contribute there," says an HP executive. "Even so, the mentality is that each company is world-class in its area. We would never be able to catch up with Canon in electrophotography."

"Canon makes final decisions about laser engines," says Doug Carnahan, long HP's lead executive, "but sometimes HP may push back if we do not agree." Adds Takashi Kitamura: "Since HP is handling a latter part of the product, Canon does not know or need to know all HP decisions. By contrast, HP needs to know more about the engine because it influences the latter part of the HP product." In the end, each company makes its own decisions in its area of expertise and on internal matters such as new manufacturing capacity for Canon, or relationships with software vendors for HP.

BUILD A GOVERNANCE TEAM

One year after a cable TV firm and a telephone company formed a JV, poor results and growing friction between the board and the CEO resulted in his being fired. I agreed to advise the board on finding a new chief executive. The first step was to meet with members individually to understand their views. Later, I shared my conclusion with the full board: They had fired the wrong person.

During the interviews, I learned that each member had distinct ideas about the venture's direction. Like travelers passing through an airport, members agreed they were on a trip but not on where they were going. Their objectives were so general and their interpretations so different that, although the former CEO had attempted to accommodate everyone and avoid conflict, he served no one.

Compare that case with the situation at Ciba Corning Diagnostics, a joint venture of Corning and Ciba Geigy (now Novartis), whose performance exceeded its parents' expectations. A key reason was that the board gave clear stretch targets to management and actively championed the common cause within their firms. "We wanted to give life to the idea that management reported to the board," said Doug Watson, a CCD board member and now president of Novartis. "So the board had to function as a team."

Under the co-leaders a governing body delivers best performance when members add to one another's thinking and move forward as a unit. "We do not always get a high level of teamwork," says Gordon Lankton, Nypro's CEO, "because this depends on each partner's culture. When we do not, we do not get the best solutions."

Highly effective boards and steering committees have a distinct style. Each meeting is a forum for open discussion where people learn from each other's views and find creative ways to combine them. This openness advances mutual understandings, reinforces teamwork, and limits polarization. Equally important, an open and constructive dialogue at the top sets an important pattern for those below.

At the best alliances I have seen, governing bodies formally critique themselves and how they handle issues. People discuss how well they reach consensus and whether they give fuzzy signals to others. Those reflections contribute to better performance at the top, which sustains ongoing improvements in an alliance.

Much of the work in formal meetings is to explore issues and options. If you have significant differences and seem headed toward polarization, agree to resolve them by the next meeting. Taking tough questions off-line gives those who share the lead on an issue a chance to confer in private and find an acceptable solution. Subsequent voting is then pro forma and demonstrates agreement on a difficult matter, which reinforces governance.

One test of an effective board or steering committee is that members come to recognize their colleagues' strengths and give more weight to these. Another is that relationships become so close that discussions are about issues, not company views. "You really could not say who worked for Ford and for ABB," says Ford's

Miller of the paint plant alliance. A third test is the clarity of two-way vertical communications with lower levels.

For instance, in the Maersk–SeaLand alliance, the steering committee oversees a vessel network planning committee and three regional committees. SeaLand's Ron Sforza, who co-leads the network committee, does not report to anyone on the steering committee. But "we constantly communicate on issues and the status of things," he says. "We have a good alignment between us on what has to be done and where we want to go."

During startup or at times of major change, frequent meetings help bring people up to speed. After this, expect to hold several formal gatherings a year. The number depends on the size and complexity of an alliance; having too few meetings creates a leadership void, while too many implies poor delegation to the operating teams or venture management.

The Canon–HP steering committee, for example, oversees a multibillion-dollar alliance and focuses on plans and relationships. Beside meeting three times annually, members keep in touch by phone, fax, and e-mail. Substeering committees, which are more operational and concentrate on product lines, meet more often. At Ford–ABB, leaders held monthly project reviews, which is normal for a one-of-a-kind, major plant project. And though Nypro's joint venture boards meet quarterly, members are expected to monitor monthly performance.

Be sure to grade board or committee members on alliance success or failure, placing the heaviest weight on the joint leaders' shoulders. At Nypro, having team skills is seen as important for promotion. Membership on boards gives people an opportunity to demonstrate their abilities beyond the confines of their regular jobs. Accordingly, boards are an important source of future managers. Nypro members get recognition but are not financially rewarded.

SEPARATE A STEERING COMMITTEE
FROM OPERATIONS

In direct cooperation, day-to-day leaders do their best if they are not included in governance, a task that is distinct from operations.

The purpose of governance is to provide guidance and support, and to clear the political roads in both firms for the operating teams.

Asking day-to-day leaders to serve on the steering committee blurs their role and spreads their obligations. It also reduces by two the number of policy-level people you can include on a committee and still keep it small. The operating leaders should report to the committee and may sit in on meetings. But do them and their companies a favor by letting them focus on their jobs. That is how HP and Canon, Ford and ABB, Maersk and SeaLand, and other successful direct cooperation alliances work.

GIVE A JV BOARD FULL CONTROL

When planning a board, be sure that its members control all policy links between their firms and venture management. At Global One, the alliance of Sprint, Deutsche Telekom, and France Telecom, the top three executives reporting to the CEO come from the respective partners and maintain close ties there. To serve Global One they ought to be loyal to their boss, who should be getting his marching orders from the board. Yet they often bypass him on difficult issues, taking them instead into the upper reaches of their own companies.

Those separate ties into the parent firms have weakened the board and CEO by compromising their roles. The bypass also has created conflict at lower levels. Believing that he could get what he wanted for his firm, each of the three senior executives has rigidly protected his turf. That this telecom venture has neither performed as expected nor kept a CEO for long illustrates what happens when an alliance rich in talent lacks clear direction at the top.[4]

It is appropriate to expect people who move from either parent into a joint venture to apply their firm's values and experience. But it is always a mistake to use executive positions as side channels for parent influence. Before they move to the JV, make clear that staffers are expected to be loyal to the venture. Reinforce this directive by arranging for JV management to conduct their performance assessments, basing these on venture objectives.

The attention JV governance requires depends on your expectations. Less effort is necessary when your objectives have fewer dimensions. For example, Dow Chemical and Eli Lilly set return on investment targets for DowElanco and defined a scope that separated the venture from other Dow or Lilly interests. Guided by those parent expectations, management set the direction with appropriate board review and approval.

By contrast, the objectives of Tasty Wares (the retail business owned by two food companies) include reaching a defined position in the market, with attractive returns. At the same time, Tasty must coordinate its evolution with each parent's advancing marketing and distribution plans. Venture management works closely with those functions through board subcommittees. The full board monitors overall progress. Tasty's board members have consequently been far more involved in their venture than have those at DowElanco.

> DETAILS ON GOVERNING FULL EQUALITY, POLICY EQUALITY, AND LEAD PARTNER JVs ARE ON PAGES 253–258

When you govern as equals, all policy and operating matters not delegated to management—from appointing the CEO and deciding executive compensation to approving plans, budgets, obligations, asset sales, dividends, and reviewing progress—come before the board. By contrast, in JVs where one firm has the lead, the board must agree on major issues, while the lead partner handles operating reviews and much of the monitoring, advising, and routine approvals.

MAKE YOUR VENTURE TOP PRIORITY

For several minds to speak as one, board members must put other matters aside. "We tell them to forget their other jobs when they have their board hats on and do what is best for our joint venture," says Nypro's Lankton. "With some people I have to keep emphasizing this point."

As the voice of both partners, the board owns their mutual objectives. Through the board's actions, it confirms the importance of those objectives and sets priorities among them.

An example: Plans for DowElanco called for blending the Dow and Lilly agrochemical units into one smoothly functioning organization. Because integration would be essential to the venture's success, a board subcommittee composed of senior human resource executives from both firms worked with DowElanco HR management and oversaw the process. Periodically, the board asked for an update.

In a joint venture where your firm and its partner have equal roles in policy and operating matters, it should be easier to raise issues on the board. However, when neither firm is wholly responsible for a venture, board members—busy with other matters—tend to skirt complex topics. An effective chairman counters this attitude by routinely probing for issues and asking how specific synergies are really working.

Parent equality also leads some to believe that not having a controlling vote means the JV deserves less of their firm's attention than do majority-owned activities. Such attitudes make these ventures low priority in their parent firms in critical areas like staffing, capital budgeting, and systems integration.

"We still face the problem of some people saying that since we own only 50 percent, the JV deserves only half of our normal attention," says Barry Potter, a Nypro executive. "We have to remind people that we only make half the investment so our returns are at least as good as internal operations or we would not have the JV. Someone has to beat the drum occasionally to get people to pay attention." Because board members are accountable for success, they must be the drummers.

SEPARATE BOARD AND MANAGEMENT

In planning a venture board, avoid any temptation to model it on how governance works at most companies, perhaps including your own. Although the practice is changing toward board autonomy, management at many firms still dominates their boards. Further, any dissent is stifled by an etiquette that leads directors to vote for a CEO's proposals even when they disagree.

A joint venture is not like that. It exists only to advance parent interests. To do its work, a JV board needs its own perspective separate from management. You can help, and avoid confusion, by defining a boundary between board and management that describes what each is accountable for. Topics usually within a board's sole purview include the scope, duration, and direction of the venture. Also under the board's umbrella are partner-related matters, items the board must approve, and management performance evaluations.

While management should attend meetings to stay informed, they should not serve on the board. Instead, fill seats only with full-time partner employees. By the same logic, third parties such as outside attorneys and people from other firms should not be on these boards. It is hard enough to get alignment between two companies.[5]

Part of the needed separation between board and management is political. In the Kaleida software joint venture of Apple and IBM, Michael Braun, the CEO, was given the power to break board ties except when a significant matter was involved. This role brought him into parent politics, which is always dangerous. Also, it led some members to avoid grappling with tough issues, since they thought Braun would handle them. Consequently, a number of issues ended in deadlock.[6]

Unlike Kaleida, Nypro and its partners limit management involvement in partner politics to minor issues. "We don't want them to get caught in the middle," says Lankton.

The point is that, while management should be aware of parent politics, they should not get involved. "I do too much guessing," comments the CEO of one joint venture. "While I don't want to get immersed in their politics, which could shorten my career, I do want to understand the context better. If I know what the issues are, I can present matters in a way that helps get them resolved. It is never smart to argue with one parent against the other," he adds. "If I see such a situation developing I always say 'this is a partner issue—you guys tell me what you want.' I win their trust by always taking a 'what's best for the joint venture' attitude."

With clear separation between board and management, and

board members being part time in this role, the CEO has more freedom than many executives who report to full-time bosses. This autonomy gives management room to set its own course. A strong management that is not firmly placed in the parents' orbit becomes master of its own universe. Those with less gumption who lack clear signals from above hide in a corner, fearing the directionless darkness. I have seen each response often enough to believe that both are common; neither serves the parents' interests.

These possibilities demonstrate the importance of the board being clear about objectives and tying executives' rewards to them. In the BestBank–Consumers JV, that did not happen, and the venture suffered. The CEO was incented on the first year's sales growth, not on the equally vital but more challenging and longer-term task of organization building. Further, he was a short-timer with a one-year contract. Given these circumstances—and an inattentive board—the JV almost collapsed. Although one could point fingers at the CEO, the real culprit was the board, which failed to make him accountable.

For best performance, build a strong board that will set and reinforce clear stretch objectives. Complement it with a strong CEO who can deliver on those objectives and suggest alternatives when he sees a better way. Having strength on each side may create tension between board and management, but that can be constructive if it is based on solid relationships and serves the partners' objectives.

Effective CEOs nurture one-on-one rapport with all directors. Their purpose is not to pursue a separate agenda, which could frustrate governance. Instead, by spotting issues that concern individual board members, and by responding to their interests, CEOs build confidence in their own leadership.

At Nypro, DowElanco, and other ventures that have enjoyed effective communications between board and management, the lead representatives meet often with the CEO to stay on top of issues, discuss personnel matters, sort out any rough spots in board-management relationships, and generally keep up to date. Such visits also give the CEO an opportunity to test the waters on board matters.

CREATE AN EXECUTIVE COMMITTEE
WHEN GOVERNANCE IS TOUGH

Regardless of how well members work together, there are limits on what a board can do. When plans for a JV call for significant separation from the parents and substantial coordination with them, governance requires more attention.

For the board of Tasty Wares, the challenges were overwhelming. Members learned, almost too late, that it was impossible for a board of six busy people meeting a few times a year to digest a wholly new context, keep up with the many policy and operating topics involved, and build consensus on every question.

Because their firms were not otherwise involved in retailing, board members lacked depth in the business. Governing Tasty required them to learn about the market, which called for more time than they had, while overseeing the coordination between Tasty and each parent. Sensing a policy vacuum at the top, each parent pushed its own agenda on the venture. That led to serious problems and Tasty's near-death. At the last minute, its parents initiated a repair (for details, see Chapter 8).

Part of the solution included more attention to governance. Tasty's parents replaced the old board with a new slate, and created an executive committee consisting of the firms' two lead representatives. They, in turn, got more time from their companies, learned the business in depth, and met regularly as an executive committee of the board with the CEO. The committee's first task was to define short-term objectives, which the full board ratified. Setting longer-term goals required more clarity from the parents about their separate objectives. With the lead representatives more involved and a forum for them to explore the options, those objectives got needed attention.

At Tasty, creating an executive committee facilitated other tasks as well. The committee, which meets twice as often as the board, began conducting operating reviews and summarized these at board meetings. Doing that gave the board more time for strategic and coordination issues. The board also delegated some authority to the committee, which sped decisions on matters where management previously had to check with everyone.

Like other competent JV executive committees, Tasty's shares with management the responsibility of selling other board directors on specific items. Since committee members are more involved and better informed than other directors, they help the board reach consensus. They also keep the board posted about unresolved issues on which they are working off-line. To further their role as facilitators for the full board, committee members always reach consensus before forwarding a proposal. Regular executive committee meetings involve the full Tasty management team. At times, the committee visits only with the CEO to review people issues, compensation, and other sensitive items.

CHAPTER 7

TAKE NOTHING FOR GRANTED

■

In what may be one of the great alliance mistakes of all time, MCI and British Telecom had a misunderstanding that fundamentally changed their futures and the structure of the world's telecommunications industry. Their joint venture, named Concert, was widely seen as the leading global carrier serving businesses. Having decided to move closer together, they agreed that BT would acquire MCI.

Just before the purchase, MCI announced losses close to $1 billion, which depressed its stock. BT shareholders suddenly found they would be paying a hefty premium for MCI, and were outraged. BT management claimed it was surprised by the news; MCI management said it had kept BT informed.

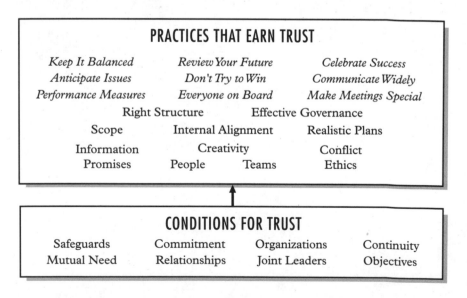

PRACTICES THAT EARN TRUST

Keep It Balanced	*Review Your Future*	*Celebrate Success*
Anticipate Issues	*Don't Try to Win*	*Communicate Widely*
Performance Measures	*Everyone on Board*	*Make Meetings Special*

Right Structure	Effective Governance

Scope	Internal Alignment	Realistic Plans

Information	Creativity	Conflict
Promises	People Teams	Ethics

↑

CONDITIONS FOR TRUST

Safeguards	Commitment	Organizations	Continuity
Mutual Need	Relationships	Joint Leaders	Objectives

When Worldcom—then a second-tier player—made an unexpected bid for MCI, BT's angry owners foreclosed a higher offer by their firm. The alliance ended when Worldcom bought MCI, becoming a major force in the global business market.[1]

An alliance is like a foreign body that has been grafted onto separate organizations. To keep it alive you have to guard against rejection by each one. Doing that includes getting a solid start, managing meetings differently than you might normally do, and preventing breakdowns—a tactic BT and MCI could have used.[2]

Because alliances differ from normal practice, mistakes will be made. In troubled alliances people publicly ignore and privately recall their errors. In successful alliances, people admit when they stumble and learn together how to avoid repeating that in the future.

DEFINE PERFORMANCE MEASURES

Between negotiation and implementation, two additional practices will make the passage a smooth one: developing ways to monitor progress and bringing everyone on board.

To be confident that you and your partner are advancing as expected—and to spot problems early—make shared measurement the foundation of joint management. One set of measures should compare alliance progress with what market transactions could do. Without superior results there is no basis for an alliance.

Another set compares results with your objectives and plans. To illustrate: In the Wal-Mart and Procter & Gamble alliance, the interface team created a formal scorecard covering their chief objectives for growth, profits, and inventory turns, which is used to track monthly progress. Once a year, the team sends a report to both firms. Contents include results overall and by region and function, and comparisons with Wal-Mart averages across its whole business. Also included are plans for the next year and important issues to be addressed.

Developing those tools took a lot of work. Since P&G has many products and customers, gauging the alliance means subtracting from whatever business it creates any volume the alliance reduces at other customers. This careful analysis quieted doubters by showing that the alliance has been a major net contributor to P&G's bottom line. Wal-Mart has a less complex organization and uses simpler metrics, which showed that the alliance added significantly to profits.

Because cooperation depends heavily on behavior, regularly use the trust conditions and practices to assess this dimension of an alliance and to surface potential problems. These habits are typical of alliances discussed here: P&G/Wal-Mart team members monitor how well they are solving problems together; the HP–Canon steering committee observes teamwork, communications, and relationships.

You can foster acceptance for an alliance within your firm by including it in internal operating reviews. Add progress in trust building to the agenda. It will encourage such practices within your company.

Periodically and objectively confirming that your organizations are doing well together fortifies trust. San Miguel, a Philippine food and beverage enterprise, has brewing alliances in China and the Philippines with Malt Europe, a French company. Although they have been partners for two decades, they still regularly assess whether this match is best for each of them.

Says Cesar de Larrazabal, a San Miguel vice president: "We have been building trust over the years, one step at a time. Now whatever we say to each other is completely credible. But we still benchmark prices, quality, and other key factors around the world. This reinforces our trust, because it shows us we are doing our best for each other."

In multiunit alliances, internal benchmarking will help you monitor performance and encourage progress. Maersk and SeaLand illustrate. At their semiannual alliance meetings the container shippers compare regional performances, using the results to spur improvements. The firms also benchmark with each other on vital cost components in operations and customer service. "Whenever

FOR MORE DETAIL ON PROGRESS MEASURES, SEE PAGE 267

we see they are doing better in some area, we ask ourselves why we are not as good," says an executive.

GET EVERYONE ON BOARD

When newcomers join a company, they need time to learn the routines; in fact, their confusion may linger for a long time. The task of understanding one's role in an alliance is more demanding. During negotiations different groups from both firms—executives, operating-level people, planners, attorneys, and human resource and financial experts—work on separate tasks. Few are involved in the whole undertaking, yet all are expected to invest in its success. To encourage their efforts, help them understand the reasons for the alliance, how it is structured, where it is headed, and how they fit in.[3]

Consider what happened in a pharmaceutical alliance that ignored this principle and launched in a fog. While only a handful of people were involved in the negotiations, many others would be called on to support implementation. All they knew from a brief announcement was that the alliance had started. Said one manager: "It was cloaked in mystery. People did not understand why we had it, there were conflicting rumors about it, and we were unwilling to back it." The alliance was short-lived.

For a strong beginning, invest in time up front to start everyone together. In a group meeting, explain the reasons and objectives for the alliance. Discuss how you have built trust so far, what must be done to reinforce it, how to recognize signs of potential trouble, and what to do if problems occur.

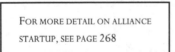

FOR MORE DETAIL ON ALLIANCE
STARTUP, SEE PAGE 268

An open forum like that would have prevented some early grief for Maersk and SeaLand. "We agreed on communications," says an executive, "but did not have a joint meeting where everyone came together. Anything we could have done to improve collective understandings would have enhanced wider acceptance."

Ford and ABB did things differently in their paint plant alliance and reaped the benefits. At launch, they held a day-long alignment meeting aided by an external facilitator. Some twenty-five people attended, including leaders from both firms and from Fluor Daniel, the construction contractor. This was the first chance the full project team had to observe the comradery and joint leadership of Ford's Vince Coletta and ABB's Tom Mark, who sat next to each other and guided the discussion.

The agenda covered alliance objectives, scope, schedule, and who would make what decisions. Coletta and Mark opened the meeting by setting the tone for how they wanted people to work together. They described the centrality of trust, as well as the role of the steering committee and how it would support the operating teams. They also explained ground rules, including how key issues would be resolved, and procedures for handling unanticipated problems.

Importantly, Coletta and Mark spoke in detail about the difference between the firms' prior working relationship, which had been unpleasant, and what was expected in the alliance. "It was almost like a sermon," says Ford's Larry Miller. "Tom and Vince made a joint speech on what they expected from us—they sounded like identical twins."

MAKE YOUR MEETINGS SPECIAL

Alliance meetings are distinct from those within a firm. In an alliance, meetings help keep two firms stretching together. That creates a need for mutual learning and raises more issues, which present a higher risk of polarization. Also, you and your partner may have conflicting styles.

As the steward of an alliance, the board or steering committee must set the course, encourage creativity, monitor progress, reinforce trust, and keep adversity at bay. In substance and style, its formal meetings are especially critical.

Everything you know about good meetings applies to alliances: developing and circulating agendas and information beforehand, stating objectives at the start and being guided by them, developing a list of issues needing more attention, and communicating the results to others as soon as the meeting is over. But because alliances are different, you have to do more.

To encourage participation, make every meeting agenda a joint product. "We work hard to avoid surprising each other," says an HP executive. "Issues are identified very early, often going to a subcommittee before they come to the full steering committee. We even go over our slides together the night before a meeting, so that everyone knows what is coming. Our agendas are developed and circulated well in advance and often modified at the last minute, based on inputs from others. If an unresolved issue comes to us from a subcommittee, they will have worked out how to explain it so neither partner will be embarrassed."

Well before a meeting date, apprise each other of any issues and decide which topics are appropriate for the full group and which ones should be addressed in private. At a joint venture with difficult labor relations issues that also affect its parents, one manager who shares the lead on labor matters says, "It is important that my counterpart and I come forward with a range of options we have agreed upon. The issues are complex, and our firms' positions have to be worked out quietly."

"In the past, when two views were brought into the full team we got six opinions instead of one solution. Now, we explore and agree on possible outcomes before presenting them to the board. Once we have their feedback, we may have more homework to do before we have a proposal to sell them. But by getting our act together first, we create a platform everyone can build on."

While getting ready for a meeting, discuss within your firm what you believe your partner's views are on the topics, as well as your own. "Doing this helps us appreciate their perspective and makes us more sensitive to what they have to say," observes Nypro president Gordon Lankton.

However, don't set fixed positions in advance. Otherwise, joint sessions will be polarized at the start and someone will have to back down. "I like to think of all board members as being individuals, rather than representing either party," says Lankton. "We get the best ideas out this way." Nypro board members usually vote alike, but there is no stigma if they do not.

Before one steering committee meeting, HP and Canon agreed to approach the issues with open minds and no fixed positions. "It was a breath of fresh air," says John Stedman, a member. The experience encouraged a more open style, and led to similar behavior at lower levels. Now, joint engineering teams more often focus on developing better products, rather than division or company positions. Though such views still exist—such as in each firm's philosophies about what is best for the customer—they are a more subtle influence.

If you have ever been involved in a brainstorming session, you know that certain principles—like building on others' ideas and not being critical—make it more productive. Even if all team members know this, by reviewing the principles when a meeting begins you keep them fresh in everyone's mind. Similarly, articulating the shared norms developed in your negotiations helps make these common ground.

At Wal-Mart and P&G, interface team members bring a statement of their norms to every meeting. People point to relevant norms when they get to a tough point, to remind one another of how they promised to collaborate.

To foster ongoing joint improvement, emphasize mutual learning. After each meeting, briefly review what was supposed to happen, what actually happened, why they differed, and lessons learned. Then agree on how to work more constructively together the next time. Similar reviews, typically for about a day at the close of each joint project, enhance succeeding projects.

The better your joint leaders' relationship, the more effective your meetings will be. For instance, as Doug Carnahan and Takashi Kitamura grew more comfortable together, they were better able to guide the steering committee when discussions got too tense. Whenever either one sensed imminent polarization, he left the table—a signal for the other to follow. Then, visiting privately, they discussed the issues and background matters in their firms. Informed by these insights, each then met with his own people to guide them on a more constructive path.

With their bond as a model, similar relationships have grown among others on the steering committee. That has made it easier to focus on improving how the committee functioned. "In the past," says one member, "we did not trust their response on a topic if we did not agree with it. Today, we are much more accepting."

Now, when really tough meetings are over—and even if some issues are undecided—everyone knows these will be resolved. That is trust at its best.

ANTICIPATE TOUGH ISSUES

Take a major opportunity away from a partner and you'll likely destroy your alliance or damage it badly. Yet that did not happen when Hewlett-Packard turned away from Canon in color printers and went to Konica, a new partner. That HP and Canon continued together in black-and-white printers illustrates how to manage through difficult times.

In the late 1980s, HP concluded that the market was ready for color laser printers for high-volume applications. Canon also recognized the opportunity, and the partners began working toward that objective. However, HP wanted to get to market fast with an acceptable printer, while Canon sought higher quality and could not meet HP's schedule. Well before his firm decided to go to Konica, Doug Carnahan, HP's lead executive, explained the problem to Takashi Kitamura, Canon's lead. Carnahan said HP believed the window would be missed if it did not move soon. When Kitamura did not agree, Carnahan observed that HP did not want to breach the firms' relationship, but explained that the opportunity was important to HP and it would have to start buying from Konica.

Though Kitamura was very unhappy, he and Carnahan had built a foundation of trust. Further, the companies had previously reached an understanding about going separate ways in defined areas. And HP had prepared the ground for its color decision by keeping Canon informed of its thinking all along. "I understand your needs and constraints," Kitamura responded. "Although I do not like your decision I accept it."

Most negative surprises—unexpected actions by one of you that injure the other—can be avoided. One way to do that, as HP's and Canon's color printer experience illustrates, is to agree in advance on what might divide you and how you will handle it. P&G and Wal-Mart, for example, accept that each firm has the right to decline any initiative that is not in its best interest.

Because new issues surface all the time, make it a habit to review potentially divisive matters frequently; then settle them early or have contingency plans. SeaLand and Maersk learned that the longer they went without doing this, the larger issues became. "Things we could have easily fixed when they were small got bigger and harder to correct if we did not work on them right away," comments Dick Murphy, who leads the alliance for SeaLand.

DON'T TRY TO WIN EVEN WHEN YOU'RE RIGHT

As tempting as it may sometimes be to press your views on a partner, be sensitive as to when to back off. One firm's enthusiasm is easily weakened by another's insistence on doing things its way. Since you choose a partner out of need, you must respect its people's thinking and respond to their interests. It isn't possible for every decision to support your views. If it were, you wouldn't need a partner.

By the time you get to implementation you probably will have used some of the techniques for conflict resolution described in Chapter 3. Those are as valid now as they were at earlier stages. However, once an alliance is under way, there is more to lose. So make constructive problem solving a shared habit. On those infrequent occasions when you cannot agree, give your partner's thinking more weight if the issue is more important to that company.

"We always try to understand each other's views," says Nypro's president Gordon Lankton. "If something is more compelling to our partner than it is to us we might say, in effect, 'if this is really important to you we'll go along, but if it was our choice we would not do it.' If they decide they want to do it anyway, they know our position and it gives us psychological credit for another time."

On the rare occasions when Nypro and its partner can't agree, they look for a creative solution. For example, in a joint venture with Mitsui, Nypro proposed buying four injection molding machines but Mitsui was skeptical about the market. When they still could not concur after exploring their differences, Nypro bought the machines and leased them to the venture.

COMMUNICATE WIDELY

Think about how hard—yet essential—it can be to keep people current on events within your firm. In alliances, good communications are more important because you don't share the kind of fabric that connects companies on the inside.

At P&G/Wal-Mart, as in many alliances, bad news travels by itself. If leaders want good news to be known, they have to make it happen. Through oral and written means, employees in both firms learn about the alliance's successes and that the results would not have been possible separately.

Both Canon and HP widely communicate their progress together within their organizations, from the highest levels down through the steering committee, substeering committees, and below. Each also has internal facilitators for the laser printer business who make sure everyone is up to date on relevant matters. There have been a few unpleasant surprises, usually caused by busy people forgetting to communicate.

When you have internal meetings on company issues, provide an update on your alliances. Discuss the pluses and minuses of each, including concerns anyone may have. This is particularly useful for people who are not directly involved and may not appreciate what is happening. By acknowledging when things are going well and when teams have resolved tough issues, you reinforce success.

Because the SeaLand–Maersk alliance spans eighty countries, top executives make a constant effort to send the same message widely in each firm, and see that it spreads to lower levels. Much of that message focuses on cost reduction, a major objective.

In opening remarks at one semiannual alliance meeting, for instance, John Clancey and Ib Kruse, the container carriers' CEOs, described how the firms' cost effectiveness together was more important than ever because ocean freight rates were dropping fast. They emphasized the need to set even tougher targets and find new ways to lower costs. Following Clancey and Kruse, each pair of regional committee executives made joint presentations on progress and plans to lower costs. Breakouts then focused on specific cost-reduction tasks, further drilling the message into operating levels.

KEEP IT BALANCED

Sooner or later you are likely to face a storm when you do something a partner doesn't like. When it hits, your best chance for remaining secure will be that your partner trusts your firm enough to let it blow over.

To build a partner's confidence, be sensitive to any imbalances that might reduce its commitments. Identifying these early and resolving them before they fester sends a powerful message that you can be counted on to support the other firm's interests.

Looking out for a partner is not done just to build credit for a rainy day. "We need Canon to stretch for us," says Doug Carnahan. "They would not be likely to do this if our benefits were lopsided. Together, we make sure we are fair and respectful about how each of us wins in an overall balance." Both firms try to do every project on a win-win basis, but this does not always happen. On several occasions HP has given its partner substantial funds because Canon had a problem in a particular area—such as a plan that did not work out as well for it as for HP.

Similarly, the Japanese firm makes special efforts to help its American partner. For example, Canon discovered that a component already in the market was failing under high stress. The firm notified HP and stopped its own production until the problem could be fixed. To avoid embarrassing HP, Canon arranged to retrofit printers that had been sold, at its expense. On another occasion, Canon made a big concession in laser engine prices when HP decided to keep a printer in the market longer than planned, until HP's next product was ready. Such actions have helped the firms stay together through rough times.

The kind of fair balance Carnahan refers to comes from candid conversations about your respective situations and a shared understanding of what is reasonable for both companies. Such transparency and fair play typify best practice in any relationship.

"I have to win occasionally for each sector in our firm,"

observes a lead executive in an airline alliance. "I discuss our internal realities frankly and privately with my counterpart. These conversations include my problems with certain individuals on our side and what must be done to get their support. I can't do that often because it detracts from our shared objective. Besides, this would not be fair to our partner, and I have to be willing to help it the same way."

The attitude that keeps a partner with you through difficult times also comes from diligently improving on the trust conditions and practices discussed in earlier chapters. I have never seen an alliance where everyone behaved as they should. But in the best ones, the leaders regularly set new stretch objectives, keep their organizations aligned, strive to keep a fair balance, and emphasize relationships.

Says a division president involved in a publishing alliance: "I have several inputs from different parts of my firm as well as from my partner. I use this information to try to judge personality matches, discuss these with my partner, and coach my team on styles that will facilitate our cooperation." Adds someone on his staff: "He has a hands-off style, but he wants to know where I am going on a topic and gives me useful suggestions, such as encouraging me to be more open-minded with my counterpart."

"We have both worked on building more rapport between us," notes an operations manager from a health care group about his colleague from the partner organization. "We have taken time away from the office to do this. Having a quiet meal or a beer together gives us a chance to explore our thinking and concerns, and helps us understand each other better. As we have gotten to know each other, we are exploring more together. This openness allows us to be more creative and find more constructive ways through tough issues."

REVIEW YOUR FUTURE

Unlike a marriage, an alliance exists only for economic reasons. Even if things have gone well, should either partner find a better way to meet its own objectives, its enthusiasm for the relationship will decline and the alliance should end.[4]

Though HP and Canon have been linked for many years, HP periodically assesses possible transition points where it might go alone or with someone else. "We owe it to our stockholders and employees to remain competitive," says an executive. "With rare exceptions, such as color printers, we have concluded that Canon technology is the best way forward for us."

Each company knows it would lose if the other walked away. To prevent that, each strives to become more valuable to the other through continuous improvement—Canon in laser engines, HP in software, quality, and distribution.

CELEBRATE SUCCESS

When you win together, visibly confirm it. Nothing beats a shared sense of accomplishment to encourage people to do even better.

After Ford and ABB completed the Oakville paint plant, the groups were so pleased with the results that Paint Finishing's parent group within ABB held its annual board meeting at the new plant.

Outside HP's laser printer headquarters in Boise, Idaho, and near Canon's offices in Tokyo, identical one-ton redstone rocks were placed, marking the celebration of 20 million printers shipped. Identical plaques on each read "*Kyosei*—living and working together for the common good."

People at the interface between Wal-Mart and Procter & Gamble prepare sweatshirts they wear to celebrate milestones, as when they passed $1 billion in sales. The firms also recognize, in alliance annual reports and other ways, those who took risks and who supported the behaviors that led to their success.

CHAPTER 8

REPAIR BROKEN TRUST

■

The KLM–Northwest alliance—a flight to nowhere—changed course only after both firms realized that backstabbing was causing them to fall behind their rivals. Key shifts at the top of each company also helped. Northwest co-chairman Al Checchi left to pursue a political career, while KLM chairman Pieter Bouw retired. Fortunately, Bouw's successor, Leo van Wijk, had built healthy relationships with other Northwest executives, despite years of constant battle surrounding them, which became a platform for launching a broad-based renewal.[1]

How these airlines got a fresh start together illustrates a cardinal rule: Whatever undermines any of the eight conditions for

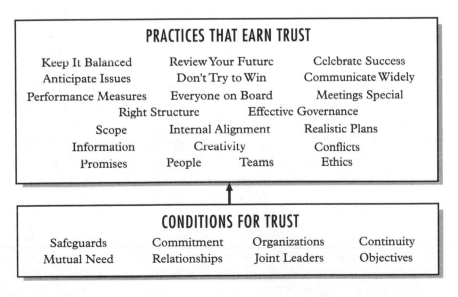

PRACTICES THAT EARN TRUST

Keep It Balanced	Review Your Future	Celebrate Success
Anticipate Issues	Don't Try to Win	Communicate Widely
Performance Measures	Everyone on Board	Meetings Special
Right Structure		Effective Governance
Scope	Internal Alignment	Realistic Plans
Information	Creativity	Conflicts
Promises	People Teams	Ethics

CONDITIONS FOR TRUST

Safeguards	Commitment	Organizations	Continuity
Mutual Need	Relationships	Joint Leaders	Objectives

trust must be eliminated before trust can be revived. In the KLM–Northwest alliance, mutual need had been overshadowed by conflicting objectives, and individuals who should have been joint leaders did not assume that role. The alliance could not be salvaged until those roadblocks to trust were removed.

If you are involved in an alliance in which trust has failed, an early step toward repair is to recognize that problems with any of the trust practices—such as poor teamwork or dysfunctional governance—may be symptoms, not causes.

No amount of team building will produce superior results without joint leadership; governance has no value if relationships have become hostile and cannot be turned around. In short, if the trust conditions can no longer be satisfied, rather than try to rebuild what cannot be, it is time to thank your partner for its efforts and move on.

You cannot write a contract for enthusiasm, or one that will force another company to assign its best people. Regardless of your success together in the past, should an alliance lose its rationale for either firm, the internal commitments needed to sustain it will end. Though momentum may keep things going, if the need is gone and can't be rekindled, an alliance becomes a drag on both firms.

Damaged trust is distinct from the occasional friction that happens in every alliance. Intermittent conflict is a natural offshoot of cooperation. When you settle issues constructively, as Chapter 3 notes, performance improves. However, if you let irritation grow to impair an alliance, the only sensible remedy is to review the fundamentals with your partner and seek a better understanding together.

As with building trust, mending damaged trust usually involves internal change at both firms. Repair may have to wait until people are ready for that. A general rule seems to be that reform happens when it becomes less painful than the status quo.

Problems in Tasty Wares were evident to many people for several years before they were addressed, yet no one wanted to take on the tough issues involved. The turning point came when Tasty had a serious problem with regulators. Its parents had to resolve their differences first. In the interim, Tasty suffered great losses and almost went out of business.

HOW TRUST GETS DAMAGED

Probably the most common reason for weak trust is that there was no effort to build trust in the first place. As an alliance proceeds, if initial expectations collapse, people may feel that trust was broken when in fact it never existed.

Trust may also be damaged through inattention. If you stop working on relationships, a likely fallout is that issues needing better understandings don't get settled. Then, you and your partner lose faith in being able to solve problems together. The larger your collection of open questions, the less you can count on trust. Take the example of a pair of auto parts firms that served different market segments.

Originally a cross-licensing deal, the alliance evolved over the years as the firms added shared development and combined marketing to their activities. Each expansion required new objectives, adjustments in both organizations, redefined boundaries, and wider teamwork. Those new tasks raised more issues which, unhappily, were not addressed. For example, conflicts between development programs led each side to conclude its interests were being ignored. Further, one firm excluded its partner from sales visits to customers, which irritated that partner.

What went wrong? Beneath their conflicts were distinct customer needs in their respective markets. These differences called for separate development tasks and selling methods in each case— contrasts that could have been resolved by working through the issues. Rather than try to understand and reconcile their differences, they chose to endure the growing discomfort and muddle through. That alliance is now history.

PREPARING TO MEND AN ALLIANCE

No matter what may have caused a breakdown, repairing weakened trust must begin by attending to the most basic trust conditions that have failed. Repair is like building a fresh alliance, only now you carry the added burden of misgiving.

If mutual need is unclear, that question must be addressed first. Or, if those involved recognize mutual need but have grown apart, relationships must be worked on before you can assemble the other building blocks of trust. If joint leaders are unwilling to guide a repair, someone has to convince them of the necessity and get them involved—or bring in new leaders. If those three trust conditions are met but your shared objectives are vague, that is the place to start. The more conditions that are violated, the more you will have to work on repair.

The steps to be taken in repairing trust are equally fruitful with any structure—direct cooperation, joint venture, or minority investment. To illustrate, if you have a problematic joint venture, it may be tempting to fault management. Don't yield to that view; you might as well blame the fox for noticing the henhouse door is open.

If management is not doing what you want, first look at the board. Have its members been attending meetings? Do they agree on objectives? Do they give management clear guidance? Do they monitor performance? Have they provided needed support from their firms? If any answer is no, management is just a symptom; the board is the problem. A competent board will fix any difficulties with management.

When you search for the roots of weakened trust you have to consider the practices that earn trust. But rather than stop there, examine the underlying trust conditions. Those must be met to support the practices.

For instance, Tasty Wares, now a thriving business, went through fire before it got on a productive path. During Tasty's last five years before its near-collapse, the board dismissed three general managers and watched performance deteriorate until members confirmed to each other what some had known individually: They had hired each executive, given each one mixed messages, then jettisoned each when he could not deliver. But a deeper problem was that Tasty's parents had never defined their objectives for the venture.

One essential in any renewal is that someone on each side must be willing to take the initiative. Whoever they might be, those individuals who will jointly lead the repair must get involved early on, and continue in that role as the rebuilt alliance proceeds.

If your firm and a partner share a hostile past, you will not be able to renew trust until you discuss the cause and agree on what to avoid in the future. Otherwise, people may feel that whatever created problems before may do so again. If the underlying issue was a misunderstanding, probe for how it happened rather than just promise to understand one another better in the future.

Be aware that the alliance you get when trust is restored may differ from your original plans. You may find, for instance, that renewed trust has expanded your firms' shared horizon. But if your original ambitions exceeded what revived trust will support, you may have to cut back.

MENDING TRUST WHEN CHANGE IS EASY

Having journeyed this far in *Trusted Partners,* you know the alliance between BestBank and Consumers Group was designed to fail. It had vague objectives, no joint leaders, little operating support, the wrong structure, and board members who were preoccupied with other matters.

The partners' immediate reaction when they could not respond to customers' requests for the new insurance product was to fault the venture's president for having built a weak organization. There was also some finger pointing within and between the firms. But the interviews I conducted at a board member's request soon after the debacle exposed the real causes of this alliance's problems: It had come together without several of the components of mutual trust.

Even with so much lacking, the alliance remained a priority for both firms. When asked to reflect on alternatives, each still saw the other as its best option. Key people did not have candid, constructive relationships with their counterparts, but they admitted they had not tried to develop them. In fact, the outlook for such relationships was promising. Most individuals had solid interpersonal skills, no one was polarized, there were no entrenched positions, and almost everyone was eager to improve the situation.

The venture had been put together by financial staff at Best-Bank and planners at Consumers Group, with few inputs from other areas. Deeply embarrassed by the problems, developers welcomed wider participation. Although the partners' objectives needed work, it seemed likely that these would cut across a number of functions in each firm, all of which reported to the respective CEOs. Given the potential, the CEOs were the logical candidates to take the lead. Each executive accepted that role when I went over the interview data separately with him. The next step was to firm up their joint leadership.

Over a long dinner, the CEOs reviewed the data with each other, discussed their thoughts and concerns, and listed issues needing attention. The following morning I joined them to answer their questions, to cover what joint leadership involved, and to plan the next steps. We also talked about the venture president, and criteria for selecting a small group of people who would become a repair team and continue as the newly constituted governing body. Another topic was that the JV's structure was inhibiting important teamwork between the parent firms.

From that point on the repair was mostly straightforward. The CEOs assembled the new team, briefly reviewed past difficulties, and laid out an agenda for moving forward. A discussion of problem-solving methods and the development of shared objectives topped the list. Conversations were candid, and people took time with their counterparts to better understand their views. The revitalized alliance was built on that foundation.

But the existing structure could not be changed. Creating the joint venture had required hard-won regulatory approval. No one wanted to repeat that arduous and uncertain process. Still, the venture was in the way of needed direct links between its parents' product development, sales, and service staffs. To reduce the venture's interference, many tasks were reassigned to the parents. Before the alliance was repaired, it was losing $5 million a month. A year later, it was producing that much in earnings.

REPAIRING TRUST WHEN HOSTILITY DOMINATES

Compared with the BestBank–Consumers alliance, Tasty Wares was in worse shape. Tasty also had vague objectives and a listless board. But its parents were rivals—a fact that caused no problems when Tasty was first created because competition then was weak. As the market grew more demanding, the parents' rivalry also grew until it eclipsed their common interests.

Encouraged by their own senior managements, individuals in each firm used the venture to defeat suggestions made by the other, even when doing so hurt them both. Relationships became so poor that, in one key meeting, parent company executives were so angry they shouted at each other.

Often, Tasty's employees got caught in the middle. Sometimes they played one partner off against the other to serve their own interests. Mostly, staffers resisted new initiatives, believing these might help either firm against the other and make matters worse. The stress got so bad that, while each parent knew it needed the other, each was actively reviewing its options for termination.

Early Leaders Initiated the Renewal

It was in this context of mounting crisis that a man I'll call Rick White became vice president for human resources at one of Tasty's parents. As a newcomer, he had not been involved in the hostilities. His counterpart at the other parent, Bill Porter (also a pseudonym), had wanted to improve the situation but needed a colleague on the other side.

Soon after White arrived, the two began discussing the alliance and whether a repair was feasible. To better understand each other and the state of affairs between their firms, White and Porter took a weekend ski trip together. For much of the time they discussed their careers, Tasty Wares, and personalities and politics in their firms (staying away from proprietary topics). By the end of their trip, the two had enough confidence in each other to go further.

At that point they asked me to review the matter with them. We discussed the issues and developed a tentative agenda; they arranged for interviews in each firm and in the joint venture. We agreed to work together as an ad hoc repair team. We also knew that higher-level executives would have to get involved. White and Porter were taking personal risks. If senior management from their firms chose not to participate, the HR executives might be seen as having gotten too close to the enemy.

Senior Leaders Were Recruited

The interviews pinpointed those trust conditions and practices requiring attention. Among them, interpersonal relationships were prominent. Everyone with whom I visited knew the firms needed each other, confirmed there were no common objectives, and agreed that Tasty's board was dysfunctional. But ill will and a well-founded concern about hidden agendas led most people to believe that a joint meeting would be fruitless.

After going over the interview data with White and Porter, they concurred with my findings, agreeing that relationships had to be addressed early. They also recognized that only joint leadership from high levels of both firms could bring people together. The HR executives then enlisted their division presidents in the cause.

This was a critical step. The presidents had never met, and their chairmen were said to have had a longstanding feud. But the timing was right; each president wanted to resolve the affair one way or another. To help prepare them for a meeting, White and Porter got analyses from their firms showing costs and income losses caused by the hostilities. Both firms concluded that the difficulties were taking at least $50 million annually away from their respective bottom lines.

In separate discussions, I went over each firm's interview data with its president. We had concurred beforehand that no further steps would be taken unless both executives agreed with the findings and wanted to proceed. In the meetings, each asked questions about the interviews, and each said the conclusions rang true. Buttressed by the financial analyses of their HR executives, both indicated that they wanted to proceed. We then discussed possible steps forward and confirmed that, as the heads of their units, they would have to take the lead.

Next, the two presidents visited privately for several hours to be sure they understood each other and to start discussing the road ahead. Each shared the interview data from his firm with the other, as well as their respective cost-benefit analyses. The fact that a pair of their executives had jointly prepared the ground gave the presidents reason to hope that the proposed repair had a chance.

Recalls one of the presidents: "At first, neither of us was sure we were being sincere with each other. But when we discussed the findings and possible remedies we found we were looking at the same picture. After the meeting, we followed through on tasks we had agreed to do—such as making joint communications to our respective troops. That made it easier for us to go into the repair process. We understood that if we did not lead the repair with integrity our organizations would not follow with integrity."

Others Were Included

The interview data indicated that pervasive attitudes in each firm would have to change. Accordingly, the repair process had to involve the senior managements of both companies.

The ad hoc team suggested three days off-site to reconfirm mutual need, review what had gone wrong in the past, build relationships, and set a new pattern of joint leadership. If those steps succeeded, we could start working on shared objectives, governance, and the other elements of trust. Along the way the partners would either have to assemble a new board or reinvigorate the old one.

However, many failed to see the value of investing in relationships or of revisiting old battles, and so were not interested in the proposed meeting. Several were reluctant to sit down with their adversaries. White and Porter lowered this resistance through one-on-one visits, in which they focused on the level of pain in the current situation and asked each person if it was worth trying to overcome that. Eventually—and with the divisions presidents' backing—enough people agreed to take part that everyone else went along.

To prepare for the meeting, each firm reviewed its objectives for Tasty Wares and analyzed the consequences of keeping the alliance versus breaking it up. The division presidents met again to review plans and draft a joint letter inviting meeting participation, reiterating how important it was for both companies.

Meanwhile, the HR duo kept the pressure on, encouraging people to be candid and ready to discuss tough issues constructively. The fact that they were now being supported by their presidents gave their message more force.

The Off-Site Meeting

The division presidents launched the meeting with a joint presentation about desired results and the need for candor. Following a briefing by an attorney who reminded them of topics that as rivals they could not discuss, White and Porter reviewed their joint analysis of what the firms would lose if the repair failed. This was the first time most people had understood in detail how and why their firms needed each other. The message helped set the tone for the meeting.

Then things got rough. The ad hoc team had encouraged both firms to avoid taking a fixed position while preparing for the meeting. That concern now seemed naive; fragmentation in each company prevented many people from seeing the whole picture. Those narrow views produced tough issues about what the objectives should be, with wide disagreement within and between the firms. But the presidents refused to back down. They kept pushing for clarity and consensus, visibly conferring with each other all along. When an agreement was finally reached, they were seen as having produced it and gained stature as joint leaders.

As the meeting moved into matters of organization and governance, participants said they wanted to take more time on earlier problems they had with each other and on how to avoid repeating them in the future. Though it had been hard to get this topic on the agenda, the group's recognition of mutual need, its accomplishment in clarifying objectives, and effective joint leadership created a feeling of confidence. People were now comfortable enough to address their difficult past. The old problems were seen as inhibiting repair, and participants wanted to get them out of the way.

Throughout the meeting, the division presidents jointly led the proceedings, and were seen chatting about issues over meals and at every break. After a long walk the first afternoon, they presented a joint plan that addressed some troubling questions constructively. Encouraged by their open cooperation and displays of mutual respect, others from both firms spent time together.

During the review of the past, several people said they were concerned that higher levels of both firms might still expect their troops to use Tasty Wares in ways destructive to the other partner. Both presidents agreed that could happen and promised to review the matter with their respective chairmen. In a later meeting, the presidents briefed their chairmen on what happened at the off-site, including the report on what poor cooperation cost. Both chairmen acknowledged that their firms had used Tasty to foil one another, and that those actions had weakened their venture. They promised each other to prohibit such behavior in the future.

With that final indication of support from the top, both firms aligned on the inside to better support Tasty Wares. For awhile, some people tested whether the change was real. Each time one of the presidents or HR execs stopped the initiative. One other change proved necessary. Tasty's general manager had become so used to fighting political battles with its parents that he could not adapt to the change and had to leave. Under the joint leadership of the two presidents, Tasty ended its losses and regained market share. Each parent added more than $50 million to its annual profits.

CONSIDER THE CONTEXT, NOT JUST PEOPLE

In some troubled alliances particular individuals are seen as a cause of the problem—perhaps because they fuel polarization, appear unwilling to yield turf, or for other reasons. Before concluding that they must be moved out, though, consider the forces on them and their performance in other settings. The reason for taking this wider view is not just to retain top talent. By focusing only on people, you may overlook deeper causes of mistrust.

For instance, during my review of Tasty Wares, a number of staffers in both parent firms told me that one board member—let's call him John Lowman—had aggravated the situation. Lowman chaired the board's finance committee and often took rigid positions against others' wishes. At times, he used Tasty to help his company at its partner's expense. A repair, they said, would involve his departure.

Understanding Lowman's attitude requires knowing something about the context. Though his behavior made him an obvious target for blame, Lowman was not the root cause of Tasty's difficulties. More basic problems included personal friction between the partners' chairmen and rigid turf boundaries within each firm, as well as board members who were busy with other matters. Lowman, whose bonus depended entirely on progress in the venture, believed that the only way he could get things done was to resist others' disjointed efforts.

Lowman had been one of his firm's stars before joining Tasty's board, and he knew more about the alliance than others. Still, his rigid style had jelled attitudes against him. Any effort to mend trust would have to overcome that. And if Lowman stayed, he would have to become a team player.

Lowman told me he was frustrated by rancor within the alliance and by mixed messages from his own firm. On the one hand, his marching orders had been to use Tasty against his firm's partner. On the other, he was measured on Tasty's performance, which required cooperation.

Newfound joint leadership above Lowman changed those ground rules. No longer at loggerheads the two presidents, in preparing for the off-site, reviewed Lowman's style and discussed the merits of his attendance. They decided to invite him since he was so knowledgeable. Further, Lowman's boss told him that expectations had shifted from adversity to cooperation and coached him on more positive behavior. Lowman was cautioned that his tenure would be short unless he changed.

Lowman saw the off-site as a way to improve matters without being in the spotlight. During the meeting he displayed a new style. Rather than dominate, he occasionally asked questions and made constructive comments. At a difficult moment when his job as finance committee chairman was being questioned, he suggested eliminating the position because it interfered with governance. The presidents agreed and did just that. Some people suspected a hidden agenda; I am confident that Lowman had no idea of what was ahead.

Following the repair Lowman was made co-chair of Tasty Wares' executive committee. He and his counterpart jointly led Tasty's rebuilding and have won wide admiration.

ALLIANCES WITH KEY PARTNERS

∎

CHAPTER 9

HOW TO TRUST DIFFICULT CUSTOMERS

■

What most firms depict as alliances with their customers are little more than transactions wearing an alliance label. Evidence for that includes the poor ratings sales executives give to such links.[1]

If your company has a difficult relationship with a customer, it may be possible to shift to a healthier course. Two examples below show how this works. In the first illustration, adversity created an opportunity for change. In the second case, the supplier converted a stubborn customer.

Among all businesses, links between engineering and construction firms, on the one hand, and clients for whom they design and build, on the other, are often the most contentious. The uniqueness and complexity of each project often mean that specifications cannot be complete. The upshot may be misunderstandings and hard feelings. Clients get upset if contractors miss major items even though these may not have been spelled out in the plans. As contractors see it, clients add tasks once a project is under way, claiming these were already understood. Another problem: In preparing

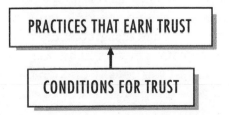

bids, each contractor must assume that others will not get in the way of its work.

Anticipating such issues and that they will not be resolved fairly, each side protects its interests. Contractors build what they think is the minimum needed to meet the specification, while clients demand the maximum. Change orders become a battle-ground. Clients see these as a way for contractors to pad their profits, while contractors regard the orders as their only way to make a decent margin. When they can, contractors protect them-selves by hiding contingency costs in their bids, which may amount to 5 percent to 10 percent of a project's total cost.

PART OF FORD BREAKS A BAD HABIT

It was in that context of traditional mistrust that Ford Motor's paint plant staff and ABB's Paint Finishing unit shared a particu-larly bad experience at a major truck finishing plant in Ohio.

Painting a vehicle is far more difficult and expensive than you might imagine. Because consumers have high expectations for quality, even tiny imperfections in a car's finish cause it to be re-painted. This leads to rejection rates at paint plants that can exceed 25 percent, with 10 percent being unusually low. Finishing conse-quently takes five of the thirty hours needed to make a car. Fur-ther, less than 80 percent of the paint sprayed on a vehicle adheres to it. The rest is waste, which requires sophisticated environmental controls. A typical paint plant consequently costs several hundred million dollars, involves a dozen or more contractors, and is ex-tremely complex.

For these reasons, when things go bad they can get really bad. Noted one Ford executive about the Ohio experience: "Our safety was not good, coordination was terrible, a lot of mistakes were made, contractors got behind schedule, and there were serious cost overruns. We had tough disagreements with the contractors regarding who owed whom money." This was one of the worst of such projects at Ford. It was equally discouraging for ABB, which had just made large investments to strengthen its paint finishing business.

Because change seems to happen when it is less difficult than standing still, the Ohio affair was a watershed. Commenting on that experience Larry Miller, Ford's purchasing specialist on the job, says: "It was painful for all of us. We did not want to go through that again." Adds Paul Bechard, ABB's vice president for Paint Finishing: "After Ohio we all had a burning desire to do something different."

Leadership at Ford

The initiative for change came from Vince Coletta, Ford's executive engineer for plant facilities. Long before Ohio, he had been thinking about better ways to build new factories, but had found internal resistance. "Our bad experience in Ohio gave me an opportunity to go forward with it," he says. But the path was rough. "It took a lot of courage for Vince to take this initiative," says one Ford manager. "He was breaking with tradition. Even some of his own people were opposed."

Coletta's idea was to replace Ford's usual practice of seeking competitive bids for each of many parts of a plant with a single contractor that would integrate everything. In the old way, each supplier saw only a small part of a whole project, so there was no chance for project-wide creativity. The same fragmentation also hurt coordination, which caused the problems Ford and ABB had in Ohio.

To get alignment within Ford, Coletta first spoke with his boss, Owen Zidar, about how a full-service contractor would be an attractive way to control these projects. Zidar liked the idea, believed it needed a strong hand from purchasing, and suggested they get leadership from that function as well. This led to a visit with a top purchasing executive, who suggested Larry Miller. Miller welcomed the opportunity.

Says Coletta: "Larry and I supported each other from the start. We talked about the project at length and understood we could succeed only by working together. Unlike other experiences, we reviewed the issues with each other openly and found practical solutions. He played a big part in the success of the alliance."

Choosing a Partner

Soon after the trouble Ohio, Ford asked three firms, including ABB, to bid on two paint plants in North America. ABB was the low bidder for one in Michigan, which was later canceled due to weak market conditions. The other plant, in Oakville, Ontario, was similar to that in Michigan and ABB seemed qualified. But Coletta and Miller wanted more than an arm's length bid.

Integral to Coletta's dream was his belief that success would depend on relationships. "Larry Miller and I both had to feel comfortable that ABB was the right group to pull this off," he says. "We knew them from earlier jobs and spoke to them at length about Oakville. In our prior work together disputes had come up, often leading to strong disagreements. But we found that we could always talk about the issues productively and reach fair conclusions."

Echoes Tom Mark, president of ABB Paint Finishing at the time: "We wrestled with some difficult issues on the Ohio project and found we both had the will to resolve them fairly. When you work through adversity with someone you see what they are made of. That is something you can build on."

Growing comfort among people who would be teamed together was reinforced at higher levels when Coletta, Miller, Bechard, and Mark met with Paul Sullivan, executive director of purchasing at Ford. Sullivan had asked ABB to lead a balanced discussion comparing how it would manage the new project with Ford's usual construction methods.

Confidence in the novel approach got another boost when Miller opened vital channels in his organization. The way things had normally worked, contract management at Ford was expected to reject creativity and favor standard practice. In fact, other vendors put political pressure on Miller and Coletta when they discovered what the two had planned.

On other jobs, Ford had always presented bidders with a set of specs. This time they were only going to give ABB key requirements, such as the need for spray painting booths, without detailed specs. Coletta and Miller sat down with engineering and purchasing and discussed their readiness to do this as a team and then got buy-in from top management. Meanwhile, Sullivan protected the two from political snipers. He understood the new opportunity and had become comfortable with ABB. Ford invited ABB to make a sole-source bid.

ABB Aligns Its Organization

As internal alignment proceeded at Ford, ABB created a new management position, a new project structure, and a cross-functional project team. Though using such teams was normal practice for ABB, the alliance was larger and involved many more ABB activities than a typical job. The task of integrating all of them thus required the new position. The firm also developed incentives for team members to encourage creativity, coordination, and integration across the project, all aimed at Ford's objectives of better safety, lower cost, and speed. ABB reviewed its proposed structure and processes with Ford, which concluded that these would work.

At ABB, the notion of committing to a firm price contract far larger than any it had taken on before was hard to accept initially. Just as worrisome, ABB would have to trust that any changes sought once the project was under way would be resolved constructively. Tom Mark's and Paul Bechard's growing comfort with the Ford people, and their knowledge of higher-level support there, convinced the two to proceed. Mark sold the project to his superiors at ABB, and he and Coletta became joint leaders of the alliance.

Backsliding—and Recovery

On the surface, the newfound partners had reason to celebrate their arrangement, which offered a welcome departure from an unhappy legacy. But experience is the only soil in which new habits grow. What had been agreed to in principle still had to pass the test of practice, and this was to be dramatically different from how the firms normally operated. In fact, at the start, both sides fell back on traditional behavior in which the spec goes out, bids come back, there is a meeting for clarification, and the award is made.

Because Ford was pressed for time, it gave ABB two weeks to develop a fixed-price proposal. When they met to discuss ABB's response, it included the usual contingencies and was rejected. Coletta was agitated. "For a few seconds I wanted to revert to the old way of slamming the door in the other guy's face," he says. "I felt they were not looking at it properly and their price was way out of line. But this had been a dream of mine for a long time and I was determined to make it work."

It was an acutely embarrassing moment for everyone. They had created the opportunity together, success was important to them, and personal commitments were growing. Suddenly, people realized they were still trapped in the past and began exploring how to escape. As was its custom, Ford had been considering various options for several parts of the plant. ABB included those possibilities in its proposal, which drove up the cost. Once they grasped what had happened, says Miller, "It was a dramatic change for all of us. It was as though we had taken our shoes and socks off right there and walked around the room barefoot."

Driven by their shared desire to make a difference, and sobered by their mistake, those in the meeting engaged in a detailed conversation to clarify Ford's objectives and judge the alternatives. To promote better understandings, Coletta commented on the importance of personal relationships. The group talked about the need for trust and to be more open. "We had to be sure we really understood each other," says Bechard. "We had to confirm how things would work and what we would do if the unexpected happened." There was also a feeling that people wanted to know each other better. "This could have been a career-ender for all of us," he adds. "We were going to be critically dependent on each other." One thing they learned was that neither firm really understood the concept of a full-service supplier. That led to more discussion and better understandings.

As the meeting progressed, Coletta encouraged ABB's commitment by stating that "we want ABB to do this project and make a decent profit on so it will be a contender for our next project."

He also told ABB to get rid of contingency costs, promising that if his firm missed something, it would pay. Everyone also agreed that ABB would pay for anything it had missed. In fact, Ford later added capacity, and paid for it.

Coletta and Mark created an interfirm engineering team and gave it three months to develop a better proposal. Thanks to joint creativity it was radically different from past designs. At the end of the engineering effort, they agreed on a fixed price and signed a brief purchase order. "It was about what I would have written to buy ten rolls of toilet paper," says Miller. Next came a detailed engineering phase, and then construction.

Joint creativity continued during construction—adding a ramp here, better airflow there. While there were few change orders involving payments to ABB, there were many no-cost changes. "We had become a team," says Bechard. "We collectively discussed the impact of proposed changes on safety, cost, time, and quality. If the team decided to add cost in one place we looked for ways to reduce cost somewhere else."

In contrast to the Ohio job, where Ford people were on the phone every day with every subcontractor to keep things on track, at Oakville the auto maker's staffers didn't have to pick up the phone. On those few occasions when Rudy Golla, ABB's project manager, told Coletta that Ford owed his firm money, Coletta simply asked for an explanation and okayed it. Formerly, even if one firm believed it owed the other money, it would try to avoid paying.

Despite the added time up front, the project set a completion record for the industry. Improvements in safety due to better coordination more than covered suppliers' insurance costs. Reject rates were cut substantially, and capital cost was 25 percent below normal for such plants. The completed facility did not compromise—and in some cases surpassed—the initial specifications. Oakville was the smoothest launch for any Ford paint plant up to that time. It had fewer problems and got to full volume in one-half the time needed formerly. Since start-up, operating and maintenance costs have been less than for any Ford paint plants built earlier. "And to think that before, we were bashing each other over the head," Miller observes.

CONVERTING A STUBBORN CUSTOMER

Adversity brought leaders at Ford and ABB to the same point si-multaneously: There had to be a better way to work together. Even if executives at your customer firm do not seem open to improving relationships, all is not lost. You still may be able to identify some-one who will spearhead change. However, if your firms historically have been at loggerheads, convincing a customer that an alliance is worthwhile will take time and persistence.

With any recalcitrant customer, the trust conditions must be met to get on a healthier course. Early steps require both firms to recognize mutual need and relationships as top priorities. Your cus-tomer must see your firm as the source of a solution to a critical problem. For your part, business with your customer must be im-portant enough that you assign your best talent. To turn things around, key people on both sides will need strong interpersonal skills.

Such was the case with Butler Manufacturing, a supplier of buildings like retail distribution centers. Butler had endured a tra-ditional adversarial relationship with SuperSave, a large general re-tailer. To Butler and other suppliers, the retailer had a long history of being dictatorial. SuperSave did not believe suppliers were com-mitted to its objectives and used power to get its way. Relationships were terrible. "We always tried to be professional with them," says Bill Johnsmeyer, president of Butler's construction unit, "but they regularly pulled the rug out from under us."

For Butler, the situation was exasperating. SuperSave was one of its largest customers, the retailer acknowledged that Butler con-structed superior buildings, and Butler was often the lowest-cost bidder. While those elements confirmed a priority mutual need, it was so tainted by conflict that Butler was close to being dropped.

Finding a Potential Change Leader

The one hope for turning things around was a man I'll call Walt York, SuperSave's construction manager for distribution centers. York was overbearing, demanded superior performance, and didn't trust suppliers. But he also was ambitious and driven to shrink cycle times for erecting new centers. The faster a distribution center went up, the sooner the new stores it supported could open.

York had been pushing Butler and his other contractors as hard as he could toward this goal. However, unlike Ford's Vince Coletta, his caustic style and lack of faith in suppliers prevented York from reaching out to them. Making matters worse, York had a long and testy relationship with Butler's lead executive on the SuperSave account. Johnsmeyer got the same dictatorial treatment when he moved into that position. Still, York's ambition presented an opportunity for change.

Demonstrating Commitment

Absent healthy relationships with his customer, Johnsmeyer and his team sought chances to display their commitment, hoping that York might see the light and return that commitment in kind. Two separate occasions provided the chance.

One was when SuperSave hired a new design firm for its distribution centers. Typically, designers and builders work against specifications with little interest in or collaboration on improving on the specs. But this time, Ralph Agee, Butler's senior project engineer on the job, helped the designer get started.

Agee coached the design firm on Butler's product and alternate ways to use it. This allowed the designer to standardize some tasks, simplifying its work and permitting Butler to lower its costs and cycle time. Soon, the design firm and SuperSave's staff architect were seeking ideas from Agee. Personal chemistry grew between them, and he became comfortable sharing more information than usual, which led to even better results. When York learned of these improvements he began seeking Agee's advice in other areas.

Meanwhile, Dennis Wasserman, Butler's field superintendent for SuperSave, had become a textbook example of how best to treat a customer. His constant attention to the retailer's needs so impressed York that he told Johnsmeyer that Wasserman was the best field superintendent he had ever seen.

These experiences thawed York's attitudes, which melted

completely after a critical experience the firms shared. On a key job in Maryland, some anchor bolts imbedded in the concrete foundation by another contractor broke when Butler was setting structural steel. Johnsmeyer told York that going ahead as planned would be unsafe. If more bolts proved to be brittle, the steel might collapse while being erected. York doubted there was a problem; he said Butler was just looking for an excuse to be late.

The traditional approach to a broken anchor bolt was to shut down the job until the issue was resolved. Then, if testing showed other bolts to be brittle, new ones would have to be installed, requiring the project to stay shut and causing substantial delays. Knowing that cycle time was important to York, Johnsmeyer proposed that Butler keep construction on schedule by installing special braces to hold the steel in place. In his usual intimidating style, York accepted but said if the bolts were later determined to be sound, the breakage must be Butler's fault. He would then expect Butler to pay the added costs.

Some days later, Johnsmeyer called York at home. The anchor bolt test had just come back indicating the bolts were brittle. Butler would continue to use the special braces to erect the building to stay on schedule. York abruptly dropped his abrasive style. Finally, the accumulated experiences had convinced York that Butler offered the opportunity he sought. "Our relationship changed dramatically," Johnsmeyer recalls. "Never again did Walt throw things in my face. From then on, he believed we were always looking out for SuperSave's interests."

York's and Johnsmeyer's newfound relationship encouraged cooperation at lower levels and facilitated changes in Butler's organization to better align with the retailer. People grew so close that what had before been unthinkable became normal. To illustrate: A Butler field supervisor was best man in the wedding of a SuperSave construction manager. As relationships grew information sharing and joint creativity rose apace. Together, the firms cut the cycle time for erecting distribution centers from an initial 180 days to 28 days.

YOU MAY HAVE TO CHANGE PEOPLE

Faced with intractable hostile attitudes, relationships may not be repairable. In such cases, if the other trust conditions can be met you will have to bring in new people. Recall that Walt York's discord with Bill Johnsmeyer's predecessor kept Butler stuck in an unhealthy relationship with its customer. Johnsmeyer's personal style and commitment to changing how the firms worked together made the difference.

New faces at the top may not be enough. Ralph Agee's early success with SuperSave's design firm and staff architect happened because each was new in his position and open to fresh ideas. "All three of us were starting together," says Agee. "We were not part of the history and knew adversity was not going to help us. We faced a major challenge and needed each other to meet it."

CHAPTER 10

HOW TO SELL ALLIANCES
TO CUSTOMERS

■

As a supplier, the closest relationship you can have with a customer is through an alliance. Yet despite clear benefits—including more value for your customer and healthier revenues and margins for your firm—many customers aren't ready for such intimacy. By using the eight trust conditions as a guide to selecting customers and selling them alliances, you have a better chance of reaping the rewards.

To appreciate why some firms aren't prepared, consider the leadership dimension of trust. At many customers, purchasing executives are second-class citizens. Typically, their performance is evaluated based on prices they pay suppliers, rather than on total cost or value received. Because of their limited authority, they can't spearhead internal changes needed to ally with suppliers. In such cases, someone else in the firm has to fill the void. For instance, none of the customer-supplier alliances described earlier—Hewlett-Packard and Canon, Ford and ABB, SuperSave and Butler, Wal-Mart and Procter & Gamble—was developed or led by purchasing people.

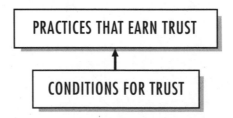

Similar leadership gaps exist at many suppliers. Like their counterparts in purchasing, most salespeople are gauged by narrow criteria such as short-term revenue gains. Often, they lack the influence, orientation, or time needed to build cross-functional teams or align their firms with customers. Recall from Chapter 5 the early years in the Wal-Mart/Procter & Gamble alliance, when P&G interface team members had to struggle against internal resistance.

Such deficiencies in customer and supplier companies are clear impediments to alliances. Another barrier is poor understanding about how these alliances work. So few companies have true customer-supplier alliances that most are not aware of the possibilities. The results these alliances have delivered for the firms described earlier are almost unknown in the broader business community.[1]

In the commodity business, many companies I have told about customer-supplier alliances in other settings doubted that such arrangements would work with their undifferentiated products. All were surprised to learn what commodity producer Exxon Chemical Europe had achieved. By allying with its bulk carriers, Exxon cut its transportation costs by more than 20 percent without harm to its margins—or those of the carriers. Both Exxon and its suppliers expect their results to keep getting better.[2]

One consequence of these weak understandings: When you try to sell alliances to customers, they hear you asking for a more secure relationship, not proposing to deliver more value. To sell an alliance you must overcome those barriers and develop trust. No amount of entertaining, CEO-to-CEO contacts, or any other often-used sales tactics will result in an alliance with a customer if the ingredients for trust are absent.

CHOOSING CUSTOMERS

Alliances are so clearly superior to transactions that after Procter & Gamble prospered with Wal-Mart, the consumer goods maker built similar links with other customers, including Kmart and Kroger in the United States, and Tesco, the leading British retailer.

ABB Paint Finishing, flush with its successful teaming with Ford, built on that experience. Showcasing its Ford results, ABB has won two-thirds of the truck finishing market in North America by selling and successfully implementing customer alliances.

In judging candidates, P&G and ABB seek an ability to engage in the processes trust building requires. Since only forty retailers account for some 80 percent of P&G's business, the firm must consider all of them as potential alliance partners. Consequently, those who sell alliances for P&G set their expectations for each customer based on what they learn during the qualification phase.

Compared with qualifying customers in traditional selling, locating alliance prospects and judging each one takes more effort. The payoff comes from deeper customer penetration, increased revenue, better margins, and superior learning for your company, and—for your customer—substantially greater value.

To find the best opportunities, look for a priority mutual need: customers for which your product can make a significant difference, and where strategic fit and profitability are attractive to your firm. Of course, the other trust conditions apply as well. P&G has learned, for example, that when it cannot find a change leader who is in the right position, an alliance with a customer has limited potential.

If you have many possible candidates, a two-step process will help you find the most promising ones: first, marketing research to identify likely market segments, and second, company-specific analysis that examines good prospects. Companies that sell in your market, and that are not your rivals, can be useful sources of information about which customers treat their suppliers fairly, and how their people and organizations work.

Your business does not have to be as big and powerful as P&G to persuade customers to ally with you. Chicago-based Craftsman Custom Metal Fabricators, which makes a variety of custom parts and specializes in short-cycle operations, begins its search for alliance customers by identifying firms for which fast cycle times are critical. Its best prospects are electronics companies that need to get new products to customers as quickly as possible and are likely to value suppliers that can help them do this.

Within Craftsman's target segment, Al Krempels, vice president of engineering and product development, often gives half-day seminars for any prospect that expresses an interest in what his firm offers. These presentations are aimed largely at engineering staffs, who are likely to have a stake in short cycle times. Krempels reviews how cooperation in fast-response design and manufacturing works, explaining the need for creative relationships and information sharing.

Craftsman's record is notable: 50 percent of its qualified prospects convert to alliances. "We set our targets once we understand that the potential is there," says president Bruce Bendoff. "Then the expectation becomes the reality a high percentage of the time."

COVER BEHAVIOR IN INITIAL DISCUSSIONS

Once you have a list of promising companies, meet with each to assess whether its organization can perform as needed. Also determine how an alliance with your company would add unique value, explore whether the firm is open to your being a new supplier, and explain how what you are proposing will work. Companies that simply want to solicit bids shouldn't be in the running.

In your conversations, be specific. Asking for details about how leadership really functions and cross-discipline teams perform, and making other queries related to the trust conditions and practices, help you evaluate an opportunity. "Our salespeople must learn about the customer's organization," Bendoff observes.

Paul Bechard, ABB's vice president of sales and marketing, goes through the following steps. Initially, he visits people who would be involved in an alliance at the operating level. He reviews the alliance's value, learns if it would get priority, describes how it would operate, and determines if the customer's organization performs as needed.

Bechard asks who the lead executive is likely to be, and inquires about that person's ability to build teams and to support needed changes. Other questions are aimed at surfacing issues that might be raised by higher-ups in later meetings. If

Bechard finds enthusiasm for an alliance and believes needed abilities are present, the company becomes a candidate for further conversations.

Craftsman salespeople begin their alliance discussions with existing and potential customers by inquiring about what these firms want to improve in its core area of fast-response manufacturing. They also cover how Craftsman works, including its need to interface with a firm's quality, engineering, and production functions. The metal parts company delivers the best cycle times to customers that are or can be aligned in those areas.

After they have pinpointed promising situations, Craftsman's salespeople ask about the customer's internal politics, to find the right change leader for the intended project. Obvious candidates include sourcing managers above the day-to-day purchasing level who are looking for best-in-class suppliers, although the individual may be in another function.

The understandings you develop in selling alliances help qualify prospects, prepare both firms for working together, and resolve possible impediments. For instance, before joining with P&G, Wal-Mart regarded the consumer goods maker's soaps as too expensive. During early discussions P&G staffers took Wal-Mart people into its labs, demonstrating how soaps were researched, developed, and tested, and what a difference that made in cleaning power. Wal-Mart's cost concerns disappeared.

In addition to your own learning about a customer, that firm's staffers must understand how your company works. Craftsman, for instance, wants to convince prospects that it functions as its salespeople say. The company does this by inviting promising candidates to its facility to observe its operations firsthand. Since customer and supplier want to be confident about the match, staffers from both visit often enough to understand how their activities will connect and to begin building relationships. Craftsman regards the reluctance of a prospect's key people to visit its facility as a negative signal.

Echoing the need for candid understandings, "I want potential customers to know our limit points," the sales executive of a transportation firm with a number of customer alliances says. "My competitors don't share this, which can lead to problems for them. We excel in our business, but we can't be all things to everyone. If a company is attracted to our product and knows where we can and cannot stretch, having that knowledge gives them confidence in what we say we will do. If they push back and ask us for more, we brainstorm what we might do together to make it possible. Often, we find ways to avoid barriers on each side."

What your firm's salesperson learns depends on his abilities and the contact's ease in discussing such matters. People are not as cautious about their firms as they are when asked about proprietary topics. Still, you have to handle the dialogue about individuals and organizations sensitively. "It is up to our reps and salespeople to get honest answers," notes Bendoff. "They have to be skilled at this and have solid relationships to accomplish it."

BEGIN JOINT LEADERSHIP

When an initial visit uncovers a promising opportunity, ABB's Bechard meets with whoever is seen as the appropriate change leader, to start building rapport and understandings at this level. The two go over the alliance in detail and discuss how it can create benefits. "It is really a matter of selling a process," he explains. "We go through every step."

ABB's sales vice president also inquires about his counterpart's experience in leading change, and what the person hopes to gain from an alliance. In addition, he asks about who else might be involved, and explores their work style and attitudes.

With this probing, "I am really looking for a read on the chemistry of the discussion," Bechard says. "There is a lot of exploration about the organization and the individual's interests. We get into politics, personalities, internal issues that could influence an alliance, how success would affect his career, what would make him a hero, and what could cause problems. Some people are surprised by these questions, but when they realize my concern is genuine they appreciate the candor. By the end of the first meeting, we have identified the critical business issues to be resolved for us to go forward together."

The alliance-selling process helps you avoid proposing what your customer can't implement, which can damage relationships. For example, if best results will come from involving several customer functions in a team but one function won't participate, scale back your plans and get early results that you can build on.

Though your own financial and any other vital objectives must be met, the overall objectives in a customer-supplier alliance are set by the customer. That's what it means to be market-oriented. Recall that Canon's and HP's goal is to grow HP volume. Customer-supplier alliances are generally structured using direct cooperation, as Chapter 6 notes.

When a prospect shows obvious interest—and with your ideas fresh in its people's minds—be ready to move faster than you would in other selling situations. Doing so helps you build on early interest and shows how important the opportunity is to your company. Also, bring your best people to meetings and be sure they will continue through implementation. For qualified prospects "we must be willing to commit our 'A' team," remarks ABB's Bechard.

To facilitate continuity after your initial discussions, include in planning meetings at least one customer staffer with whom you visited earlier and who recommended your company. Also solicit early support from the relevant buyer and include that person in the decision process; it's easier to respond to visible objections than to a hidden sniper. In addition, include each firm's designated operating-level leader, so that they can start developing understandings and contribute to joint plans.

One early test of a prospect's interest is who attends meetings. If participants come only from purchasing when other functions must be involved, expect problems ahead. Attendance from corporate only, despite the need for substantial local involvement, may indicate little local interest. Another potential deal breaker: key people who are hard to work with. ABB ended discussions about a possible alliance when the customer insisted on including someone with an abrasive personal style.

From here on, meetings shift to assembling an interfirm team and taking the other steps described in Chapters 2 through 7. Two additional steps are—handling objections and closing the sale—have aspects that are unique to alliances.

ANSWER OBJECTIONS AND GET THE BUSINESS

As with any kind of selling, most prospects will raise concerns. A frequent issue is whether the seller's proposal can work. The best response is to describe how your firm operates, invite staffers to make site visits, and arrange contacts with your current alliance customers. ABB, which uses that strategy, considers its ability to display its experience its strongest selling point.

If a customer asks why you didn't propose an alliance earlier, answer directly. If you never took the time to step back from the daily fray and honestly explore better ways to work together, say so. For customers with whom your relationships are poor, the techniques discussed in Chapter 9 may be useful.

Many companies resist alliances with suppliers out of concern for overdependence. Explain that this misgiving can be avoided if the customer uses benchmarking, measures supplier performance, and has a backup plan. (These tactics are wise with any suppliers, not just in alliances.) A related issue for many first-time alliance customers is how they can be sure the proposal will be competitive with traditional procurement. One response is to agree on metrics that compare both approaches. Your customer will need the same metrics for benchmarking. An alternative is to offer an attractive price.[3]

For instance, though total cost is a more effective measure, most Craftsman customers evaluate suppliers based on price. So the metal parts firm must be competitive on that score. Once it has the order, Craftsman finds ways to cooperate to change the product, add value, and reduce cost on both sides. The firm's ability to make such improvements is a key to what it sells. By qualifying customers for alliances, Craftsman knows they will be able to participate in those processes and keep its margins healthy.

Another frequent question is how a customer can be certain the supplier will assign its best people to the effort. To address that concern, promise that key people will stay from start to finish—

and keep your word. In selling alliances you cannot make the pitch, close the deal, and leave. Since initial relationships are part of the underpinnings of mutual trust, they must continue. Senior executives like Tom Mark, president of ABB Paint Finishing, have scored alliance sales successes by following through on company and personal commitments that key people and resources will be involved over the long haul.

Once a prospect's concerns are resolved and it is time to close, some companies ask for sole-source proposals, initial the plan, and launch joint teams. Others call for bids. You may not appreciate the latter, which can threaten trust if it comes as a surprise. Still, Craftsman's Bendoff notes that "the customer is on top, so we have to accept this when it happens. If we bring enough to the party and the customer wants to do business with us, asking for bids is not an impediment." Often, bids are sought to stifle internal critics who claim there is no way to know whether the supplier is best unless its offering can be compared with another firm's.

Upon getting the business, the negotiating team moves into implementation. In Craftsman's case, vice president Al Krempels often becomes the lead executive. He and his counterpart recognize each other as co-leaders, and become a two-person steering committee for the alliance's duration. At both ABB and P&G, the lead salespeople and their opposites join newly formed steering committees.

WHAT ALLIANCE SELLERS REQUIRE

People who sell alliances must be able to deliver to their customers those activities that differentiate alliances from transactions. Alliance sellers not only need more authority than those handling transactions, but also must have team-building skills. Your lead executive, like Paul Bechard, Al Krempels, or Tom Muccio, vice president for customer business development at P&G, must be able to reach into your firm, draw upon its best talent, and align these people around the customer's objectives.

P&G, like most firms with account management functions, distinguishes between the traditional role of producing revenue and that of people like Muccio, who are accountable for revenue and can access multifunctional resources and influence how P&G does business.

Similarly, ABB's Bechard has enough authority to help bring about the internal realignment needed to support each alliance. While the day-to-day leader does not report to him, Bechard is in a position to ensure that alliance procedures are followed. ABB also expects each leader to include sales support throughout an alliance's life.

Another part of the alliance seller's job is to nurture mutual understandings. Craftsman's salespeople detail how the firm's tool-making facility and rapid response department cut cycle time, and describe how it interfaces with most computer-aided design systems. They also cover how the firm integrates its internal activities to meet customers' needs, describe how an alliance would work, and probe to learn about each customer's organization.

Listen to ABB's Tom Mark describe Bechard's part in building the alliance with Ford: "Paul was a window on the Ford organization for ABB and a window on ABB for Ford. That was an important role. It involved communicating attitudes, needs, and facts between the firms, and doing this in a way that people on both sides were confident was correct."

"Selling alliances is really a matter of understanding the dynamics of two social systems," Mark continues. "One needs interpretive skills to understand people and organizations. One must be able to convey in simple terms what those attributes are so that both firms can grasp the shared potential and how to organize, how the work flow would take place."

Your customer is buying a leader, a team, a process, and an organization, not just a product; the seller's job is to build comfort about all of them. "Our salespeople are selling our strategy and our culture," says Bendoff. Craftsman has replaced technically narrow salespeople with sales engineers who have solid working knowledge of the firm's fabricating and stamping abilities, and can support early design work with customers. "Now, we are selling process skills, not just products," Bendoff observes.

Few people have had a chance to develop such expertise. To sell alliances, you must find individuals who have some of the skills, and can learn more through training and coaching. Fill any skills gap by including others with complementary abilities.

When Craftsman's Krempels goes into the field with sales reps, one of his objectives is to teach by example. Among other things, he emphasizes questions that help determine not only if a prospect's organization can adopt relevant processes, but also if an alliance with Craftsman would be a priority. Often, the firm's evaluating team is joined by senior specialists such as the rapid-response manufacturing person. In situations requiring focused expertise, specialists may make sales calls themselves.

Those who sell alliances need more tenure with specific accounts than people in other sales positions. After an alliance is sold, the seller will need three or even more years to continue building trust with everyone involved. That leads to more information sharing, richer understandings of your customer's needs, a clearer appreciation in your firm about how to meet them, and ongoing improvement.

Clearly, sales compensation should reinforce desired behavior. Alliance salespeople at P&G are measured and rewarded based on revenue and profit growth over several years. The time frame helps sellers make decisions in the customer's long-term best interest. At Craftsman, salespeople make their commissions only by selling alliances to targeted prospects.

Though essential, it's not enough to develop alliance selling skills and incentives, and give people needed authority. How your organization works is equally important. Alliance sellers say their biggest obstacle to building teams is that team members have an internal, rather than a customer, focus.[4] As at Procter & Gamble, the solution is a matter of realigning incentive systems, cultures, and politics to face the outside world. That is a top management job.

KEEP STRETCHING WHEN AN ALLIANCE IS UNDER WAY

Because competitive markets keep improving what your customer can get from transactions, an alliance has to continue advancing to remain useful. Recall from prior chapters that Wal-Mart and P&G,

HP and Canon, and Ford and ABB keep moving ahead together.

But ongoing improvement is not enough. An alliance survives only as long as it is the best option for each partner. When Canon could not meet HP's needs for color copiers, HP shifted to Konica, as Chapter 7 describes.

Having solid measures helps you know where things stand. P&G and Wal-Mart, for example, developed a report card for their alliance, which helps them identify what needs attention (see Chapter 7). It has been an essential tool in their progress together. Rather than simply hope a customer will continue regarding your company as its best choice, confirm your status through benchmarking and customer surveys. Although most suppliers say they want to get close to their customers, few invest in such measures.[5]

The requirement for continuing improvement is inherent in any alliance. It is arguably more important for alliances between customers and suppliers, because customers can often turn to different suppliers; fewer options exist in other arrangements, such as alliances with rivals.

Craftsman has learned this lesson well. After winning a new account it keeps teaching the customer how to shorten cycle time. That practice educates new people, helps combat lost understandings due to staff turnover at the customer, and keeps best practice at the forefront of everyone's minds. To stay current, Craftsman advances its own skills in short-cycle production through investment and internal development. The firm also promotes an ongoing dialogue between its operations staffers and their customer counterparts.

Once a Craftsman alliance is under way, the sales lead serves as an advocate for the customer. He regularly visits with the end user—typically someone on the production line—to see how the parts are working. Other advocacy tasks include surfacing issues, bringing them back to Craftsman, and resolving them.

The advocate's ability to solve problems quickly is a key selling point in Craftsman's short-cycle business, and others in the firm have a formal incentive to support this role. For awhile after the advocacy effort began, account leadership was transferred from the salesperson who created the alliance to the advocate. Those hand-offs did not go well; transferring all the seller's knowledge about a customer to someone else proved difficult. Craftsman now has the same person wear both hats.

"Eventually, we want to be doing business only with the kinds of companies that we can help the most," says Bendoff. "We see acceptable margin opportunities only where we can differentiate and not where all we are allowed to do is quote the parts, make them, and deliver them. At the end of the day customer companies are going to recognize that they have to get close to their suppliers as well as to their own customers."

CHAPTER 11

HOW TO TRUST A RIVAL

■

Politics has long made strange bedfellows, but it wasn't until recently that competitive markets began to create odd couplings. Who would have guessed a decade ago that bitter rivals like Visa and American Express, Coke and Schweppes, Kodak and Fuji Photo Film, Unilever and Procter & Gamble, the *Wall Street Journal* and the *Financial Times,* and countless other rivals would have reason to cooperate?

Today, the logic is sound: Markets keep demanding better performance; companies find they cannot excel on their own at everything they must do; alliances are a natural consequence; and rivals have so much in common that they are natural partners. Enemies have become allies—albeit in ways that are carefully limited.

Visa and American Express, for instance, needed to create one global system for smartcards; incompatible electronic card systems would fragment the market and lower its appeal to everyone. Coke and Schweppes saw an opportunity to save costs in Britain by combining their distribution, and by sharing a bottling plant with a larger scale than either could justify alone. The soft drinks rivals invested those savings in advertising across their entire portfolio of brands, boosting their market share by 17 percent in the first year.

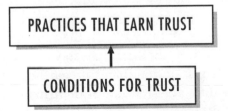

PRACTICES THAT EARN TRUST

↑

CONDITIONS FOR TRUST

Kodak and Fuji Photo partnered to develop an advanced photo system that would use the same newly developed film. Their objective was to permit dealers to stock one type of film for both firms' cameras, making each camera more widely marketable. Unilever and P&G cooperate in product safety because any problems with either firm's products are seen by consumers as implicating those of the other. For the *Wall Street Journal* and the *Financial Times,* starting a business newspaper in Russia was a risk that neither wanted to take alone. So they did it together by launching a paper that draws from each publication, with one section printed on white paper and the other on the *FT*'s standard pink.[1]

Dresser Industries and Ingersoll-Rand separately made compressors for the oil and natural gas industry. Together, in Dresser–Rand, they produce more compressors than they had manufactured individually, for the same total investment.[2]

How can shareholders, managers, and ordinary employees overcome their natural resistance to such opportunities? What are the risks and how can they be managed? How do you build mutual trust with an adversary? Before answering these questions it is worth understanding how a context of hostility affects cooperation and shapes the attitudes of those involved.

HOW RIVALRY AFFECTS COOPERATION

An obvious issue regarding links between opponents is the legal one. Because some combinations will reduce competition, they are prohibited by governments. Even certain discussions are suspect and can lead to problems. For these reasons it is always a good idea to seek legal advice about what may and may not be included before you enter discussions with a competitor.

The same principle applies once an alliance is under way. For instance, the parents of Tasty Wares, the food retailing joint venture, are competitors. To be sure they stay on the right side of the law, each firm sends all documents regarding Tasty to its legal counsel before they are shared. Both firms are also regularly guided by their attorneys on what can and cannot be discussed.

At Canon and Hewlett-Packard, rivals in the printer market, the firms' respective legal communities meet periodically to be sure all aspects of their relationship are in compliance.

Another concern is losing company secrets. You can reduce this problem by sharing data selectively. HP and Canon do not disclose their core know-how (such as Canon's laser technology), and are careful about what they reveal in other areas. To their advantage, most of each firm's business outside their alliance is unrelated to the other's. H&P doesn't make copiers, and Canon doesn't make computers. By contrast, typical relationships between large companies in Japan are much broader in scope. Takashi Kitamura, Canon's lead for the alliance, observes that on a person-to-person level trust between his firm and HP is the same as in Japan. But on a company-to-company basis there is more trust with HP, because there are fewer overlaps and less chance for damaging information flows.

FOR DETAILS ON INFORMATION SHARING, SEE PAGE 240

Because container shippers Maersk and SeaLand compete in sales, marketing, and pricing, they only see one another's containers but do not know the contents, to whom they belong, or the prices charged. Still, since the firms cooperate in operations, each learns by observing the other's functioning in that area. The exposure not only helps both companies improve but makes them more alike in operations, assuming they adopt what they learn at the same rate. The result is more strength to combat others and less differentiation between them, which could be problematic for both if the alliance ends.

This potential for learning underscores the need to determine whether what you will gain from an alliance with a rival clearly exceeds what you might lose. Volkswagen's auto manufacturing alliance with Ford in Latin America exposed VW to its partner's cost-management practices and was a turning point for the German company's global operations. "We learned how to be leaner," says Miguel Jorge, acting president of Volkswagen of Brazil.[5]

A third issue in this kind of alliance regards rationalization. In any alliance, shifting work from one firm to the other may be hard to reverse when the relationship ends. The problem is more difficult with rivals, because rationalization could leave one partner at a competitive disadvantage compared with the other. This possibility has limited what Maersk and SeaLand can do together, as Chapter 5 notes.

Despite the drawbacks, there is a decided advantage in moving quickly to consider the merits and, if they are attractive, team up with a strong rival before another competitor does so. Let's say that your firm's best choice for a partner in some area is either of two competitors. If they see the opportunity before you do and join with each other, you may be left with no options. For example, once Maersk and SeaLand formed their global alliance, other carriers had no ready alternatives for matching the coverage attained by the Danish-American pair in some markets.

SEE PAGE 274 FOR HOW TO ASSESS HIDDEN RISKS IN ALLIANCES WITH RIVALS

RIVALRY ALSO SHAPES ATTITUDES

The prospect of a partnership with a competitor can alarm your work force, provoking resistance to cooperation. Here is one example. On our way to an alliance planning session between two rivals, several of us were disconcerted to find many signs that literally spelled trouble. Much to our host's dismay, someone who was obviously upset by the proposed alliance had posted messages in hallways, in the refreshment area, on bathroom and stall doors, even on toilet seats, stating in gutter language that a demon was present and Armageddon was near. A program of constant communications with all employees about the benefits of the alliance has since lowered people's concerns, but the problem hasn't disappeared.

Clearly, the idea of cooperating with a rival creates a psychological issue: Why help someone who intends to hurt your business? Even if you see past the negative and recognize the positive, others in your firm may not, which creates political resistance. The weight of such attitudes depends on whether your firm and a rival see each other as major foes, as was the case at the company with unpleasant signs. To appreciate that point, compare Maersk and SeaLand with Canon and HP.

Because the two container shippers remain arch rivals around the world, resistance to their alliance persists in both firms despite regular top management reminders that they need one another to combat other carriers and alliances in their industry. Further, says SeaLand's Ron Sforza, "We tend to compete more against each other due to our increased mutual visibility. For example, if Maersk gets a SeaLand customer, our aggressive juices flow faster. It causes us to look closer at our own performance. It is not healthy for Maersk or SeaLand if we focus so much on fighting each other that we take our vision away from other competitors."

But the situation could be even more difficult. SeaLand has a higher market share in trans-Pacific shipping, while Maersk has more share in the Asia-Europe business. "The alliance would be harder to manage if we were nose-to-nose in every market," says one executive.

By contrast, though Canon and HP compete in the market for bubble jet and ink jet printers, they do not cooperate in any aspect of that business. The two are also rivals in the laser printer market, but Canon's share is far smaller and the firms are not each other's chief opponents. Consequently, they have less resistance to cooperation in the laser field than Maersk and SeaLand do in container shipping.

BUILDING TRUST WITH A COMPETITOR

Where cooperation with a rival is logical and legal, you can build mutual trust and a winning alliance by satisfying the trust conditions and adopting the trust practices described in earlier chapters. Taking those steps also lowers psychological and political resistance to bonding with a rival, as Tasty Wares shows.

One cause of Tasty's near-death experience was that the firms' top managements had never actively supported the venture. Only when calamity was imminent did people on both sides question whether they might be better off together than apart, as Chapter 8 describes. The ensuing analysis by each company led the division presidents, and then the chairmen, to confirm that making Tasty successful was an important objective for each of them. With mutual need sanctioned at higher levels, resistance to cooperation began to decline. Taking the other steps toward mutual trust—establishing joint leadership, building relationships, and the rest—gave Tasty a new life. Of course, the best way to develop an alliance with a rival is to work on trust from the outset.

As Always, Start with a Priority Mutual Need

Like any successful alliance, one with a rival must begin with mutual need. General Electric and Pratt & Whitney, competitors in the aircraft engine market, illustrate.

In 1996, at the annual Singapore Air Show, staffers from GE and Pratt were griping with one another about how neither firm's current products could meet Boeing's demands for an operating cost reduction for a new version of the 747 aircraft. Those complaints led to joint speculation that only a new engine could do the job, a near-billion dollar expense neither firm was willing to take on alone. Someone suggested they do it together. Soon after that, people met to discuss the opportunity, with attorneys present to guard against legal problems. Succeeding visits focused on more details. An agreement to build a new engine together came just two months after the original Singapore meeting.[4]

A year later, Boeing canceled that version of the aircraft due to uncertain demand, production problems with its current products, and the challenge of integrating its McDonnell Douglas acquisition. But GE and Pratt continued collaborating on the new engine, now aimed at a proposed Airbus model having the same requirements.

Since the two companies compete in making engines for 767s, 777s, current 747 models, and several Airbus models, they have found cooperation awkward. Even so, their alliance continues because each firm regards it as the best way to develop the engine. Further, the potential value is widely recognized in each company.

"It's not uncommon in this day and age to partner with a competitor," observes one GE manager. "People here accept this as a matter of course."

Interpersonal Relationships Are Essential

Rivalry does not stand in the way of close personal ties in business any more than it does between members of opposing professional sports teams. If anything, relationships are more vital in alliances between competitors than in those involving nonrivals because rivalry creates more opportunities for misperception and conflict.

Canon and HP, for example, are prevented by antitrust considerations from sharing cost data. That constraint makes pricing agreements difficult to reach. "In many cases we may very generally touch on cost drivers," says Doug Carnahan, for many years HP's lead executive in the alliance. "But we do not reveal our costs to each other, which may leave a negotiating gap that has to be closed. We might claim that we need a certain price from Canon for its engines to cover our investments and they would make similar claims, often with each of us knowing the other was overstating its case. But we know each other so well we can always tell if things get to the point where one of us is not winning."

Listen to one of the lead executives in Tasty Wares describe his relationship with his counterpart. "Since the first time we met I have felt a high degree of empathy with him. Possibly it is just that we have similar jobs. I know he cannot say everything that is on his mind. But I believe what he says and know he will not mislead me. Our comfort with each other helps us defeat the conflicts that tend to surface in our alliance." Similar relationships between others in both firms help make teamwork effective at most interfaces.

Joint Leaders Have More to Do

Cooperation with a rival is a balancing act. There is a danger of overcommunicating and one of undercommunicating. There is a risk of overstepping legal boundaries and one of being overly restrictive and lowering your potential together. There is a need to encourage people to take the initiative yet prevent them from taking inappropriate advantage of the situation. And there is a need to make certain that benefits are shared fairly, because perceptions of inequality are more damaging in this kind of alliance than in any others.

Getting the balance right depends on clear guidelines about information sharing, legal limits, and the boundary between cooperation and competition; regular communications about those matters with your partner and throughout each firm; and constant reinforcement of them.

"I have a very competitive team," observes the president of one Tasty Wares parent, "and there is always a drive to look for leverage points over our rivals. This is appropriate, except within the boundary where we have agreed to cooperate. I have to nip in the bud any initiatives or ideas here that may be contrary to our agreed relationship." For example, even though Tasty is off limits for both partners' sales forces, some aggressive salespeople oppose the alliance and keep looking for ways to use the venture to their advantage.

"We need to remind ourselves that to avoid misunderstandings, which plagued us in the past, we must have clear communications about our shared expectations," notes the president's counterpart in the other firm. "We are all working to better Tasty Wares. If either of us feels that someone on the other side is playing games, we have an obligation to share this observation with each other. Each of us needs to feel comfortable that we will each stop any inappropriate behavior."

In the Maersk–SeaLand alliance, rivalry plus organizational mismatches and an inability to fully separate competition from cooperation, as noted in Chapter 5, create resistance at some locales. In those cases, employees are more aware of their rivalry than of savings from the alliance. Where benefits are unevenly matched, there is also a feeling that one firm is taking advantage of the other. Such factors complicate the leadership task. At times, lead executives have to step in to get things done.

Commitment Requires Equal Access, Not Equal Benefits

Many alliances of rivals involve a shared asset, like Maersk's and SeaLand's jointly operated fleet of ships, or Tasty's food retailing business. The benefits from using such resources come from their being equally available to both partners.

It would be impractical and probably impossible for the entire global network of container ships or even for a single vessel to carry an equal number of Maersk and SeaLand containers. In fact, the number of each firm's containers involved depends on how each markets its service. Even if an equal number were feasible, the shippers' profits from their alliance would not be the same because each negotiates its own pricing. So long as there is equal access to every ship, each company's financial benefit is its own business.

During Tasty Wares' dark days, its parents' solution to equality was trying to have the same amount of shelf space in every store. Each kept the other from adding new products unless both could do so. The results: an inefficient use of space, which lowered the parents' margins, and a dearth of new items from them, which hurt their revenues.

Today, the firms agree on the total space required. Each partner pays for the space it needs, within defined upper and lower limits. Each also has complete freedom to introduce new products. Further, Tasty has accumulated a great deal of food marketing and distribution information that is not proprietary to either firm. Each partner has full access to the data; the user covers relevant costs.

Maersk and SeaLand follow the same principle of paying the actual cost each incurs for using a shared facility. But unlike Tasty's parents, which know its costs, the carriers cannot disclose their vessel operating expenses. So they have agreed on rates for container slots. For port terminals, rates are based on the open-book true cost for each carrier. Due to varying costs around the world, the firms have developed a formula for each region. They pay each other whatever is owed, without trying to net it out to zero.

Safeguards: Prepare for Instability and Termination

One problem unique to alliances between rivals can end a relationship. These links require consensus decisions on many matters. Yet if either partner uses a shared asset significantly more than the other, the dominant firm will want more influence—which is untenable with a rival. To avoid that issue, Tasty Wares' parents have set limits on how much their capacity use can vary. Should it go beyond the agreed amount for more than six months, either partner may seek termination.

It is always smart to concur on termination before launching an alliance, as Chapter 3 notes. Even with a prenuptial, unless your firm is ready to move ahead on its own, that agreement will not forestall all damage.

Autolatina illustrates. The rationale for this Ford–VW venture in South America was to help the auto makers cope with an economic crisis there. Once the Argentine and Brazilian economies regained their health, new competition entered the market. In late 1994, VW chose to go its own way. But Ford, which had not kept up with changes in the local market, lacked the smaller cars that accounted for the most volume.

Autolatina's ending exposed a serious weakness at Ford, paving the way for VW to capture market share. "Things turned out very well, even better than we hoped," said Norberto Dubar, president of Volkswagen Argentina. Ford, by contrast, lost $645 million in its South American division in 1995.[5]

MANAGE THE BOUNDARY

To encourage cooperation, you have to separate alliance activities from conflicting ones in each firm. Recall from Chapter 4 that Apple's and IBM's failure to insulate their Kaleida joint venture from competing projects led to its defeat. The same kind of separation is necessary in alliances between rivals. Here, effective boundary creation and management deserve added attention. There is greater resistance to cooperation, more potential for strife, and a larger incentive to use an alliance to undercut the other firm.

The most creative and productive joint behavior is possible only when you can fully sort out cooperation from competition at the day-to-day level—which is not always feasible. To appreciate the effects of a vague boundary, compare again the Canon–HP alliance with that between SeaLand and Maersk.

In the laser printer business, Canon and Hewlett-Packard cooperate in product development and compete in sales, marketing, and pricing. Each firm is structured so that the competitive parts are organizationally separate from those that cooperate. Canon's sales and marketing are handled by independent units like Canon Domestic Sales Company (in Japan), Canon U.S.A., Canon Europe, and similar arrangements elsewhere.

Further, though many early product development tasks are performed jointly, each firm develops its final product on its own to support its distinct business strategy. Consequently, there are few conflicting interests and strong feelings of mutual need among those who collaborate.

By contrast, while the container shippers cooperate in operations and compete in sales and marketing, it has not been possible to compartmentalize those functions in some offices. At those sites the ensuing conflict causes problems. An example is unequal treatment of each firm's customers at port terminals, which are at the interface between joint ship operations and the partners' separate container trucking systems.

There are many ways to define a boundary: by tasks, products, functions, projects, budgets, market segments, business units, or structures. Any scheme is effective if it clearly separates conflict from competition at the operating level. Above that level, however, there will be some managers whose scope covers both sides of the boundary. For them, separation is a matter of mentally compartmentalizing their mutual interests from their competitive instincts.

Listen to the president of one computer firm in an alliance with a rival: "I must understand the part of the business we share, its importance to my constituents, and its boundary. In this area it is appropriate to manage it in a noncompetitive way. Everything outside this sphere is competitive."

When your rivalry is intense, or the line between cooperation and competition is blurred, pay particular attention to the practices described in Chapter 7. In all alliances, it is important to communicate regularly and to anticipate and resolve issues early. But in partnerships with rivals, where avoiding conflict and staying aligned are especially challenging, these activities are vital.

Internal communications should not only showcase an alliance's benefits, but also should remind employees about its boundaries. SeaLand and Maersk have learned this lesson well. By keeping their staffs posted on gains achieved together, they have curbed discord at terminals and improved customer service. Similarly, by informing everyone about how the alliance has enhanced shipping schedules, each firm has helped its salespeople pitch its own container service more successfully.

Activities that might cause misunderstanding also deserve a heads-up. TastyWares provides an example. As a matter of course, on the side of the boundary where both parents cooperate, they inform each other beforehand about any major initiatives. On the side of the boundary where they compete, however, it's a different story. Like sports teams, they understand the rules of the game but remain arch rivals. If one firm takes a divisive action, it discusses it immediately with the other to make certain it hasn't broken those rules.

Take the time one of Tasty's parents, as a competitor, ran ads undercutting its partner's products. Knowing these would cause hard feelings, an executive from that firm called his counterpart after the ads appeared to affirm that their understandings hadn't been violated. His counterpart grudgingly agreed. The conversation was necessary but awkward. Both men knew some of their colleagues would not condone their talking so soon after the attack ads incident.

The moral of the story is that even when both sides clearly benefit from an alliance, cooperating with a rival isn't easy.

CHAPTER 12

HOW TO BUILD TRUST
BETWEEN INTERNAL GROUPS

■

Reason might lead you to expect divisions within a company to be natural allies, and links among them to be frequent and friendly. After all, most multiunit firms consist of closely related businesses. Experience, of course, tells a different story. Alliances within a company are subject to the same rivalries, suspicions, and behavioral differences that inhibit those with outside partners. In fact, internal alliances depend on the same principles of trust covered in earlier chapters.[1]

As valuable as internal linkups can be, don't assume that your company's various units should always be one another's priority partners. Most units in multibusiness firms were put there to serve particular markets, not to be each other's best match.

An alliance between internal units is appropriate only when it

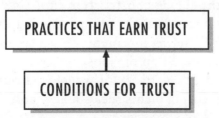

PRACTICES THAT EARN TRUST

CONDITIONS FOR TRUST

is the best way for each unit to achieve its objectives. Similarly, when an internal supplier errs, or becomes less attractive than an external source, its customer should be free to go outside. Protecting units from their own mistakes, or insulating them from the market, weakens them.

Petrochemical firms like BP Chemical and Exxon Chemical get most of their raw materials from their parent firms, because co-location with internal supplier plants offers low logistics costs. But to be competitive in their own markets, the units go outside for feedstocks whenever pricing there is better.

Three cases illustrate how to build alliances between groups within the same company. One describes an internal customer and supplier at Butler Manufacturing. The second shows how an American multinational's business unit in Brazil teamed with the local office of a corporate staff function. The third explains how internal units at J.P. Morgan collaborate to serve the same outside customer. In one case, the units first had to overcome friction between them. Results in each situation include more value for customers, increased market share, and healthier profits. Taken together, all three experiences describe how to create a culture that fosters trust.

ALIGNING AN INTERNAL CUSTOMER
AND SUPPLIER

Soon after Butler Manufacturing and SuperSave had put mistrust behind them, as Chapter 9 narrates, the retailer asked Butler to erect six distribution centers in twenty-eight days (less than half the time needed for previous jobs) and at a lower price. Stringent safety and quality standards also had to be met. The only way Butler could meet these objectives was to abandon business-as-usual.

Normally, the firm's construction unit sources proprietary building components from its manufacturing unit on an arm's length basis. While the arrangement was acceptable for small volumes, it proved difficult on big jobs, because manufacturing also had to serve Butler's network of franchised builders. Further, Butler's manufacturing plants seek stability and predictability for efficient production, while construction wants flexibility to meet changing site conditions. These differences caused coordination problems between the two units, added time and costs, and created discord when internal priorities conflicted. SuperSave's latest request involved a huge volume and could be more disruptive.

Early Elements: A Priority Opportunity, Joint Leaders, and Relationships

Bill Johnsmeyer and Dick Jarman, respective heads of Butler's construction and manufacturing units, regarded the new Super-Save opportunity as important for their businesses. Without that impetus, getting support for needed internal changes would be difficult. Still, Jarman's plant people feared their profits could suffer, and believed the new demands might compromise their ability to serve other customers. To plan their response the two executives agreed to co-lead a joint effort of their units.

In communications to their staffs, they both emphasized that the opportunity was important for all of Butler, and that the units had to find a way to meet SuperSave's objectives. Johnsmeyer told his people he expected them to work as a real team with manufacturing. Jarman informed his managers that he and Johnsmeyer wanted a review of all aspects of how their units worked, individually and together. In a note to his staff, Jarman observed "there has been enough complaining here about 'who did what to whom.'" He asked them to support Bill Johnsmeyer with their most qualified people.

Next, the co-leaders launched an interunit team. Because SuperSave was construction's customer, construction had overall lead. Johnsmeyer designated Bob Knapp, one of his direct reports, to head the team. "I chose Bob because of his technical strengths and because he has a unique ability to build relationships across organizations and bond with people," recalls Johnsmeyer. The entire effort was strongly supported by Bob West, Butler's chairman, who observed that "anyone who thinks we do not want this business does not need to work here."

The first team meeting got off to a rocky start. People argued about past conflicts until Knapp reminded them of the magnitude of the opportunity, and confirmed that the plan they produced would have to be acceptable to both units. With that, attitudes began to shift, the group developed a list of issues, and they agreed on assignments and a completion date.

As work progressed, Knapp encouraged team members to better understand each other. That, plus his own style and obvious good chemistry between Jarman and Johnsmeyer, encouraged candor and creativity in the group. People discussed their units' needs, costs, and constraints, and explored ways to meet SuperSave's objectives. Those discussions produced many ideas for change, among them fewer part numbers, more standardization, better plans for deliveries to job sites, and timelier shipping manifests. They also agreed to move some work to the normally slow first quarter, to reduce scheduling conflicts at the plants.[2]

Some ideas required SuperSave's acceptance, which Johnsmeyer and Knapp sought and won. For example, once the firms agreed on a schedule, any change would impose a cost on the plants. In the past, with Butler's units working at arms' length, construction did not fully appreciate (and could not explain to the retailer) how schedule changes affected manufacturing. This time, construction made the case for stability and SuperSave agreed to pay a penalty if it sought unilateral changes. Construction also won the retailer's agreement for more standardization.

Looking ahead to implementation, Knapp understood that close coordination between Butler people at the job site and in its plants would be essential, and healthy relationships were a key to that. To help build those ties he changed the venue of a semiannual job site supervisors' conference to Butler's main plant. The schedule included a golf tournament for all field and plant supervisors, most of whom had never met. Careful pairings matched people who would be working together.

Knapp also invited key plant people to participate in a half-day of the meeting, and included them in an awards dinner, where they were recognized for their cooperation with construction. In a dinner talk, the plant manager observed to the assembled group that the new SuperSave opportunity was important to the plants, and noted that the proposed schedule adjustments would avoid their having to make traditional seasonal layoffs.

Over the two months needed to prepare for implementation, joint leadership, a wide appreciation of the size of the opportunity, a recognition that each unit's needs would be met, and constant emphasis on relationships caused a turnaround in attitudes. "Instead of managing divisional outcomes, as before, we were managing shared outcomes," says Knapp.

Managing Internal Alignment

To meet SuperSave's demanding objectives, Butler's manufacturing and construction units redefined their processes, changed their work scheduling, integrated a number of their activities, and modified part designs to better align with each other.

Each distribution center required steel deliveries by more than two hundred flatbed eighteen-wheel trucks within the twenty-eight day schedule. To save time, each truck was to be unloaded where its steel would be erected, rather than at a central location as in the past. At times, as many as thirty trucks would arrive each day. With 250 iron workers on site plus capital equipment, a one-day delay would cost Butler the wages and benefits for that day, plus equipment rentals.

To meet the schedule, the plants replaced their normal objective—meeting shipping dates—with meeting delivery times, in a defined sequence. While manufacturing chose and oversaw the steel carrier, on-time deliveries called for seamless coordination of plant departures and site arrivals by manufacturing and construction.

Other changes helped meet SuperSave's objectives without compromising Butler's work. To protect the needs of its franchise builders, Butler found a way to give them more lead time than was normal. Butler's own suppliers and SuperSave also contributed to meeting the new objectives. Steel companies were given more time to fill orders and cut their products to needed lengths before shipping to Butler. For its part, SuperSave sped the completion of building foundations and integrated other contractors' plans with Butler's schedule.

To encourage alignment, Jarman and Johnsmeyer included

the objectives for the six distribution centers in all contributors' performance measures—a first for Butler. People from both units say it vastly improved teamwork and communications between them.

The plants' early assurance that their needs would be met won their support. For an equitable sharing of the benefits, construction and manufacturing lowered their respective prices by 2 percent from prior SuperSave jobs. Equally important, the two leaders wanted their units to succeed together. So they looked for and found ways to lower their separate and joint costs, by improving scheduling and deliveries, and pushing standardization beyond their initial plans.

With their objectives and incentives aligned, and knowing that benefits would be shared fairly, each unit took initiatives to advance the common cause. One time, for example, Jarman sent his research engineers to a site to solve problems that had slowed roofing construction. On another occasion, construction's engineers redesigned a steel beam so it would be easier for manufacturing to make.

A Focused Structure and Clear Governance

With overall responsibility for the SuperSave account, Johnsmeyer created a small hierarchy within his construction unit that reported to him on a dotted-line basis. The structure served to coordinate the six projects, support the new processes, and interface with SuperSave. Within that framework, Johnsmeyer was the final decision maker for construction, while Jarman played that role for manufacturing. The two leaders also acted as an informal internal steering committee to keep their units aligned.

In principle, either executive might have taken issues he could not handle to Don Pratt, their boss and Butler's president. But they enjoyed an excellent relationship and preferred to work things out between them. The two had been college classmates, Jarman had hired Johnsmeyer into Butler, and their relationship continued to grow. Further, Pratt had made it clear that he wanted issues to be resolved at the source.

Lasting Benefits

Butler met all of SuperSave's objectives for the six distribution centers, as well as its own profit targets. Since then, having learned the value of cooperation, the construction and manufacturing units continue finding ways to be more effective together.

Now, before a new job begins, the designated project manager and superintendent visit the plant to coordinate all aspects of the work. New workers and managers and even veteran employees prepare for a new job by reviewing each other's needs. "They try to accommodate us and we try to accommodate them," says one manager. "These discussions contribute to trusting relationships between us, which help us get through thorny issues."

REPLACING HOSTILITY WITH SYNERGY

A company I'll call PrimeBrazil is the Brazilian branch of Prime-Crops, a specialty chemical unit of an American global company. PrimeBrazil was losing business in the Brazilian farm market for many years, because it was at loggerheads with the local corporate treasury office.

The parent company's corporate treasury function in the United States, through local offices around the world, determines financial policy for all subsidiaries, including PrimeBrazil. That arrangement led to problems in Brazil, where credit terms can be more important than product price. Although its rivals control the terms they offer, PrimeBrazil must work with local treasury staff, which follows corporate policies designed primarily to serve the parent's core commodity chemical business. Consequently, rivals offered better terms and left PrimeBrazil with a small and declining market share.[3]

Under pressure to grow faster and profitably, PrimeBrazil sales personnel asked treasury's local office for freedom to decide credit risks—a move the office saw as a request to write a blank check. When the request was denied, PrimeBrazil staffers became irritated and complained to their headquarters, which in turn complained to corporate treasury. Corporate told its Brazilian office to find a solution that worked for both groups.

Each local treasury unit around the world is expected to contribute to business growth in its area, and its people are rewarded for doing so. Local offices have some authority to adjust their policies; but having been treated poorly and bypassed, those in the Brazilian office were not in a mood to cooperate. Instead, they responded rigidly and bureaucratically.

That was the situation Andres Montoya (not his real name) found when he moved from another country to become general manager of PrimeBrazil.

Joint Leaders Diagnosed the Problem

Soon after Montoya assumed his new position he met with the director of treasury's local office Paulo Ferriera (also a pseudonym). Each had been in similar jobs in Chile, where the business was smaller and simpler. The two had developed a candid and constructive relationship, which created an opening for change in Brazil.

Talking with their staffs and each other, Montoya and Ferriera probed for the underlying cause of the conflict. In addition to learning of the bypass and the ill will that followed, Montoya found that treasury had earlier made a number of valuable contributions to PrimeBrazil in taxes, imports, and cash management that treasury people felt were never acknowledged. Further, the PrimeCrops unit had not followed through on past promises it had made in areas where treasury had control. Consequently, the unit was not trusted.

In looking for deeper roots, Montoya and Ferriera reviewed how their groups interacted. They found considerable confusion, caused by improper connections and poor intergroup communications. "Our talks exposed feelings on both sides that each of us had bad people," says Montoya. "What we learned was that our groups' habits were bad. We had been making the wrong links, we were not trying to understand each other, and we were reaching the wrong conclusions."

Montoya and Ferriera then built a shared view of the situation and discussed ways to repair the damage. They also reviewed their authority limits, and the political and personality issues that would be involved in any change.

By combining their units' separate objectives the joint leaders defined a mutual objective. With PrimeBrazil's desire to boost sales and earnings and treasury's goal to limit the unit's financial exposure and help it grow, they set their shared purpose: increasing business without a corresponding rise in exposure.[4]

Jointly Leading Change

Montoya and Ferriera began building a team from both units to develop and implement joint plans. Their first step was to replace negative attitudes with more constructive behavior.

Initially, they met considerable resistance from angry staffers on both sides. Some people even refused to participate in the change. To encourage acceptance, the two leaders told their staffs that neither group could succeed without the other. They acknowledged mistakes, such as inappropriate initiatives and asking people to do things they were not in a position to do. Both leaders observed that such issues had to be resolved.

They also said they were unwilling to discuss whether individuals were good or bad. They asked their people to focus on the issues, and coached their staffs to be more open and to listen better. "I don't expect you to make friends," each said, "but I do want you to be professional."

Separately, Montoya visited treasury staffers to thank them for their past support. And he invited them to a meeting of his people where he thanked them again. He also organized dinners for workers from treasury and his own unit to encourage more discussion and to build relationships. With new understandings came progress. Those who had been particularly difficult began to feel left out and asked to participate.

During all of this Montoya and Ferriera continued discussing the nature of the problem and relevant issues. "Our relationship was critical in working through this and to our being candid with each other about all aspects of the situation," says Montoya. "I also promised to prevent further interference by our headquarters or by corporate treasury. We agreed that it was up to our two groups to work it out."

The Realignment

To develop joint strategies, the combined PrimeBrazil–treasury team reviewed each unit's policies and practices and brainstormed changes that might help them reach their shared objective. Team members discussed their units' boundaries of authority, as well as changes that could be made in individuals' roles to delegate more decision making to the customer interface. They also examined parameters such as assets that customers used as collateral, to better judge credit risk.

Those discussions, jointly guided by Montoya and Ferriera, led to the development of credit mechanisms, such as third-party drafts, which were new to Brazil. Other arrangements the team made included having the relevant treasury credit manager work directly with the appropriate PrimeBrazil sales manager on individual opportunities, to judge the prospect's financial position and set credit limits. The team also agreed on customer analyses and other pre-work to be done by each unit.

Another task established appropriate communications channels and conflict resolution practices. Montoya and Ferriera placed a heavy emphasis on resolving conflicts at the lowest managerial level.

Results and Outlook

The new approach was first used in a product market representing one-third of PrimeBrazil's volume. Under the old way, sales had proposed customers to treasury without adequate supporting data, and credit terms were consequently inflexible.

Under the new approach, PrimeBrazil and treasury salespeople and credit analysts work with each customer, profile its sales and credit potential, develop a credit package that fits the situation, and make final decisions together. If they want to go further, they bring the opportunity to the credit manager and sales director to decide. Few issues get escalated.

Within the first year, available credit and sales volume more than doubled. PrimeBrazil rose from being a minor player to become one of the top three suppliers in the market. Even though total exposure increased, no money was lost, thanks to a better shared understanding of how to tailor credit packages for customers.

GAINING WIDE COLLABORATION

Ranked by the esteem of its customers, J.P. Morgan is either first or second in the world in the fixed-income products and services it provides. Internal cooperation deserves much of the credit for those results.[5]

In what is a routine exercise at Morgan, the bank developed a product that allowed an oil company to invest in a politically troubled country. Such project financing, which must be raised from private investors, is often stymied by political, interest rate, and oil price risks that together investors don't understand. Morgan overcame this barrier by forming a team from units that specialize in each risk area. The team divided the risks into distinct investment packages and offered them to investors who were comfortable with each kind of risk. This approach worked: The project was funded and all parties profited handsomely.

Thanks to such collaboration, the bank has displaced well-entrenched competition in the fixed-income market to become a leader there. "We often come up with a brand new collective product," observes Peter Hancock, chairman of the firm's risk management and capital committees. "This is important because we can offer something unique for our customers. Our rivals cannot match us, which reduces our need to compete on price."

Morgan aims to provide as many as twenty different services for its best clients, and must integrate across its various disciplines to do so. Opportunities for joint projects surface in internal planning, a critical part of which requires collaboration focused on each client in turn. Further, individual unit heads are always looking for new opportunities together. They first seek generic areas—such as complex investment risks in the oil business where the payoff will be high—then use brainstorming and analysis to pinpoint individual targets.[6]

Criteria for picking opportunities come from the units involved and reflect demanding performance expectations. Since collaboration is time consuming, and it is hard to make ad hoc teams seamless in front of clients, potential benefits must be high. Individual units reach their own conclusions in each case.

Leaders for chosen opportunities come from as many as four participating units and build an interunit team. Depending on who is best for a task, the leadership role often shifts during the course of a project. Unit heads support the fledgling alliance by adjusting their internal priorities so that the right people are available. Every team has the authority to follow through on day-to-day matters.

Each team begins by defining its objectives, which focus on creating more value for the customer and an attractive gain for Morgan. Unit heads act as an informal steering committee, monitor and support progress, and resolve issues as needed. Usually, cross-unit teamwork strengthens personal relationships, which often leads to teams re-forming around the same people for new opportunities.

Benefit sharing is determined once a product is developed and each unit's contribution can be assessed. "We have a collective sense that the allocation will be fair," comments one staffer. "We avoid haggling over spoils that do not yet exist, which can be destructive." The final price for a new product sums individual unit's prices. Those, in turn, are guided by internal and external benchmarking, and reflect the value added by each unit.

Conflicts are resolved according to what is best for the overall benefit. At Morgan, it is widely understood that those involved will settle issues directly. Another option is for those who disagree to present the pros and cons to the steering committee in a jointly written memo. Without an integrated presentation, there is no access to the steering committee.

CREATING A CULTURE OF TRUST

Alliances within a company will proliferate and prosper only if its culture encourages them. At J.P. Morgan, "people would rather brag about their results from collaboration than what they have done within their groups," observes one manager.

Compare the bank's style with that at PrimeBrazil. Though Andres Montoya and Paulo Ferriera made major gains, they got little recognition. "Part of the problem here," notes Ferriera, "is that our leadership was not seen with favor in our parent company. We upset how things are supposed to work. No one seems to care as much about better results as they do about protecting their own functions."

An organization's ability to form alliances on the inside provides the skills needed to do so on the outside, as I noted in Chapter 1. Consider that being able to recognize and build on mutual need is a skill that works anywhere. Consider also that people adept at joint leadership within a firm can apply those same strengths in collaborating with outsiders.

If your company's culture does not now foster cooperation, you may be able to nudge it in that direction by appointing leaders with strong relationship skills to positions where ties between their groups are important. Even better, do that with leaders who enjoy a solid relationship. (Montoya and Ferriera were matched serendipitously in Brazil.) However, if your firm's style is not consistent with the trust conditions, it will be hard to find and support such people, and cooperation will be rare.

TASKS FOR DEVELOPING A CULTURE OF TRUST ARE SUMMARIZED ON PAGE 282

Earlier chapters described how the cultures of Canon, Chrysler, Hewlett-Packard, and Nypro contribute to their success with outside partners. Because of their cultures, those firms also benefit from alliances on the inside. J.P. Morgan has emphasized internal alliances, and seems to have gone farther than other companies in making that normal behavior.

Mutual Needs and Objectives Should Define Opportunities

Creating a bias toward cooperation requires more than simply rewarding people based on firm-wide results. In essence, you have to develop internal habits that support the eight conditions for trust.

Take the condition of priority mutual need. J.P. Morgan encourages this with top management leadership, incentives, and training, among other tactics. For instance, chairman Sandy Warner not only participates in most of the firm's annual course for newly appointed managing directors, but does some of the teaching. His remarks focus on strategic thinking from the perspective of the bank as a whole, reinforcing the need for cooperation to realize the benefits he describes. Other elements of the three-day course also emphasize cooperation.

Alliances at Morgan are intended to serve its objectives of delivering the most value to customers and earning healthy returns. To make its units attractive to one another, every Morgan unit is held accountable for staying at the cutting edge in its field. That expectation is framed by a top-to-bottom objectives hierarchy that keeps all groups aligned as they individually strive to advance. The bank also makes the benefits of allying widely known.

Bank managers are expected to inform their people on a regular basis of Morgan's capacity, resources, and reputation, as well as what other units have to offer. Managers are also expected to make certain their staffs understand and appreciate how people in other areas contributed to the bank's success.

Making people aware of their need for each other does not imply that cooperation is automatic. Morgan units team up only when mutual need is a priority. When a unit needs help and judges outside skills to be best, it may use them.

Now, take the trust condition of mutual objectives. Having a consistent set of objectives on the inside makes internal connections that much simpler. To illustrate, Hewlett-Packard and J.P. Morgan use objectives hierarchies that extend from business-wide objectives at the top down to objectives for individual units.

Among other benefits, HP's objectives for its printer business keep its product lines aimed at their markets, speed cycle times by aligning activities at all levels, and bolster collaboration in quality and technology across product lines. At Morgan, a consistent set of objectives helps units find mutual opportunities and avoid working at cross-purposes.

Emphasize Leadership and Collective Behavior

Fragmentation at the top of any company guarantees battles below. Internal friction at Motorola, the electronics maker, was so rampant for so long that staffers labeled the company "a federation of warring tribes." The tribes often fought for turf and resources, repeated each other's mistakes, stymied cooperation with outsiders, got badly out of step with one another, and lost track of their markets. For instance, the wireless systems group sold digital gear to customers two years before the wireless phone unit had phones that matched.

When Christopher Galvin became CEO in 1997, he observed in an internal memo that the firm had become "arrogant and dogmatic, and was slower than it should have been in adapting new ideas."[7]

Underlying these troubles was a practice of emphasizing independence and entrepreneurial machismo in selecting people as business heads, and a mistaken belief that individual managers could not both lead and cooperate. Unit heads were rewarded only according to their own results, and top management did not encourage collaboration. Meetings of the internal management board were often fractious. "You always knew when a meeting ended, because the number of mixed signals coming from high levels rose sharply afterwards," says one manager.

The upshot at Motorola was a culture in which executives had personal empires, did not want to risk their bonuses by working for the benefit of the whole, and were unwilling to share the limelight or yield any control.

By contrast, in a culture that emphasizes cooperation, teamwork and fairness among senior executives set a pattern for the entire organization. In these cases, people readily cross internal boundaries looking for opportunities to share. They see higher-level objectives as a step in that direction. "Our loyalties are to the firm," says a Morgan staffer, "and our collective benefits are greater than what individual groups can get alone."

Bank senior managers engage in healthy debate and dissent, but are always in concert on company-wide matters. For example, when a key staffer is being recruited by a rival, executives who might gain from the departure nevertheless rally to keep that person. Says a member of the top management team: "When we learn of the possible loss, we see that as threatening the whole company.

We look for what caused the person to think of leaving—such as a barrier to his or her continued growth—and try to lower it. This is J.P. Morgan at its very best."

At bonus allocation time, every Morgan business unit head makes a case for his or her cause. Occasionally, if one unit feels strongly that it was not treated fairly, another will share its allocation on its own initiative. "Such events open our eyes to our larger purpose. We talk about them to remind ourselves of that," notes an executive.

As leader of the firm's top management team, Sandy Warner actively encourages collaboration among his direct reports. Though cross-unit cooperation was initiated before he became chairman, Warner has reinforced it.

It All Begins with People

With higher-level managers setting the teamwork example, cooperation at lower levels begins with new employees. J.P. Morgan, and other firms like Canon, Hewlett-Packard, and Nypro that prosper from cooperation, recruit people who have the dual traits of leadership potential and an orientation to reach out to others. Individual initiative and group behavior are reinforced through training, rewards, and management attention.

Keeping both traits balanced is important. "We actively promote individuality, and expect collective behavior, but not at the expense of stifling individual perspectives and thinking," says Nypro president Gordon Lankton. "We get people to stand up and take the lead by rewarding individual as well as group behavior, and by recruiting and promoting people with leadership as well as collective traits," adds a Morgan executive.

At Morgan, every college graduate entering employment anywhere in the world goes to New York for five months of intense training about the firm's clients and disciplines. All are housed in the same building. Most of their learning occurs in teams that must synthesize members' views and make integrated presentations. Team performance is judged for content and cooperation. The new hires develop solid and lasting personal relationships. Constant contact and an intense focus on collaboration forge an internal network that persists for decades.

Listen to John Bradley, the bank's managing director of human resources, summarize this orientation to people: "Our continuing concern is not only that we have the best talent, but that they also do things the J.P. Morgan way."[8]

As people progress through the ranks, the bank reinforces desired habits through further training, promotion criteria, management attention, and incentives. While younger employees tend to have more transaction-like relationships than more seasoned people, they are surrounded by teamwork and quickly see the benefits of investing in relationships and trust. Consequently, as they mature they seek opportunities for collaboration. Senior managers encourage that through coaching and by setting personal examples.

Morgan's top management regularly creates cross-unit opportunities for people to socialize away from work—such as company sports events. Units having a lot of potential together are co-located on the same floor to increase contact, mutual learning, and cooperation.

Managing directors co-lead the bank's intergroup teams. Criteria for promotion to that position emphasize relationship and networking skills. Of fifty typical new appointees, the few who are weak in those areas made the grade because their other competencies were off the chart.

Alliances within the bank are further encouraged by a compensation plan that reflects both unit and firm-wide results and individuals' contributions. Bonuses are based on evaluations by peers and subordinates as well as by superiors. When stock options are awarded for exceptional performance, more goes to those who earn high marks for leadership, teamwork, and people management.[9]

Other banks have star systems; at Morgan, hotshots are not tolerated. Interviewed by the *New York Times* for a piece on J.P. Morgan's role in the oil industry, Rod Peacock, co-head of the firm's global natural resources and power investment banking group, "was clearly uncomfortable talking about himself," wrote the reporter. Instead, Peacock emphasized the team effort at Morgan and named others who had contributed.[10]

Earn Commitments, Sustain Continuity

To encourage collaboration on a joint project, allocate financial gains among cooperating units based on the value each contributes. If a unit's performance is reduced when key employees are assigned to the project, account for the loss in the unit's performance evaluation. At Morgan, for example, individual units occasionally detail staff to a project with another unit, thereby compromising their own revenue for the duration. Senior management makes allowances for those losses in judging unit performance.

Like their external counterparts, internal alliances benefit from staff continuity. Butler's Dick Jarman and Bill Johnsmeyer have overlapped as heads of their units for more than ten years. That stability reinforces teamwork across their units and helps them win more of SuperSave's distribution center business. Likewise, the longer teams stay together at J.P. Morgan, the more effective they have been. Morgan reinforces internal continuity by making fewer layoffs than its rivals during periodic industry downturns. Tenure at the bank is substantially longer than industry norms.

Promote the Trust Practices

If your firm meets the conditions for trust, the trust practices described in earlier chapters will be as useful on the inside as they are with outside partners. One example is managing conflicts constructively.

Let's take internal rivalry, a problem in many firms. To be sure, rivalry can help surface different views, promote best practices, and improve productivity. It also creates opportunities for benchmarking. But if conflict or competition dominate internal affairs, people will avoid collaborating.

One way to limit conflict is to expect direct issue resolution. Recall that Butler's Dick Jarman and Bill Johnsmeyer settled all matters between them using their shared objectives as a guide. This style also sped decision making between their units, added to their mutual confidence, and improved their combined results.

Morgan also expects its staffers to resolve their differences themselves. When misunderstandings between two managers grow, the bank may rotate them to each other's position, a practice that helps them see both sides of the matter. Senior bank managers also curb rivalry through compensation, demotion, and even termination. Further, while heated private discussions are acceptable, Morgan people are reprimanded if they argue in the presence of subordinates. Another practice is used if two groups get into a destructive rivalry: They may be taken off site for two days to air and resolve their differences. A senior manager serves as facilitator.

In dealing with internal rivalry, limit management actions to coaching and facilitating; avoid the temptation to make subordinates' decisions for them. Keeping a political back door open for appeals to resolve conflicts may settle an immediate question. But it reduces people's incentive to learn constructive problem solving.

Underlying Values

A firm's culture consists of a set of shared beliefs that guide peoples' behavior. For high-trust cultures, as at Hewlett-Packard and J.P. Morgan, these values invariably include expectations of uncompromising integrity, and of teamwork to achieve their objectives. Such values are deeply and widely held, and are constantly reinforced by top management.[11]

RECOGNIZE THE LIMITS TO COOPERATION

There is a difference between temporarily sharing control of a project that helps your unit and yielding permanent control to others. It isn't likely that two units will agree on how to rationalize activities between them, or integrate to become one unit. Such decisions must be made at higher levels.

For example, isolation between salespeople and traders in J.P. Morgan's interest rate business unit prevented them from finding innovative solutions for clients. Unit management fixed the problem by delegating some trading authority to the salespeople—a step the traders could not be expected to take on their own. The change remarkably improved productivity, and produced a fivefold volume gain in the fast-growing interest rate swaps and derivatives market. Now, each salesperson can customize a product on the spot and determine final price to meet client needs.

The traders, who had dominated a subservient sales force, did not welcome the shift. Management won their acceptance by explaining the logic of the move, and by starting with a small team that demonstrated early success. That example was then used to train others. "We now have a partnership of equals," concluded one manager.

CHAPTER 13

HOW TO BUILD TRUST IN MERGERS AND ACQUISITIONS

■

So far, *Trusted Partners* has covered trust in alliances between and within companies. But the toughest challenge may be forging trust in mergers and acquisitions. Most end up as financial duds, due to a focus on deal-making rather than on implementation.[1] The lesson here: To create the most value, trust building must define all activities, starting at first contact.

Alliances of independent firms and those involving internal units join parts of each and leave the rest alone. Not so with M&A, which involves whole companies. Though rationalization, transferring knowledge, or gaining a larger scale—standard practices in M&A—may yield new value, they are one-time gains. Ongoing advances that get the most from both firms will require alliances between what have become internal units in the new organization.[2]

To produce the best results, you have to acquire or merge in a way that grows trust widely. Reaching that objective involves more than the usual exercises of carrying out financial due diligence and using integration teams. Trust building starts with the same steps used to develop alliances on the outside, and proceeds from negotiation through implementation to establish the conditions for

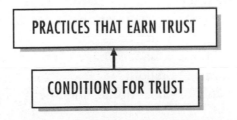

trust on the inside. How Chrysler and Daimler-Benz created DaimlerChrysler exemplifies many tasks done well, and a flaw that seems likely to make this once-acclaimed deal fall short of its promise.

UNDERSTAND EACH OTHER

The hardest aspects of trust building regard organizational behavior and developing good relationships. To manage these dimensions, do your homework. Besides reviewing financial matters, invest time in group presentations and private visits to learn how each company and its people work. When lead executives and members of their teams take time to understand one another's issues, people, cultures, and politics, fewer mistakes or surprises occur later.

Chrysler and Daimler-Benz, which combined in one of the most celebrated mergers of recent years, illustrate these points. Together, they became the world's third-largest auto company, with revenues of $130 billion and 430,000 employees. Blending two very different cultures—the champion American cost cutter and the superb German engineer—posed staggering problems. Knowing that rapport would be a key to their future, Chrysler and Daimler executives encouraged staffers to invest in relationships and monitored how that was going. Individual negotiating teams performed better when members understood each other and their contexts.

Cisco Systems, the computer firm, is another case in point. "We've walked away from companies with autocratic leaders because their employees wouldn't fit in with our team culture," observes Ammar Hanafi, director of business development.[3] And in the pharmaceutical business, traditional drug makers prefer to form alliances with biotechnology firms rather than buy them. Both sides learned this lesson the hard way, as acquisitions often led to destructive conflicts between the larger firms' highly structured styles and the smaller ones' entrepreneurial cultures. Although many of these alliances have been marked by friction, independence limits the fallout.[4]

Objectives and organizational alignment—two more trust

Acquisition   Merger

conditions—also deserve early attention. When AT&T acquired NCR, for example, the firms had different expectations about what would happen. AT&T wanted to use NCR's customer base to sell full-service networks, while NCR was interested only in using AT&T's brand name to sell its hardware. Needless to say, the deal was a financial failure.[5]

Prior to agreeing to merge, purchase, or be acquired, identify each company's priorities. Also detail how each firm works. Because much of that depends on its processes and informal networks, go into enough depth to identify these.

Before Southwest Airlines bought Morris Air, a smaller rival, in 1993, it weighed the likely effect of a takeover on everything from Morris's systems and schedule to its culture. In effect, Southwest undertook a cultural due diligence analysis and used what it learned to guide integration. The merger was profitable. By contrast, USAir's takeover of Piedmont Aviation six years earlier ignored behavioral differences. That led to years of cultural warfare, slowed integration, and kept costs high.[6]

In the Daimler and Chrysler linkup, soon after merger discussions began Chrysler's management assigned a team of senior staffers from all key departments to define the U.S. auto maker's unique traits. "We worried that the cultures would be very different," said Tom Stallkamp, president at the time.

Cost cutting—a top objective for both firms—had been a religion at Chrysler, but was almost alien at Daimler. Further, the German company was used to a single solid line on its organizational chart; Chrysler was a web of dotted lines, with reporting responsibilities crisscrossing the organization. Daimler hoped to become more like Chrysler, but the Americans wanted to be specific about what that meant because they weren't sure their counterparts understood. Chrysler's staffers prepared the ground by detailing behaviors such as its admired processes of internal collaboration, fast decisions, and ability to bring new vehicles to market quickly. Chrysler negotiators then explained to Daimler what practices had to be kept for the merger to proceed.

ALIGN FIRST AT THE TOP

Once you have identified your separate issues and priorities, use these to develop overall shared objectives. Those guideposts, plus understandings about how each firm works, will be the basis for agreeing on integration, appointing people to flesh out more detailed objectives, assembling teams, preparing your plans, and managing implementation. Settle all major uncertainties about integration, senior management positions, and other topics of major concern to either firm before getting locked into the deal.

Integration should involve only those activities that will best serve your shared objectives by being combined. Keep all else separate, to preserve and build on each firm's strengths. Recall from Chapter 12 how PrimeCrops' specialty chemical business in Brazil was stifled by the policies of its global parent, which had been honed for the commodity chemicals market.

Daimler and Chrysler planners defined their overall goals as revenue growth and cost reduction. For more detailed guidance, they developed a number of subobjectives. Two, aimed at cost cutting, were to adopt Chrysler practices in purchasing and in computer operations. Another, on the revenue side, sought to keep separate brands so as to maintain each one's distinct value. An interfirm team clarified that by drafting a "brand bible," which set rules for each brand and business function.

The document prohibits sharing vehicle platforms, and forbids dealerships that sell both Mercedes and Chrysler products. Common car parts were seen as desirable to get lower costs, so long as using them did not violate the brand separation rules. Team members identified possible conflicts and set guidelines to avoid them, such as defining when each brand gets new technology. Managers at suppliers that serve both brands must be fully dedicated to one or the other.

More than just a matter of strategy, integration depends on

culture. Larger differences require more time to assimilate. Though the process should move as fast as possible to capture the benefits and reduce uncertainties, imposing your firm's style on another's can lead to destructive conflict—as happened at USAir and Piedmont. If you intend to keep aspects of each firm's ways, plan your steps to avoid damaging the informal networks that make up much of the fabric of any organization. Be aware of what will be gained and what might be lost, give people time to adjust, keep the pressure on, and monitor progress.

Daimler and Chrysler, for example, have had to deal with sharp national and organizational contrasts. The firms planned to integrate their buying and computer operations quickly, which they believed would produce early benefits and be the least difficult. But they kept sales, engineering, and manufacturing apart to limit confusion. Integrating other functions will take at least five years. Even then, many aspects of each company will be separate, to preserve their distinct brands.

If neither company has a culture of trust, don't expect to get trust in the combination. Put two bureaucracies together and you get one that runs worse, not better. If that is your case, the best hope for gains will be through rationalization and selective access to each other's resources. Similarly, if company cultures are quite different, the best way to integrate may be to avoid doing so. Take the case of Hasbro, the $3 billion maker of Tonka™ trucks, G.I. Joe™ dolls, and other toys.

When Hasbro bought Tiger Electronics, a $400 million business whose popular items include Furby™ and Lazer Tag™, both companies wanted to keep Tiger's entrepreneurial culture. Hasbro sought no changes in management, staff levels, business functions, or in the firm's recognition and reward systems. Tiger's accounting changed because it became part of a public company. Roger Shiffman, president, says his team will have to become more aware of other Hasbro units' plans to avoid overlaps, and Hasbro suggests financial targets. But "as long as we perform as we agreed, we only expect to hear Hasbro's voice regarding the larger strategic picture."

Recognizing that cooperation works best when it is in everyone's mutual interest, Tiger is free to choose how it goes to market. At times, it divides the market for different products between Hasbro and others. "We see our role as giving Tiger access to a vault of assets," says Hasbro chairman Alan Hassenfeld. "Tiger is welcome to take advantage of those as it deems best."

PICK LEADERS WHO CAN BUILD TRUST

Appropriate leadership at the top depends on your objectives, company cultures, and on individuals' skills. If both units will remain significantly intact, management stays in place—as happened with Tiger and Hasbro. By contrast, if a purchased firm is to be absorbed into the buyer, newly arrived management will take positions there or move on.

When your objectives call for integrating both firms—which is common in mergers—joint leadership is not the best way to build a culture of trust. Though having co-leaders may avoid domination by either side, the disadvantages outweigh that benefit.

For one thing, leading as equals is more demanding than in alliances between separate companies or internal units, where each executive has his own turf. Integration is supposed to create a single turf. Having co-executives means that every issue affects both of them. Doing the job well includes agreeing on objectives, communicating constantly, jointly responding to political undercurrents, and spotting and resolving divisive issues before they fester. Another key task is selecting people based on merit, while ignoring the inevitable political jockeying for positions.

Most significantly, all of those tasks call for equality of the joint leaders—a condition that cannot be sustained during integration unless each leader represents a culture that nourishes trust. If this is not the case, co-leadership will at best achieve a blend of both cultures. At worst, it may lead to polarization. Avoiding these problems calls for a single leader whose strengths include building teams and managing organizational change. That person might be an outsider, as was the case with two drug firms.

Following the merger of Pharmacia, of Sweden, and Upjohn, of the United States, friction between top executives caused sales and earnings to drop, while rivals took the company's best talent. When Fred Hassan was brought in to be CEO of the combined firm, one of his first moves was to replace the fractious top management group he inherited with a team, including outsiders, who worked well together. Discord in lower-level ranks declined and tough cost-cutting decisions got support. Soon after that, the firm's performance turned around.[7]

Below the top, people assigned to key positions must also excel at leadership and team building. Take Daimler and Chrysler.

By combining their firms, chairmen Jürgen Schrempp and Bob Eaton sought to make the whole enterprise run more like Chrysler. Having agreed to be co-chairmen, they picked Tom Stallkamp to lead integration, even though Daimler was the senior partner in the deal. Stallkamp was a highly regarded team builder who had been a major contributor to the U.S. firm's winning style. Those traits, the leaders agreed, were what they needed in their new organization.[8]

Gary Valade, who was Chrysler's purchasing head, was appointed to lead purchasing—worth $60 billion annually—in the combined firm. Early savings were expected, and Schrempp and Eaton wanted to adapt Chrysler's noted buying practices, which built on trust with suppliers. Before the deal, Daimler-Benz had labored with dozens of computer systems that could not talk to one another. So computer operations in the new firm were centralized under the aegis of an experienced Chrysler executive.

Andreas Rentschler, a German employee of Daimler's, was tapped to head global executive management development. Rentschler had just returned from a six-year stint in Alabama, where he helped set up the firm's American operations. Part of his assignment involved integrating German and U.S. cultures. His tasks at DaimlerChrysler include nominating people for management positions and overseeing the careers of the top two thousand or so managers.

CREATE A FUTURE TOGETHER

Once the deal is done, implementation involves two sets of interwoven tasks. The first, well-known in the M&A business, includes creating teams and posting managers to smooth the transition, developing flowcharts to analyze interunit processes, and brainstorming to reach conclusions about how best to align and combine activities and accountabilities. For that, continue using your shared objectives to guide everything you do. Few companies honor this rule, which is one reason many mergers and acquisitions underperform.

The second set of tasks leads to high performance by building trust into the combined organization, using the principles detailed in Chapter 12. For instance, one transportation company smooths acquisitions—and helps make them profitable—by emphasizing relationships from the outset until long after the deal is done.

In one key step, the firm creates "buddy teams" composed of its own employees and people from the purchased firm. Team members from the parent company build rapport with the newcomers, while familiarizing them with the transportation company's philosophy and practices. Many of those early relationships continue for years.

Unless both companies have cultures that actively nourish trust, building a combination that does so will be a long-term undertaking. Tiger and Hasbro illustrate. In the year after it was acquired, Tiger's performance greatly surpassed the agreed targets. Results came primarily from the electronic toy maker's access to the larger company's international sales force. Tiger also gained from creative collaboration between its product developers and Hasbro's model service and engineering, which sped the launch of Furby™.

Cooperation with corporate engineering has gone well because "when we have a hot product, everyone wants to work on it," says Al Verecchia, executive vice president. Though Hasbro people are not specifically incented to help Tiger, the acquisition is seen as a major growth opportunity. Many employees are rewarded through stock ownership, while others may receive bonuses.

More generally, Hasbro sees alliances with corporate functions and among its various units as important to its growth. The company has license rights to many brands that it wants to build on widely. Senior people in its units recognize the opportunities, which is a step in the right direction. Corporate management understands that alliances work best when those on both sides have solid interpersonal skills, are creative, are good at teamwork, and solve problems constructively. But "cooperation is not always easy," observes Verecchia. "There can be issues of turf, personality, and priorities."

Fundamental to a successful combination is ensuring continuity—another trust condition. If just one firm has a culture of trust, its management must lead implementation over the long term. Usually, that is realistic only if the more senior partner's culture is the one to build on.

Having a more participative culture in the lead does not make such transformations easy. The style at British Petroleum, for example, emphasizes delegation and entrepreneurship; BP found a heavy internal bureaucracy when it acquired Amoco. Lawrence Fuller, Amoco's CEO, hoped the companies would combine both cultures. But "that was not negotiable for us," commented John Browne, BP's CEO. When the two cultures clashed badly, Browne stayed the course and Fuller left. Many Amoco staffers had a hard time adjusting to BP's style. "We weren't prepared for this," said one Amoco executive.[9]

Given that building a culture of trust requires strong leaders at the top who are vested in that style, DaimlerChrysler seems off to a rocky start. Jürgen Schrempp wanted to make his firm more American and more like Chrysler. He particularly sought to adopt the U.S. company's methods for driving down costs and shrinking cycle times.

Chrysler's strengths came from the remarkable degree of collaboration its top executives enjoyed, making that aspect of the company unique in its industry and a model for firms in other sectors as well. At the heart of its organization—and fundamental to its costs and cycle time results—was a matrix structure, in which the same senior executives had two roles: They served as functional heads on one side and as leaders of car programs on the adjacent side. For example, when Stallkamp was vice president of purchasing, he was also general manager of large car operations.

Within the matrix were multifunctional teams of people from engineering, manufacturing, finance, and purchasing. While each team, as a whole, reported to the executive responsible for the car program on which it worked, individual team members were accountable to the relevant functional organizations. Teamwork benefited from the same executives being on both sides of the matrix, and by cohesion among them. Trust was bolstered by Chrysler's recruitment, promotion, training, and reward systems, which were moving in the direction of those at J.P. Morgan, described in Chapter 12. By contrast, Daimler-Benz had a conventional hierarchical structure, and vertical chimneys often presented costly barriers to internal cooperation.

Chrysler's participative culture was built by chairman Bob Eaton and his management team over many years. As challenging as that was, the auto maker's people could focus on their only business: passenger vehicles. By contrast, Schrempp's empire spans many major businesses besides cars, including rail systems, truck making, aerospace, telecommunications, microelectronics, and diesel engines.[10]

Clearly, the best way to make DaimlerChrysler's practices like Chrysler's would have been to give the U.S. firm's management team the lead for building the new enterprise and to keep them there. But that would have asked a lot of Daimler, and it did not happen.

Originally billed as a merger of equals, the American unit was organized as a subsidiary of the German company. Of the eleven slots in the tier reporting to the co-chairmen, nine were filled by Schrempp's people. Compared with collaboration at Chrysler, teamwork among them has been uncommon.

Soon after the deal was completed in 1998, Chrysler CEO Bob Lutz departed. Bob Eaton, co-chairman of the new company, agreed to leave after three years, when Schrempp would take full control. Eaton's announcement upset members of his management team; suddenly, the center of power had shifted from Chrysler's headquarters in Auburn Hills, Michigan, to Stuttgart. Five months later, press reports indicated that Eaton would be gone sooner. After other top executives left, Schrempp told a reporter, "We don't need their know-how. You can quote me." That is not the kind of message that encourages trust.[11]

Within a year of DaimlerChrysler's formation, two more changes were a portent of things to come. First, to better mesh with Daimler, Chrysler's team-oriented matrix was replaced by a conventional hierarchy. Second, Stallkamp—whose authority had been eroding since the start—resigned. James Holden, his replacement, has a strong marketing background but lacks experience in those operating processes that made Chrysler unique—and attractive to Daimler.

Like countless acquirers, Daimler seems to have ranked keeping control higher than achieving its stated objectives. Time will tell whether Schrempp's team will help him adopt Chrysler's celebrated cost-management and cycle-time practices, or hold on to the past. But the original bright promise of DaimlerChrysler has dimmed.

TOOLS FOR TRUST: A GUIDE FOR PRACTITIONERS

■

This material is designed to complement the text. It should not be used to bypass the alliance-building process described in the book or for "quick-fix" solutions to difficulties. Trust must be built or repaired in a set of integrated tasks that will not work and may be counterproductive if you employ them in isolation. Be aware that trust is not the same as good will. The latter is a friendly attitude that may be due to trust, or to respect and cordiality. When the outlook for trust with another firm is poor, consider using a transaction instead.

Contents

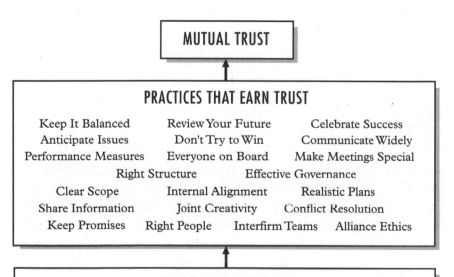

I. ANTICIPATING AND MEASURING TRUST

■

Mutual trust is a shared belief, defined in Chapter 1, that you can depend on each other to achieve a common purpose. In an alliance, where your purpose is to get results that exceed what a transaction can do, mutual trust means you can depend on each other to adapt as necessary to achieve your objective. For mutual trust to exist across an alliance, the eight trust conditions must be met and the trust practices employed at each interface where you expect cooperation.

A. DO YOU MEET THE CONDITIONS FOR TRUST?

The following chart shows how to use the trust conditions to assess your situation. The outlook for trust is good only when these conditions are met. One or more of these conditions, described in Chapter 1, are prerequisites for the practices that earn trust (see the Appendix for details).

Note that mutual need and common objectives do not necessarily go hand in hand. As an example, many university health care systems and independent hospitals have struggled to combine the universities' need for the hospitals' patients with the hospitals' need for the universities' specialists. Despite evident mutual need, shared objectives have been elusive. A primary reason is that many universities make teaching and research a priority and are less interested in patient care and cost management. The independent groups give patients and their physicians much more attention and are intensely focused on cost management.

Condition	Low Trust	High Trust
Mutual Need	We have better alternatives than working with them. This is not a priority for parts of our firm whose contribution will be essential.	Working together is the best way for each of us to reach some of our priority objectives.
Interpersonal Relationships	Our conversations do not go beyond being cordial. I am often surprised.	I have strong interpersonal bonds that • keep me informed on all matters • make it easy to raise tough issues • help us find constructive solutions.
Joint Leaders	They are ineffective together.	They always provide needed resources, get the best out of everyone, and keep us on course.
Shared Objectives	Beyond a general mission statement, we have not defined any mutual objectives.	Our mutual objectives • integrate our separate interests • are clear enough to guide our day-to-day activities
Safeguards	They have no formal way to guard sensitive information. Termination will result in an unacceptable loss for us.	They are airtight with our information. Termination will be fair and acceptable.
Commitment	There is little enthusiasm for the alliance on one or both sides.	We get high levels of policy and operating-level support in both organizations.
Adaptive Organizations	Our cultures conflict with what our objectives require.	The style we will need is identical to our normal behaviors.
Continuity	Likely changes in their people, procedures, or policies will weaken our ability to rely on them.	Any changes they are likely to make will not disrupt our relationship.

B. MEASURING TRUST

The trust practices, summarized here, can be used as a yardstick for measuring how close you are to building high trust. Where you and your partner fall on the continuum between high and low trust determines your ability to rely on each other to reach a common objective.

Practice	Low Trust	High Trust
Keep Promises	We cannot rely on what they say.	They always do what they say.
Right People Involved	They often assign people with weak relationship or professional skills.	We always get their best.
Joint Teams	Are rarely effective.	Often produce superior results.
Alliance Ethics	Their conduct suggests hidden agendas.	They always behave admirably.
Information Sharing	We get little of what we need. We do not share as much as we might.	We get all we need. We share extensively.
Mutual Creativity	We are rarely creative together.	We often combine our expertise to produce truly superior results.
Conflict Resolution	Many conflicts stay unresolved. Others are resolved through power, bargaining, or a reference to rights.	We always treat conflicts as a chance to understand each other better and be creative together.
Scope	Our alliance plans exceed the conditions for trust.	All activities within our scope meet the conditions for trust.
Realistic Plans	We are reaching beyond our ability to respond.	Our plans can be implemented with a high probability of success.
Internal Alignment	People at and behind each interface are neither empowered nor encouraged to perform as needed. Our cooperation has not been separated from conflicting activities in either firm.	They clearly and consistently support our objectives at all levels and every interface. We have completely separated cooperation from conflict.

Right Structure	Our structure prevents us from establishing the patterns we need or from securing important benefits.	Our structure clearly reinforces our essential activities and allows us to capture all meaningful benefits.
Clear Governance	The governing body often • fails to provide resources or • provides vague or inconsistent guidance.	Our governing body always • delivers needed support and • gives clear and consistent direction.
Performance Measures	Our progress measures are vague or inconsistent with theirs.	Our measures are clear and identical.
Everyone on Board	Key parts of our firms have been excluded.	All contributors are well-informed and appropriately involved.
Meetings Are Special	We are often confused or surprised. Friction occurs too often.	We understand the issues and each other's views before meetings begin. We go to meetings with open minds. We follow shared norms. We learn from and don't repeat our mistakes. We find creative solutions when needed and never get polarized.
Anticipate Issues	Too many issues cause damage before they get settled.	Our issues are always resolved before they get serious.
Don't Try to Win	They often try to get their way.	They try to accommodate us on topics that are particularly important to us.
Communicate Widely	Few people who matter are aware of our purpose or progress.	Everyone, even part-time contributors, is fully up to date.
Keep It Balanced	The next problem they cause will be the last.	They are always fair with us. We can easily tolerate their mistakes.
Review Your Future	We seem to be stuck in this alliance.	They continue to be our best way to meet an important objective.
Celebrate Success	We have never made success visible.	We confirm and enjoy passing key milestones together.

C. USING THE TRUST CONDITIONS
FOR PARTNER CHOICE

It is not possible to know how well the trust conditions will be met or if needed practices will be adopted until you are some way into negotiations. During preliminary discussions with each partner candidate, use the conditions to decide which one deserves more attention. Continue making this assessment during negotiations until both firms are convinced this course is correct. Here are some questions that will help you determine the prospects for mutual trust.

Mutual Need	What firm's skills and resources would best help you reach your objectives? Is this firm your company's best choice compared with available alternatives?
Relationships	What is the outlook for constructive interpersonal relationships at all levels?
Joint Leaders	What are the prospects for mutual understanding and confidence between the leaders? Can they deliver both firms? Can they share the limelight? Are their styles compatible? How effectively do they raise and resolve tough issues with each other? How comfortable are they with each other?
Shared Objectives	Will a prospective partner give priority attention to objectives that would be served by cooperation? Can shared objectives be defined that, if met, would satisfy each firm's objectives?
Safeguards	How effectively do they protect sensitive information? Can we agree on a termination that is fair and protects our vital interests?
Commitment	What evidence is there that each firm is willing to help the other succeed? Are both willing to make adjustments to keep it this way?
Adaptive Organizations	Is it realistic to expect the change in each firm needed for complete alignment?
Continuity	Do they maintain continuity in key activities when people leave? Will they provide continuity for this alliance?

D. AVOIDING VULNERABILITY ON
THE WAY TO TRUST

The eight trust conditions can be used to anticipate your vulnerability to loss or damage. They serve as a guide to possible remedies and to decisions about whether to stay the course or withdraw before serious harm occurs.

You can judge the consequence of an unmet condition by considering each alliance activity in the context of that condition. For example, if you hope for a six-week cycle time in an activity and the organization that must deliver this normally has a six-month cycle, your expectation is not likely to be satisfied.

Trust Condition	Consequences If Condition Isn't Met	What to Do
Priority Mutual Need	Incomplete internal support	Change internal priorities
		Change scope for better fit
Relationships	Misunderstanding, withdrawal	Coach or change people
Joint Leadership	Weak teamwork, internal support	Coach or change leaders
Clear Shared Objectives	Possible serious conflicts	Clarify objectives
		Change scope for better fit
Safeguards	Sensitive information leaks or is misused or a brand is misused	Strengthen firewalls or reduce what is shared
Commitments	Incomplete internal support	Adjust benefit sharing
Adaptive Organizations	Performance limited to how each organization normally works	Lower expectations
Continuity	Confusion, inconsistency	Install continuity policies

E. HOW LONG WILL TRUST CONTINUE?

Because competitive markets keep changing the context of a business relationship, you cannot expect mutual trust to continue automatically once you have it. Advancing markets offer each firm new opportunities, cause objectives to change, and demand better performance from everyone. Combining these facts with the eight trust conditions indicates what you must do to maintain trust, as well as how long trust will last.

An alliance's potential life span is shorter in turbulent markets because it is less likely that mutual need will stay high and objectives aligned under those conditions. Deregulation in the airline industry illustrates. A host of new entrants and growing competition caused two-thirds of the several hundred international alliances that existed in 1991 to be grounded by 1996.[1]

Mutual trust will endure so long as both firms meet the following conditions:

Mutual Need Stays High. Each firm continues to see the other as the best way to achieve an important internal objective. Alternative ways for reaching this objective remain less attractive because each firm continues to increase the value it brings.

Relationships Strengthen. People keep improving understanding, comfort, candor, and their ability to solve problems together.

Joint Leadership Improves. Leaders keep your mutual objective visible in each firm, coach and encourage teams and individuals to improve, and keep winning more internal support.

Shared Objectives Dominate. Your separate interests remain aligned and your mutual objectives keep you targeted on superior performance.

Safeguards Improve. As you share more information, your mutual ability to rely on each other to protect it grows as well.

Commitment Continues. You adjust how you share the benefits of your alliance as conditions change.

Organizations Adapt. Your structures and styles evolve to support more value creation.

Continuity Works. People transitions do not disrupt practices or understandings.

II. STEPS ON THE WAY TO TRUST

■

This material complements the trust-building process detailed in Chapter 1 through Chapter 7.

A. WHEN TO LOOK FOR PARTNERS AND HOW TO FIND THEM

The seeds for an alliance are usually planted when one firm realizes it cannot meet a key objective alone, seeks outside help, and understands that best results will come from joint creativity. Kodak, for example, wanted to improve its digital photography business and believed Intel's skills best filled the gap. For its part, Intel viewed Kodak's proposal as a doorway to a new market. The firms' separate goals suggested likely mutual need and led to explorations of possible shared objectives.[2]

For most companies, such initiatives are isolated forays born of internal frustrations—each firm has an important task it hasn't been able to accomplish alone. But seeking help from others only after concluding you can't do something alone is shortsighted. It is the traditional way to develop strategy, which came from blending market possibilities with a firm's capabilities.

There is a better approach. To appreciate it, ask yourself the following: Can your company, on its own, be at the cutting edge in all it must do? Probably not. So consider this: In a world rich in advancing know-how, why not assess the resources and expertise of other firms that might add value to yours, before your plans are set?

Pharmaceutical companies understand this. To keep their new product pipelines full, they continuously scan the world for new molecules, new understandings of genetics, and coming biotechnology breakthroughs.

Before Ford's alliance with ABB, the auto maker did extensive benchmarking to identify best practice in painting vehicles. When Vince Coletta, Ford's executive engineer for plant facilities, saw the results, he knew the potential they suggested could not be reached through arm's length bidding. He then described the opportunity to others at Ford and to ABB, fueling enthusiasm in both companies.

The manufacturing people in Motorola's Paging Products Group have a similar practice. To get ahead of rivals on cost, quality, and cycle time, a team of six full-time professionals and two dozen part-time experts searches worldwide for best practice. Whenever they find useful know-how, they bring it home through benchmarking, licensing, and alliances, using what they have learned about the frontiers to reach farther on their own and through alliances. Looking outside and linking with others as needed is one reason Paging Products dominates world markets in its business.

Proactive approaches like these aren't unique to large firms, however. Even a small-sized Dutch insurance company appreciates the merits of searching beyond its walls for new opportunities. To stay ahead in its market, the firm has assigned two full-time employees to analyze insurance products in other markets. It then adapts promising concepts to its own products and allies with others to develop new products, often reaching customers with improved coverage before its rivals. Like a small-scale version of Motorola's Paging Group, this highly profitable company dominates its specialty markets.

Said differently, your customers and stockholders don't care where you get your ideas, products, or technology. What keeps them on board is that your firm brings them more value sooner than others.

B. CHOOSING AMONG TRANSACTIONS, ORGANIC GROWTH, ACQUISITIONS, AND ALLIANCES

An early step toward mutual trust is for your firm and a prospective partner to determine separately that an alliance is the best way for each company to meet its objectives. To make this decision, compare an alliance with possible alternatives: transactions, organic growth, and acquisitions. There is little sense, for example, and not much chance for enthusiastic support, in carrying out an expensive acquisition if an alliance will yield better results. Under other circumstances, an acquisition may be a better choice.

To select the best way forward, first clarify your objectives. Next, compare the available alternatives for meeting those objectives. In doing that, consider the investments, other resources, and risks involved; desired timing and performances; and preferred rationalization and integration. Also look at your firm's need for strategic or operating control and what will be involved in meeting the trust conditions.

It is helpful to consider market trends before selecting an option. For instance, many companies are reducing the number of their first-tier suppliers and asking the remaining ones to expand their product lines. In that context, using an alliance may not provide as much coordination across product lines as would be possible through an acquisition or organic growth.

Except for transactions, the comparisons made here assume that you seek ongoing improvement. For this, best results will require mutual trust—between independent firms for alliances, and between groups within a firm for organic growth or in implementing an acquisition. In each case, the effort required to build trust will depend on your objectives and where you begin. For instance, starting with constructive prior relationships will be easier than with strangers. "A Framework for Realistic Planning," can help you think about what will be involved in each situation (see Section II.O.). The following observations are summarized and compared in a chart at the end of this section.

Transactions

Transactions are preferred under either of two circumstances: (1) continuous improvement at market rates is acceptable or (2) the trust conditions cannot be met, so success with an alliance or acquisition would be unlikely. These circumstances are most likely found in low-volume noncritical activities, where mutual need is not a priority for both firms.

Organic Growth

This mode of business development gives a firm more control over the activities and resources involved than alliances, where control is shared. The disadvantage of organic growth is that a firm's ability to develop unique value—to differentiate its products—is limited to its core competencies. Beyond that, other's core expertise is superior. Because there are more skills relevant to a typical firm's needs in other places, confining your activities to internal development will restrict your firm's growth.

Acquisitions

The advantages of buying another company include gaining control of its activities and more complete rationalization or integration than is possible with alliances. One disadvantage of acquisitions is that most reward the seller's stockholders and are financial failures for the buyers. In that respect, the premium paid above the target's market price is a gift from the shareholders of the acquirer to those of the target company.[3]

The reasons buyers do so poorly are straightforward. To justify an acquisition to your shareholders, you have to improve the purchased firm's performance enough to make an acceptable return on the investment. To do that, you must either buy and add value to an already strong firm, which is a rare skill, or strengthen a weak firm, an even rarer skill.

Another problem with acquisitions is that they often lead to executive departures. When the value of a purchased firm is in the people involved, this can be a good reason to have second thoughts.

The track record of acquisitions indicates that they perform best when buyer and target are closely related, presumably because cost reduction or value creation synergies are easier to find. Further, the challenge of earning an acceptable return on an acquisition makes this option logical only when you need most of another firm and when that firm is much smaller than yours. The latter condition eases integration and is less distracting for your firm's management.[4]

Because acquisitions can be harder to implement than alliances and usually involve larger investments, they typically are made for the long term. By contrast, the lifetime of an alliance can be tailored to the combined interests of both firms. In dynamic markets, that flexibility can be an advantage.

Alliances

In most cases where one firm has resources that are attractive to another, the need is not for the entire other firm, but rather to share certain activities. So unlike acquisitions, alliances are narrowly focused. You only have to mesh those parts of each firm that will work together.

Being free of the burden of adding value to an entire company, alliances do not have to be limited to closely related firms. Consequently, you may choose from an exceptionally wide set of possible partners.

COMPARING ORGANIC GROWTH, ALLIANCES, ACQUISITIONS

Attribute	Organic	Alliance	Acquisition
Access to Skills, Resources	Own firm	Any expertise anywhere	Only closely related firms
		Best firms make the best partners	Best firms cost more, may not be available
		Each firm needs part of the other	Need all of purchased firm
Control (operating, strategic)	Singular	Shared	Singular at the top, shared between units
Rationalization, Integration	May be complete	Partial	May be complete
			Harder in fast-moving markets
Investment	Made alone	Shared	Purchase price of firm
	Risks taken alone	Risks shared	Risks taken by buyer

Continued

COMPARING ORGANIC GROWTH, ALLIANCES, ACQUISITIONS (cont'd)

Attribute	Organic	Alliance	Acquisition
Key Risks	Individual project	Individual project	Must add enough value to justify investment
			May lose key people
			Tendency to overintegrate
			May lose momentum
Duration	Short- to long-term	Short- to long-term	Several years or longer

C. RULES OF CONDUCT FOR NEGOTIATORS

By agreeing on constructive principles at the start, you set shared expectations about the behavior that will lead to best performance. The following principles are based on the trust conditions.

- Our priority is to build an empowered, enthusiastic intercompany team that is well supported in both firms.
- We will be guided by what is best for our shared objectives.
- On every issue we will start with views, not positions, and explore to better understand.
- Candor is our style; bluffing and deception are unacceptable.
- We will use only logic, not politics or pressure, to find the best solutions.
- We will treat each other as equals in all respects.
- We will share benefits and risks in a way that encourages our commitments to each other.

D. AN AGENDA FOR NEGOTIATIONS

Here is a general sequence of steps from initial contact through implementation. Alliance design typically requires iteration among key steps such as objectives, scope, benefits, alignment, and structure.

As your planning proceeds, arrange joint presentations to both firms' management to keep them posted and help alignment at those levels. Make such presentations seamless, to reinforce confidence at higher levels that the alliance is coming together well. The best timing for these presentations is to review your mutual objectives and, later, the final plans.

Preliminary Discussions

- Confirm to each other that collaborating appears to be the best way for each of you to meet a priority internal objective for each firm.
- If you are rivals, get legal guidance on what you can/cannot discuss.
- Start developing candid personal relationships.
- Agree on whether each of you may explore the opportunity with others. Even if you don't anticipate such discussions, acknowledge that should the chance arise, you may talk with others up to an agreed cutoff point. Otherwise, if an unexpected opportunity surfaces *during* negotiations and you explore it, you must hide that from the original potential partner or disclose it. Either option could damage trust.
- Describe each firm's stretch objectives for the alliance.
- Discuss each firm's resources and the activities that might contribute to the alliance.
- Identify day-to-day and policy-level joint leaders.
- Make a first-cut analysis of the net benefits expected.
- Identify all issues to be resolved before implementation can begin.
- Disclose all deal breakers.

Initial Planning by Joint Leaders

- Agree on joint leaders' roles at policy and operating levels; confirm that joint leaders can deliver relevant parts of their firms and that they will be held accountable for the alliance.
- Discuss and agree on alliance ethics (see II.F., "Ethics for Alliances").
- Based on each firm's objectives for the alliance, define a shared

vision—a qualitative picture of what you hope to accomplish, key activities, and the scope.
- Agree on principles of financial sharing (see II.G., "Guidelines for Sharing Benefits, Costs, and Risks").
- Begin resolving issues and potential deal breakers.
- Do an alignment check: Will the alliance require making only realistic changes at both firms? By customers? By other important stakeholders?
- Identify and assign day-to-day team members, emphasizing relationship skills.
- Through presentations and discussions, build shared understandings of your separate norms, practices, unique strengths, organizations, and political and legal contexts.
- Establish guidelines for desired conduct (see II.C., "Rules of Conduct for Negotiators").
- Define conflict resolution procedures.
- Determine that both firms have adequate safeguards for information sharing.
- Begin managing expectations about outcomes within and between both firms and with other key players, including customers, employees, and investors.

Alliance Design
- Joint leaders assemble team members, review alliance ethics, cover desired norms and guidelines, and point out that all activities and decisions are to be guided by firms' mutual objectives.
- Develop mutual objectives and ratify them within each firm (see II.I., "Ten Steps to Practical Mutual Objectives," II.J., "Objectives That May Need Attention," and II.K., "Alternatives for Exclusivity").
- Set a negotiation timetable, including objectives development, outstanding issues, joint business plan, legal clearances, internal alignment, and approvals.
- As needed, perform joint marketing and technical research to clarify and confirm opportunities.

- Identify all alliance activities and cross-check for completeness with mutual objectives.
- Start planning termination agreement.
- Set alliance scope; agree on limits to integration and rationalization.
- Define activities each firm may choose to pursue alone after the alliance has begun.
- Develop joint business plan; assign activities according to the following criteria:
  –what best serves your mutual objectives
  –what requires the fewest new links within and between firms
  –what ensures near-term success (see II.O., "A Framework for Realistic Planning")
- Agree on customers, suppliers, and relationships with other outside parties.
- Start developing separate and joint financial models for the alliance.
- Agree on specifics for sharing benefits, costs, and risks.
- Align within each firm (see box).

Alignment Within Each Firm

- Define own priority objectives
- Decide if alliance is best way to meet objectives
- Affirm partner choice
- Designate policy, operating leaders
- Ratify mutual objectives, provide resources, confirm joint business plan
- Define boundary (using budgets, plans, structure, rewards, and recognition) to separate alliance activities from internal conflict
- Develop plans to support joint business plan and facilitate transitions to alliance
- Delegate final authority across full scope of alliance to governing body members
- Align performance measures, rewards of groups, individuals expected to contribute
- Delegate operating authority from governing body to day-to-day leaders
- Plan for people continuity

- Select the structure (see III, "Details of Alliance Structures and Governance").
- Create the governing body; decide who will make what decisions.
- Resolve remaining deal breakers and other issues that could inhibit implementation, considering both what is best for your mutual objective and necessary to win each firm's ongoing commitment.
- Agree on how to make pricing and other adjustments.
- Set implementation priorities considering essential timing sequences; strategic priority; ease of implementation; and early wins to build confidence, trust, and momentum.
- Arrange for ongoing joint product/process development.
- Define milestones for releasing preapproved funds.
- Agree on minimum continuity of key people.

You are prepared for alliance launch when the above tasks are done and the teams are ready to go. (As a check, see II.Q., "Early Warning Signs Detectable During Negotiations".)

Letter of Intent/Memorandum of Understanding
- Helps ensure clear understandings, surfaces conflicts; used for approvals in each firm.
- Summarizes key points of intended alliance; done before final issues are resolved if resolution would require a major effort.
- Confirms that neither company is still considering alternatives and defines conditions under which either firm may withdraw.

Alliance Agreement
- Formal commitment is made (see IV, "Benefits of Attorneys and Contracts").

E. CRITERIA FOR SELECTING JOINT LEADERS

The individuals your firm and a prospective partner assign to leadership positions determine your potential together. Their qualities are early indicators of each firm's views of the alliance. It is best to select the right people at the start. Once joint leaders are designated, any changes may seriously disrupt your plans.

Policy-Level Joint Leaders (One from Each Firm)

Main tasks: assembling resources, providing overall guidance, building and leading the governing body.

- Exceptionally strong interpersonal skills.
- The alliance must be highly important to the person's job and career; formal position must be close to (i.e., not several levels above) the day-to-day interface.
- Recognized as a successful organizational change leader in own firm in area of alliance.
- Has substantial experience in matters that will be in forefront of the alliance.
- Through authority and influence must be able to deliver all skills and resources of his or her firm relevant to the alliance. Often, achieving this requires internal delegation and changes in authority. The person must also have or be given final authority for day-to-day aspects of the alliance.

Day-to-Day Joint Leaders (One from Each Firm)

Main task: building and leading interfirm operating teams.

- Exceptionally strong interpersonal skills.
- The alliance must be highly important to the person's job and career.
- A successful track record in building, leading, and motivating interdisciplinary teams.
- If you expect the alliance to last for several years, each company must commit its joint leader for a minimum of two years.

F. ETHICS FOR ALLIANCES

Ethics is an accepted code of conduct of a group or society. If the code is broken the act is deemed to be so offensive that the violator is punished or ostracized. In the community of alliance practitioners such rules reflect the need for trust. Based on my own experience, here are six of the most widely accepted ethical rules for alliances.

Conflicting Objectives Are Acceptable; Deception About Them Is Not. Conflict is a natural part of working together. The best way to resolve it is to be sure your shared objective is so important that both of you are motivated to find and implement constructive solutions to difficult problems. By contrast, deceit is like maggots—it will infest and consume an alliance.

Identify Any Deal Breakers at the Start. Never back a partner into a corner if you want to be trusted. This will happen if, during a negotiation, you raise a new imperative when the other firm thought everything was settled. Instead, disclose all your deal breakers—those items that really must go your way—at the outset. You may not be able to resolve these until discussions are further along, but honest and early disclosure builds shared understandings of what lies ahead, which is essential for trust. A deal breaker may be any of your objectives, such as a need for a certain price or exclusivity.

In contemplating your deal breakers be flexible. What you may at first think is critical, such as a desire for control, may seem less important when you understand their situation and how the alliance will actually work.

Honor Other Obligations. A new alliance is not consistent with trust if it will compromise either firm's understandings with its other partners. Building an alliance that causes such problems raises the prospect that the offending company might violate trust again. You and your prospective partner should agree that the expectations of your other partners leave both of you free to enter the new arrangement.

Respect Their Proprietary Interests. Alliances bring firms close together, which increases the chance that sensitive information will inadvertently be disclosed. When that happens, trust requires that it not be used in any way. Information sharing is discussed further in II.L., "Share Know-How Intelligently."

Do Not Take Their People. Alliance negotiations expose you to some of the other firm's best talent. Recruiting or hiring them reduces your prospective partner's ability to perform and suggests a hidden agenda.

Disclose Pending Issues. Factors like anticipated litigation or negative press coverage that would affect your firm's image, finances, or ability to commit needed resources could influence another firm's enthusiasm for working with you. To avoid damaging trust, inform each prospective or current partner of all such issues promptly.

G. GUIDELINES FOR SHARING BENEFITS, COSTS, AND RISKS

The best way to reach a benefit-sharing arrangement is to agree early in your discussions on the principles you will follow to define a specific formula. As with all other aspects of alliance negotiations, early steps toward a sharing agreement include mutual exploration, deepening understandings, and creative problem solving, while avoiding bargaining.

During the formation of a firm I'll call Yampa Creek Resources, a coal mining joint venture, part of the plan was for one prospective partner to sell its property to the venture. Doing so required an agreement on a fair price. Both would-be partners agreed, first, to concur on the evaluation method and assumptions to be used about future coal prices, demand, capacity use, and other variables. Next, the firms suggested parameters that both regarded as fair and reasonable. By offering the pros and cons of assumptions that would benefit each of them, the firms reached an agreement that they saw as fair and encouraged their cooperation.

Having agreed on the principles you will follow, use your joint business plan and financial model as guides to develop a specific sharing formula. Bear in mind that choice of structure can affect the benefits that are shared (see the discussion in Chapter 6 and III.A., "Comparing the Three Basic Structures").

In general, the more complex the formula, the harder it will be to understand and the more opportunity people have to suspect that it hides some unfairness. Suggested sharing principles are described below and applied to common alliance situations.

Eleven Sharing Principles

1. Discuss your views and agree on assumptions you will use about market and economic trends, and pertinent regulations.
2. Agree that your arrangement must encourage each firm's commitment to your mutual objectives.
   - –Each company must believe it is getting its fair share of the benefits.
   - –Attribute gains and losses to those business units expected to contribute to success.
   - –Tie gains and losses to corresponding performance.
   - –Favor an arrangement that encourages continuous improvement (e.g., use revenue sharing rather than cost sharing).
   - –Each firm must be satisfied with its own business case for the alliance.
3. Include significant costs, benefits, and risks within the alliance's scope that contribute to its performance. All else is a separate matter for each firm. Any agreed costs that either firm incurs for the benefit of the alliance (e.g., reducing capacity in one firm) should be included.
4. Share gains and losses according to the value of each firm's contribution.
5. Whoever controls a risk should take the risk.
6. Each company should benefit from its own separate efforts (e.g., internal cost reduction).
7. Sharing does not have to be equal to be fair.
8. Seek overall and local fairness.
9. Design a sharing formula that remains fair over the likely range of outcomes, including expected changes in alliance pricing to customers.
10. Make periodic adjustments as necessary to reflect changing circumstances and to sustain each firm's commitment.
11. Sharing post-alliance costs, benefits, and risks must be seen as fair during the alliance.

How to Judge Fairness

Usually it is not possible to quantify all value created by an alliance. The general rule is to measure significant costs and benefits and consider important nonquantifiable items to judge whether what each firm gains is a fair balance. Chapter 4 describes how British Airways and USAir became polarized, in part due to perceptions within USAir of unfair benefit sharing in areas like promotions and European market access.

In assessing what benefits to consider, include only those that can be attributed primarily to the alliance. For example, between 1990 and 1996 Canon's stock price doubled while Hewlett-Packard's grew eightfold. Some people in Canon believed that HP's increase was due to its success with printers and thought that their firm was not getting enough from HP. But in reality, differences between the firms' stock prices reflected their total businesses, which are quite distinct.

Whenever possible, use benchmarking to assess the appropriateness of prices paid to a partner. Another useful practice is to develop models of each other's costs, and use those as guides for benefit sharing.

In sharing a facility, fairness means equal access. For instance, Maersk and SeaLand have benefited from improved shipping frequencies they can offer their respective customers. Separately, Maersk gained container slots in the Brazilian and Central American markets, while SeaLand got additional slots in the Asia-Europe market. However, gaining more slots does not automatically create a benefit if the company getting them cannot sell them. Each firm pays for its additional slots, which increases its costs. So the true measure of gain is each firm's bottom line results, which are not available to the other company. As long as each partner has equal access to the alliance's resources, the benefits one realizes are of no concern to the other.

Early in the container shipping alliance there were perceptions in both firms that benefit sharing was unfair. To address that concern, staffers from both partners jointly developed and presented at an annual meeting a picture of the benefits available. That shared perspective enabled each company to conclude that it had equal opportunity to gain from the alliance. Of course, there have been perceptions of unfair sharing at local and regional levels, due to structural differences between the firms, as noted in Chapter 5.

Regarding asset valuations, if you cannot concur, have an expert third party perform the task.

Sharing Costs

Agree at the outset on what will and will not be shared, how cost is defined, and what the specific charges will be. To permit desired flexibility, consider allocating costs based on each firm's use of a facility. For some items you may be willing to share open book costs; others may be too sensitive.

For personnel costs, rather than discuss actual costs, which can cause problems, agree on a figure for a full-time-equivalent for both firms and use that as a basis for your calculations.

When capital usage is expected to vary, build that into your plans. For instance, Tasty Wares' parents developed common shipping containers for moving food between their plants and Tasty's retail outlets. At first, they tried to ship on a full truckload basis to reduce costs. But that proved to be unworkable due to different sales volumes for each partner in each outlet. They thus agreed to allow swings between defined upper and lower limits, as well as how they would pay for any differences in capacity use.

Sharing Risks

The general rule here is that whoever controls a risk should take the risk. To illustrate, by charging deductibles and making claimants bear a portion of any losses, insurers encourage those they cover to lower their risks. By the same logic, pilots who guide ships into ports are legally liable for accidents that happen on their watch.[5]

Any attempt to separate integrated risks encourages destructive behavior. In the case of Canon and Hewlett-Packard, the printers they develop involve a high degree of interaction between the firms in both design and components. When a problem occurs, it can be difficult to say it was caused by one company's input because that might have been influenced by the other's. To avoid finger pointing and go straight to problem solving, the firms see any product problem as a shared responsibility.

Canon and HP have agreed that an annual failure rate above a defined amount requires discussion. More generally, any failure can trigger joint probing and root cause problem solving to find and eliminate the source. Generally, each company pays its own costs in such exercises. But if one firm faces a particularly large cost, the other might agree to share it.

Benefits Sharing in Customer-Supplier Alliances

In these relationships pricing is the primary determinant of benefits sharing. Pricing is derived from the customer's own market price, benchmark pricing data, and general knowledge of the supplier's costs. A customer may agree to share more with its supplier if the supplier's performance exceeds defined milestones.

Open or Closed Books?

Some people believe that opening a firm's books to a partner is an act of trust. However, the merits of such actions are outweighed by the disadvantages—particularly in customer-supplier relationships. For example, when a supplier shares such information it gives the customer an opportunity to use it. To compete and remain independent, every firm must be free to manage its costs and allocate its resources. Consequently, giving cost information to a customer may lead to the customer's second-guessing those costs inappropriately.

A customer can and should learn about a supplier's key cost-drivers through benchmarking, quality audits, and value engineering. In fact, these tactics are necessary to monitor supplier performance. But going further can weaken suppliers and reduce competition among them, which is not in the customer's best interest.

Sharing Benefits in Joint Marketing

The simplest way to set customer prices in joint marketing is to add each firm's separate prices. To avoid later conflict, you should also agree on how to manage joint price reductions.

If both firms' contributions will be combined so that separate pricing is not feasible, you can use a markup based on each firm's costs. However, that reduces the incentive for cost reduction. A better approach is to share the combined revenue, which gives each firm an opportunity to improve its margins. In general, revenue from an alliance is allocated according to the value of each firm's contribution.

As an example, Airbus, the European consortium, for many years added each partner's separate prices, which gave each an incentive to maximize its profits by claiming inflated costs. Pricing meetings came to be known among the partners as "the Liar's Club," for that reason.[6]

Here is how revenue sharing works. First, the partners agree on the activities and percentage of the total for which each firm will be responsible. Allocations are then made on an agreed basis like benchmark pricing, or on activities involved like direct labor hours, capital use, and material costs. For example, in jet engine alliances, it is common for each company to consider one person equivalent to one person at equal functional levels, regardless of pay, in each firm. Each partner's representation is taken on faith by the other. The firms usually don't know each other's actual costs. Negotiations are intended to put each in a position to make a profit the best way it can. The partners share the risk of the deal in two ways—through each firm's ability to make its allocated parts efficiently, and through the marketing risks for the final product.

Revenue sharing is easier when partner firms are in the same business. That simplifies agreement on the value of each firm's contribution—and thus its revenue share—with its work share. Moreover, firms in the same business can usually estimate each other's costs with some confidence.

In a joint marketing alliance where one firm takes the lead role, it may be expected to disclose more program information. This can limit the appeal of revenue sharing between rivals.

Sharing in Joint Ventures

In general, sharing arrangements in JVs depend on the specific JV structure. For example, revenue sharing is generally best if a JV primarily serves to coordinate activities that remain in the parent firms. In that case most of the costs will be in those firms, and revenue sharing creates an incentive to lower costs. By contrast, if most costs are within the JV then profit sharing is appropriate. However, you still must agree on the balance of retained earnings versus dividends.

So long as the sharing method is consistent with JV and parent performance incentives, parent income from a joint venture may be any mix of royalties, technology fees, dividends, and payments for goods or services that is acceptable to each firm. Since dividends are discretionary, they can be omitted when a venture is strapped for cash, which often occurs in startups. For established ventures, it is best to set minimum dividend requirements to encourage management discipline and to ensure parent benefits.

The payout scheme you use for each parent's inputs to a JV must align that parent's efforts with the JV's objectives. Say, for instance, parent A earns income by selling its goods to the venture and gets a share of the venture's profits from sales to others. Such an arrangement encourages parent A to push the venture to charge others less, thereby stimulating sales of A's goods. However, the reduced pricing might compromise the other parent's income from the venture. One way to avoid this kind of problem is to pay a parent for what it sells a JV based on an agreed discount from the JV's own prices. A variation on that theme is for each parent to cover its share of the JV costs in proportion to its share of the business.

Usually, continued know-how support from both parents is not paid for. The idea here is that this is part of each firm's ongoing commitment. Yet if such inputs are clearly unequal, the venture may be expected to pay. An example is when one partner has substantial R&D expenses associated with the JV, while the other partner does not.

Management fees paid to either parent are generally inappropriate, except for joint ventures run by one partner without the other's involvement. A fee sets a precedent that any contributed management time must be paid for, which lowers the spirit of cooperation. Besides, a venture's own management is compensated by its parents through their share of the costs. When both parents make continuing contributions their benefits should come from dividends, royalties, and payments for services.

To complete your sharing arrangement, agree on the accounting practices and outside auditor the JV will employ.

Sharing Between Large and Small Firms

In alliances involving firms with substantial size differences, smaller firms are often concerned that their partners may use their power to retain benefits unfairly. To avoid such perceptions, pay particular attention to the processes involved.

Research in a variety of contexts finds that due process—the fairness of a company's policies and procedures for dealing with vulnerable partners—affects relationships more than distributive justice—the amount each partner gets. One reason is that only some of the factors that influence how much a firm shares with its partners are under its control. However, the more powerful partner is always assumed to have control over its policies and procedures.[7]

H. CHOOSING KEY PEOPLE

Here are some attributes of personal style and skills that contribute to healthy relationships and successful alliances:[8]

Competent	Has relevant business expertise
Internally Effective	Can get things done within own organization
Innovative	Explores differences creatively, finds common ground, adopts different approaches according to situation
Pragmatic	Seeks realistic solutions
Humble	Accepts others as equally worthy
Communicates Well	Has the flexibility to be understood in different contexts

Helpful	Takes the initiative in meeting others' needs
Perseveres	Keeps going when the challenge is great
Accepts Ambiguity	Comfortable in unfamiliar situations; does not push for closure when the situation does not warrant this
Courageous	Willing to make mistakes
Repair Skills	Able to rebuild damaged interpersonal relations
Integrity	By nature honest and reliable
Sensitive	Can listen and observe, glean subtle cues from verbal and nonverbal communications, know when and how to raise issues
Tolerant	Ignores petty or irritating matters
Curious	Displays an abiding interest in learning about others
Networks	Looks for and links needed people, resources
Facilitates	Promotes understandings and agreement
Personal Growth	Learns from the past but is not constrained by it

I. TEN STEPS TO PRACTICAL MUTUAL OBJECTIVES

This material summarizes and expands on the discussion in Chapter 3. Setting mutual objectives in an alliance requires more breadth and clarity than is typical for internal activities. Once your objectives are set, you can use them to plan joint activities and align your organizations to support them.

Be aware that a mutual objective may not be an obvious combination of your separate objectives. Sometimes creativity helps. In alliances between airlines, for example, each typically wants to increase its revenue from those links. To do so, partners define their objective as increasing passenger flow between them at shared gateways. This gives each carrier the most passenger miles from the alliance and the best revenue opportunity. The steps below can help you develop mutual objectives.

1. Begin by having each company define its own priority stretch objectives for working with the other. Be sure to

identify any objectives that are so much a part of each firm's culture they are taken for granted.

2. Together, define your shared vision—a qualitative summary of both firms' priority stretch objectives.

3. Derive mutual business and financial objectives that, when met, will achieve your shared vision.

4. Check: Meeting your mutual objectives must satisfy each firm's separate objectives.

5. Rank mutual objectives in terms of priority and desired implementation sequence.

6. Derive subordinate mutual objectives for each function and activity to be involved in the alliance (e.g., objectives for customer selection, value proposition, sourcing, cycle time).

7. Go into enough depth to ensure that your operating-level objectives have the clarity to guide day-to-day actions.

8. Define future objectives, such as those for development, that will need attention soon.

9. Identify each firm's objectives that must be met separate from your mutual objectives (e.g., one firm may want to retain the lead for certain customers even though your mutual objectives would be better served a different way).

10. Define organizational boundaries in each firm that separate shared objectives from conflicting internal objectives.

J. OBJECTIVES THAT MAY NEED ATTENTION

Use the objectives detailed here to determine whether your discussions have covered all of each firm's interests. In most companies, some objectives have been accepted for so long that they have become implicit. That creates a risky tendency to ignore them during alliance discussions. For more on mutual objectives, see Chapter 3.

Market   What are your priorities regarding market share, segments, customers, geography, market knowledge?

Distribution   What are your preferences regarding channel capacity, distributor expertise, customer access, other channel characteristics?

Individual Customers	What are your criteria for customer selection, priorities to serve, turnover, revenue/margin per customer, delivery, education? Do your objectives include learn ing about customer needs, building relationships, or retaining customers?
Value Proposition	What are your objectives regarding product attributes, availability, and pricing; product line width and depth; presale and postsale service?
Behavior	What style—in making decisions, pursuing opportunities, innovating, and in other areas—will you need to continue or adapt to succeed?
Sales	Do you have objectives for your sales force—such as size, learning, or customer contact? Is pull-through of your products an objective or a nicety? Do you have specific revenue, margin, or other selling expectations? Must your alliance selling mesh with or be distinct from other sales activities?
Operations	Do you have objectives for capacity use, cost, speed/timing, productivity, quality, safety, environment? What do you want to be the focus of performance improvement (e.g., individual equipment or entire site or system)?
Technology	What are your goals for performances, costs, timing, interfaces?
Learning	What data or know-how do you want from your partner or the alliance?
Financial	Do you have a preferred and minimal revenue gain, hurdle rate, return, cost, cash flow, capital limit, book value, EVA, payback, or productivity target? Is consolidation an objective? Are there any limits on funds available, dilution of ownership, acquisitions by a joint venture? What financial risks are acceptable? Do you have expectations for sharing arrangements with alliance customers, others?
Human Resources	Is job creation or retention an objective for either firm? If so, for whom—employees, family members, political appointees, others? For joint ventures: Does either firm have specific practices it expects to maintain for recruiting, training, evaluation, promotion,

	mobility, diversity, compensation, or benefits? How will labor market or union issues affect staffing? What must be done to attract and keep needed people?
Multiple Units or Locations	How much coordination do you want on strategy, pricing, technology, design, quality, service, capacity use, sourcing, logistics, IT, inventories, or customer relations?
Timing	When do you want to start, get results? Do you have objectives for key sequences or cycle times?
Limits	Do you have preferences regarding the product, market, or geographic scope?
Independence	Do you have objectives regarding policy influence on or investment in the other firm? Would you be willing to have another firm influence or invest in your firm?
Direction	What is your firm's desired longer-term growth path?
Development	What are your priorities for ongoing improvement in products, services, sales, marketing, operations, technology?
Safeguards	Do you have constraints on others' use of your know-how or other valued assets? Any preferences about when and how the alliance will end including payments, ownership of rights, assets, know-how, continuing obligations?
Organization	Your desired limits on change (e.g., to avoid disrupting other activities)?
Image	Will you want to develop or maintain any brands or particular company image?
Business Practices	Do you have preferred codes of conduct and standards regarding the environment, safety, employment, third-party payments?
Key Suppliers	Are there priority sources to be established or maintained?
Other Links	Does your firm have or seek links to labor unions, associations, universities, others that will affect your alliance?
Governments	What approvals, support, funds are sought?

Partner Inputs   What partner resources, skills, personnel do you want to be devoted to the alliance?

Exclusivity   Do you want the sole right to pursue a particular activity? Do you want to limit your partner's freedom in any activity?

K. ALTERNATIVES FOR EXCLUSIVITY

Anything that restricts a partner may reduce its enthusiasm and compromise its performance. So be careful about seeking exclusivity. For instance, asking a supplier not to sell a jointly developed technology to anyone else might prevent the firm from gaining the volume needed to pay for its investment.

The best way to solve this kind of problem is through candid discussions about each firm's needs, leading to a creative solution that works for both of you. As a general rule, granting exclusivity is useful if the benefits for both parties will outweigh expected gains from going nonexclusive.

In weighing the benefits of various options, bear in mind that a partner may need some exclusivity to protect a large investment to build on what you have done together. In that case, a nonexclusive arrangement would make the opportunity unattractive. To illustrate, this is why distributors that are expected to make substantial investments unique to products they are handling seek an exclusive territory.

Whenever possible, back up exclusive commitments with expectations that your resources will be used productively. For example, you might set minimum performance standards, such as targeting cumulative sales for a certain level in five years. Nonperformance would allow you to add other partners. This kind of performance expectation, rather than a minimum royalty, helps ensure the growth of the alliance.

Exclusivity may be expected of one or both firms. Two-way exclusivity is appropriate only when it serves your mutual objectives and does not discourage either firm's commitment.

The following list summarizes the pros and cons of exclusivity and ways to tailor it for specific situations.

Reasons for Exclusivity

- Provide an incentive for exclusive partner to innovate, make unique investment
- Nothing else would work—there is just one source for a desired item
- Need to reach scale economies
- Require substantial integration (too difficult to integrate with more than one firm)

Reasons Against Exclusivity

- Confines granting firm's options
- May reduce incentive for continuous improvement

Options for Achieving Exclusivity

- Limit exclusivity to a specific time frame.
- Require minimal performance.
- Limit the scope (product, market, geography).
- Limit the number or kinds of other partners.
- Limit market entry (where legally permissible).
- Limit conditions under which other partners could get rights.
- Grant right of first refusal for continuation of exclusivity.
- Limit sharing of future technology.[9]
- Limit or delay using know-how produced by the alliance.
- Limit use of know-how received from outside the alliance.

L. SHARE KNOW-HOW INTELLIGENTLY

Information is always shared when people work together. Before agreeing to cooperate, you have to disclose enough to judge each other's potential. Later, during joint planning, each firm learns more about the other's skills and interests. Even observing a partner's mistakes may teach you what not to try on your own. Or when someone describes a novel technique without saying how it works, the fact of its being different gets you thinking about new ways. However, certain know-how is too vital to expose and may not be protectable with patents. Share other information only if doing so adds value. A drawback of information sharing is that the quicker learner may have an edge over its partner firm, creating an imbalance in benefits.

To earn the right to use a partner's sensitive information, you have to display the ability to protect it. Relying on faith alone is inadequate because leaks can do great damage. When you share information, be clear about what is proprietary and what is not. Inside another company it is not always clear which part of what you have shared is proprietary.

Never seek information you are not supposed to have or use data that your partner inadvertently exposes or shares. Expect the same from your partner. Listen to Chuck Walter, a manufacturing manager at Hewlett-Packard, describe his firm's experience with Canon: "I cannot think of anyone in either company probing to learn what they should not learn. You never even dream of finding out what you should not know."

On one occasion an HP manager received a fax from Canon that was intended for an HP competitor. He immediately picked up the phone, called his counterpart at Canon, observed that a mistake had been made, and said he was taking the fax to the shredder at once. No one else in HP saw it or learned of its contents. Separately, Canon and HP people have been officed at each other's facilities, and no one has ever abused the access this provides.

Here are some general principles regarding what and how to share.

Do Not Share Core Knowledge

Know-how is part of a firm's core competence if it provides significant competitive advantage. Never share such knowledge; its use by others could undermine your own business. Examples of core knowledge are Canon's skills in laser engines and Hewlett-Packard's in user-friendly printing and manufacturing for reliability.

Core know-how can be used safely in an alliance so long as sharing is limited to results and not methods. Such sharing can include having adequate control of the know-how on another firm's premises. As an example, Japan's NEC holds under 30 percent of a chip-making venture with China's Shanghai Hua Hong Microelectronics. But to avoid leaking its advanced manufacturing technology, NEC has full management control of the venture.[10]

Protecting Sensitive Know-How

Any sensitive information (including core know-how) can be protected by creating a "firewall" around it. This entails:

- Hiring only people with impeccable integrity
- Assigning different people to separate projects
- Physically separating places where others' critical information is used
- Granting access to information and where it is kept on a need-to-know basis
- Marking confidential documents and locking them up when not in use
- Requiring those with access to these data to sign nondisclosure agreements
- Periodically reminding all employees about what is off limits to outsiders (HP employees receive a reminder with every paycheck)
- Monitoring what others request and receive
- Having a respected third party audit each firm's security systems before sharing sensitive data, and following up with regular audits to be sure security remains effective
- Reprimanding wilful violators
- Destroying outdated materials
- Performing exit interviews to remind employees leaving the firm about their obligations

When it is not practical to separate know-how physically, you have to rely on people's integrity. For instance, product designers at Motorola may work with several suppliers on a critical part, but in no case do they share one supplier's designs with another.

Ownership of Joint Inventions

The best time to negotiate the ownership and use of joint inventions is before a project begins. Within the scope of your core competence and in other areas where an invention can make a critical competitive difference, full ownership is best. Otherwise, deciding who owns joint inventions requires weighing the pros and cons for both firms.

For instance, in customer-supplier alliances the customer may want to own joint inventions if they enhance its competitive advantage. However, this can harm the supplier by preventing it from capitalizing on an advance it helped create. It may also raise the customer's costs by preventing the supplier from gaining volume sales. Various ways to manage exclusivity are discussed in II.K. Since know-how may have value for other parts of your firm, questions about rights transfers to others should go to the corporate level for final decisions.

When particular inventions are worth owning separately, the issue of joint ownership can be avoided through early development. This involves pursuing some projects far enough to solidify your proprietary rights before starting a project with another firm.

M. CAN EACH ORGANIZATION RESPOND?

Cooperation between organizations requires alignment around your shared objectives. Because the potential for that is rooted in a firm's politics, culture, and structure, there may be limits on what each firm can do. To determine the outlook for alignment, one general question concerns the amount of change required in each firm. More specific questions, outlined below, focus on topics that frequently cause alignment problems. If either firm has had related experiences with similar changes, such as significant rationalization or integration, one way to judge the outlook for an alliance is to determine how well that worked.

Management by Objectives. To what extent does each firm manage by clear and consistent objectives? Companies that truly manage by objectives on the inside make better partners because they are accustomed to that style and their internal objectives are more easily linked to their alliance objectives.

Teamwork. How effective is teamwork among each firm's participating individuals and units? Is teamwork part of the culture?

Delegation and Empowerment. Will teams and others at the operating level have enough authority and motivation to take the initiative and follow through on day-to-day matters?

Control. Is each firm willing and able to share control? Is doing so normal within each culture, or will this take an exceptional effort to achieve and sustain?

Vertical Connections. How well are policy initiatives and policy-level commitments to others implemented? How effective are vertical communications and coordination?

Horizontal Coordination. Can each firm maintain internal alignment over time and through significant changes, in all activities relevant to the alliance objectives? If the alliance will be multisite, can each firm keep alignment in all relevant activities at each location?

Matrix or Hierarchy. How flexible is each company? Companies that perform under a matrix or other structure that facilitates links among the parts can more readily adapt for alliances than can those with rigid hierarchies.

Problem Solving. How do issues and conflicts normally get resolved? Through power, politics, escalation, a reference to rights, or root cause problem solving at the source?

Response Times. Does each firm normally respond (decisions, new initiatives, implementation, etc.) in the time frames needed by the alliance?

Continuous Improvement. Alliances remain so by continuing to produce more value than alternatives available to either firm. Such performance requires ongoing mutual creativity and adjustments by the partners. If this behavior is part of each firm's normal style, it can be expected in an alliance. The opposite is also true.

Resources. Are needed skills and resources available? Have they been allocated for the alliance? What will it take to get more if they are needed? Why is this alliance a priority in each firm? What might lower that priority?

Context Expertise. In what markets, technologies, and other key areas is each organization competent? What are the boundaries of this competence? In what specific activities has either firm shown a lack of competence?

Change Management. What is each firm's ability to change in areas relevant to the alliance? What is its track record in related multi-unit activities such as rationalization, integration, reengineering, total quality?

Local Flexibility. How readily can participating units or functions adapt to support what the alliance requires?

Management Systems. Are each firm's formal and informal recognition and reward systems consistent with alliance requirements? What about each one's information system used for monitoring and decision making?

Internal Continuity. Does each firm now ensure continuity in key areas such as major programs and major account management?

Energy Levels. Are people overburdened by current activities? Is energy available for new initiatives?

Business Practices. How well does each firm meet social, safety, and environmental norms desired in the alliance?

N. DEFINING THE SCOPE OF AN ALLIANCE

The wider your early commitment to another firm, the more you foreclose other opportunities. Broader commitments also make your firm more dependent on your partner's performance. To avoid these problems, define an alliance narrowly at first, expanding it based on growing confidence and success.

If you agree to share future technologies with current partners, you may be unable to build alliances with other firms that want to restrict how their own technology is used.

More generally, use the eight trust conditions to set the limits of effective cooperation. Include in an alliance only those products, markets, technologies, and activities that meet all of the following criteria:

- The opportunity is a priority for both companies and they are each other's best way to achieve it.

- Interpersonal relationships of those to be involved are constructive.
- Joint leaders can build and support creative interfirm teams.
- Mutual objectives can be defined, and unresolved conflicting objectives can be excluded (for example, if your firm wants to retain the lead with certain customers even though yielding it might be best for your mutual objective, address this issue separately or exclude it from the alliance).
- Each organization can be aligned to support your mutual objectives.
- The alliance will end before damaging staff discontinuities occur.
- Both firms can treat each other fairly.
- Information sharing and termination safeguards will permit each firm to do its best.

O. A FRAMEWORK FOR REALISTIC PLANNING

Trust is strengthened by a belief that your plans are realistic and weakened to the extent they are not. Use the framework below to predict the difficulties you may encounter in an alliance. First implement those tasks that are easy to do and produce significant benefits. As a rule, behavioral and organizational changes are the hardest. Whenever possible, select tasks that do not require making such changes until you have a track record of success.

Least Difficult	Most Difficult
High trust in past relationship	Adversarial past relationship
Key people have strong relationship skills	Weak relationship skills
Joint leadership can deliver everything needed	Joint leadership cannot deliver
Objectives are within easy reach	Objectives will require substantial stretching
Insignificant cultural differences	Major organizational, national contrasts
Firms are not rivals	Major competitors
Begin with single project	Multiple projects at start

Low market, economic, technology, government risks	High risks
Realignment within each firm will be easy	Realignment will be difficult
All activities will be separate	There will be substantial integration
Strong political support exists in both firms	Weak support, dangerous snipers present
The firms will be separated by one clear interface	There will be multiple interfaces
One unit will be involved from each firm	Multiple units will be involved
Required behavior is consistent with firms' cultures	Behavior not consistent
No competitive response is expected	Major rivals will be catalyzed

↑ **Increasing Benefits**

Do First	Do Later
	Do Later
Do Later	Avoid

Increasing Difficulty →

P. WAYS TO MAINTAIN PEOPLE CONTINUITY

This section summarizes relevant parts of Chapter 4 and draws on material from other chapters.

Key People's Careers

- Keep them in positions longer than normal.
- Create career ladders at the interface to compensate for less job rotation.
- Develop transition plans for people who will take key alliance positions.

Training, Recognition, and Rewards
- Build into performance evaluations expectations about desired conduct.
- Have joint training in trust practices for newcomers from both firms.
- Give key people mentoring roles after they move on to other positions.
- Arrange for people who will be joining an alliance to attend meetings as observers.

Management Tasks
- Reduce staff turnover by making employment more attractive
- Coach new arrivals in expected behavior.
- Discuss candidates for key alliance positions with your partner to be sure of a good match.
- Include future contributors in social gatherings with people who will be their colleagues.
- Articulate shared norms at all alliance meetings and actively use them as a guide.
- Expect and encourage newcomers to start building relationships as soon as they arrive.
- Regularly and visibly remind everyone that even when people change, continuity is expected in partner relationships.
- In regular internal operating reviews, include alliance progress and emphasize the importance of continuity and other trust factors.

Q. EARLY WARNING SIGNS DETECTABLE DURING NEGOTIATIONS

In each of the following areas, certain factors predict an alliance's failure or underperformance. This checklist draws on material in Chapters 2 through 6.

Key Individuals
- Lack relationship skills.
- Are not the best from each firm.

- Do not have enough time to invest.
- Are not enthusiastic about the alliance.
- Local stakeholders are not champions for the alliance.

Negotiating Process
- Joint leadership does not guide the process.
- Negotiators will not be the implementors.
- Bargaining gets priority over joint creativity.
- Alliance development is separated from team building.
- Relationships are not emphasized early at all relevant interfirm levels.
- People who will cooperate cannot make day-to-day decisions
- Understanding each other's situation or concerns is not emphasized.
- All deal breakers are not identified at the start.
- Internal negotiations get inadequate attention.
- Latecomers have different negotiating agendas.
- Either firm misleads the other.
- Tough issues have not been raised or resolved.
- Cultural differences are not addressed.

Alliance Design
- Shared objectives did not guide all aspects of the process.
- Alliance activities have not been separated from conflict in both firms.
- There is no clear agreement about scope, exclusivity, information sharing, termination.
- Implementation will be too difficult (see II.O., "A Framework for Realistic Planning").
- Internal support and alignment are incomplete or inconsistent
- The chosen structure does not support alliance objectives or needed behavior.
- Either firm believes negotiations produced a win-lose outcome.

III. DETAILS OF ALLIANCE STRUCTURES AND GOVERNANCE

■

This material expands on Chapter 6 and refers to source material on various structures.

A. COMPARING THE THREE BASIC STRUCTURES

As you might expect, each basic alliance structure has a number of advantages and disadvantages. These are compared below.[11]

Feature	Direct Cooperation	Minority Investment	Joint Venture
Possible Differentiation	Modest	Modest	Substantial
Consolidate Financial Gains or Losses	Automatic	Automatic for operating income; not possible for equity income	Not possible for both firms
Activities Are Transparent to Each Partner	No	More than with direct cooperation	Yes
Separates Cooperation from Conflict	Not always	Not always	Can be easier than with other structures
Integration Potential	Partial	Partial	May be complete
Time, Cost to Set Up	Fastest, lowest cost	More than direct cooperation	Most legal, regulatory work

Continued

Feature	Direct Cooperation	Minority Investment	Joint Venture
Duration	Short to long term (days to years)	Longer term (years)	Longer term (years)
Secure Access to Jointly Owned Asset	No	Possible	Yes
Visibility to Outsiders	May be zero	May be evident from public filings	May be evident from public filings, or ties to customers or suppliers

If your primary interest in a joint venture is to share benefits more effectively, first consider doing that through direct cooperation. For instance, you could agree on a transfer pricing protocol. Or you might create "accounting walls" in your firms and make the books available to outside auditors. An agreed-upon formula can then be used to adjust payments.

B. CHARACTERISTICS OF MINORITY EQUITY INVESTMENTS

Recall from Chapter 6 that the minority equity investment structure is designed to support cooperation at the smaller firm's policy and operating levels. The arrangement is distinct from passive minority investments made primarily for financial gain.[12]

Rationale

- Strategic value gets priority.
- Smaller firm gets capital needed for the alliance.
- Investor gets policy influence and possibly key resource access.

Conditions

- Smaller firm must have a narrow business scope.
- Smaller firm must be solid.

- Other major investors may have to depart.
- Investment may be one-way or two-way (in which case firms must be of comparable size).

Board Role
- To preserve smaller firm's independence, investor gets narrow veto rights (e.g., changes in management or strategic direction, entry of other major investors).
- In some jurisdictions (e.g., the United States) board members must represent all investors equally.
- To avoid conflict, separate the policy and operating roles in investor firm.

Capital Access Alternatives to Minority Investments
- Use project or debt financing or pay for capital equipment.
- Consider the differences between equity and debt financing.

Equity	*Debt*
Facilitates policy role	Does not
Benefits from partner growth	Does not
Promotes psychological bonds	Does not
Permits financial flexibility	Does not

C. AN EXERCISE IN CHOOSING THE RIGHT STRUCTURE

Use this case, based on an actual alliance, to test your understanding of alliance structures. To see how you scored, see the endnotes.[13]

Two telecommunications firms are discussing an alliance to pursue the global business market. The alliance will use technologies from both firms to develop new service offerings, which will be marketed separately by each parent in its geographic area. For both firms, the business market is a growing and substantial source of revenues and margins.

The companies intend to provide their customers with easy global connectivity, as well as to serve communications needs that are in some ways distinct in each geographic area. At present, discussions are focused on a 50/50 joint venture. Short cycle times for product introduction and improvement will be a key success factor for each company.

As international group president for one of the prospective partners, you will be involved in designing the joint venture. Here are some questions you should consider:

- What resources should be under the JV's control?
- What functions from each firm should be on the JV board?
- What key tasks will the board perform?
- How much autonomy should the JV have?
- What key attributes should its CEO have?

D. COMMON FEATURES OF BOARDS AND STEERING COMMITTEES

Governing bodies for direct cooperation and joint ventures share the following traits.

For Local Teamwork and Fast Alliance Cycle Times
- Give final authority to the governing body and day-to-day authority to each interface.
- Decision-making processes must be understood by all involved.
- Overcommunicate—keep everyone informed.
- When consensus is not required, assign decisions by expertise.
- Anticipate issues and future constraints; resolve them early.

Within Each Firm
- Delegate alliance decisions to steering committee/board.
- Hold committee/board accountable for results, with most weight on joint leaders.
- Always inform your partner before making decisions that affect the alliance.
- Partner-to-partner communications that substantively affect the alliance must go through steering committee/board.

Membership Criteria

- Strong interest: alliance is important to person's position.
- Needed authority: must be able to make internal and joint decisions that bear on alliance.
- Relevant skills: members have expertise needed by alliance.
- A facility for teamwork.
- Six is the best number.

Style

- Driven by shared objective.
- Give clear, consistent signals derived from shared objectives to people below.
- Model teamwork desired at lower levels.
- Make decisions by consensus.
- Resolve toughest issues.

Tasks

- Set recognition and reward systems based on shared objectives and monitor progress.
- Champion the alliance and provide needed support in own firms.
- Select operating team members, venture executives.
- Define and monitor internal boundaries; shield alliance from conflict.
- Manage people discontinuities.
- Review and adjust benefits imbalances.
- Set priorities within alliance.
- Define delegation to lower levels.

Vertical Relationships

- All partner policy matters should flow through the board or steering committee.
- Board or committee members give the alliance priority when in this role.
- Operating-level staff should attend meetings but not serve on board or committee.
- Define a clear boundary between board and JV management.

E. JOINT VENTURE GOVERNANCE

Use this material with IV.D., "Common Features of Boards and Steering Committees."

BASIC ARRANGEMENTS

Participation	Responsibilities and Ownership	When to Use
Full Equality	Partners are equals in all policy and operating matters.	Both will make ongoing critical know-how inputs, or
	Ownership is usually 50/50.	Ongoing coordination will be essential, or
		Partners are rivals.
Policy Equality	Partners are equals in all policy matters.	JV business is closer to one partner's. Both have needed expertise.
	One is responsible for operations.	
	Ownership is usually 50/50.	
Lead Partner	One partner has the lead on most policy and all operating matters.	Different styles inhibit close cooperation, or
	Management systems are designed to meet its needs.	No ongoing know-how flows, or
	Other partner may veto specific items.	Minority partner's interest is operational, not strategic.
	Ownership depends on circumstances.	

How Differentiation and Coordination Affect Governance

The effort required to govern a joint venture rises as the JV becomes more differentiated from its parents and as the need to coordinate activities with them increases. Further, the governance challenge grows in proportion to the complexity of parent objectives as when, say, the parents specify financial performance and strategic direction, rather than just financial targets.

One example of a JV with low differentiation and significant coordination is that involving Farmland Industries and Ernst & Young (see Chapter 6). Another is the GE–SNECMA jet engine JV, which depends on its parents for all activities—including engineering, manufacturing, sales and marketing, and field service (see Chapter 4). It employs fewer than two dozen professionals, whose role is to manage that coordination.

Joint ventures having little differentiation and little coordination with their parents typically provide access to shared facilities. Often, such JVs involve no ongoing stretching by their parents, so are not true alliances.

GOVERNANCE TASKS

High	Govern as a separate business	Govern as a separate, coordinated business (most demanding)
Low	Compare results with budgets	Guide coordination

Differentiation from Parents (High / Low)

None — *Substantial*

Coordination with Parents

F. FINANCIAL CONSOLIDATION IN JOINT VENTURES

Because the 50/50 form of joint venture prevents financial consolidation by both parents, some firms seek 51/49 structures. However, before deciding to use an unequal arrangement, recall from Chapter 6 that it can inhibit both parents from doing their best.

Another view of 50/50 is that, by preventing consolidation, it allows parent firms to keep significant losses off their books. This can be a key advantage in some research and development ventures, and in minerals exploration JVs.

As joint ventures have become more widespread, a growing number of securities analysts know how to assess nonconsolidated data that are included in public financial statements. So the need for consolidation may be declining.

G. COMMON ISSUES IN EQUAL GOVERNANCE JVs

Without specified rights on policy matters for each parent, full equality and policy equality JVs have more potential for board imbalance than the lead parent form, leading to conflict or to one firm's withdrawal. Among the causes are outside events like market or technology changes that give one firm a stronger role. If such changes make the other company less valuable to the JV, a shift in control may be inevitable.

Imbalance may also result if one parent carries more weight in board discussions by being better prepared or persistent on particular issues. Usually, this shift occurs gradually. Eventually, both firms conclude that the more forceful partner deserves its clout. To avoid this situation, do your homework before board meetings and take a more active role.

Another cause of imbalance is frequent turnover of one firm's representatives on the board. This can be avoided by adopting the continuity practices detailed in Chapter 4 and II.P., "Ways to Maintain Continuity."

Some companies try to prevent polarization under equal governance by having one firm hold a tie-breaker vote—a tactic usually reserved for emergencies. Wherever I have seen this used, it has created superior and subordinate attitudes, even if the strategy isn't often employed. One executive summed things up: "You always knew that if it came to a showdown you would lose. We chose to avoid raising difficult issues to prevent blowups."

H. GOVERNANCE IN LEAD PARTNER VENTURES

When one parent has the lead, you still need trust to ensure cooperation and ease reaching a consensus when this is necessary. A lead parent should thus keep its partner well informed and give it a chance to be heard. The list below outlines ways to structure board decisions.

Topics Requiring Unanimity
- Define major issues that could substantially affect either firm.
- Include substantial commitments, withdrawing from the market, significant changes in products or employment practices.

Topics Requiring Majority Approval
- Define secondary matters of concern to the minority partner and on which it wants to be heard at the board level.
- Require majority approval to give the minority partner a chance to present its views before board action is taken.
- Include annual profit and capital investment budgets, operating plan, borrowing program.

Topics Requiring Board Discussion
- Include any items to be discussed before management acts.
- Define other issues significant to either partner that should be aired before making a decision.

I. STAFFING JOINT VENTURES

To do your best together, agree on job descriptions for key positions and recruit competent people to fill them, regardless of which firm brings the most business or the most value. Job descriptions should include those key attributes that serve your priority objectives. One such objective—though not always made explicit—is for integration, which calls for team building and organizational process skills. If the right people are not available, the venture may have low priority in their firm.[14]

Parent companies should not use JV management positions to exercise control. Doing so weakens the board's role and inhibits management teamwork. Typically, most senior staff in a JV should come from the parents, to ensure know-how transfer.

The CEO

A venture's top executive is accountable for building the management team, delivering results, and maintaining relationships with the parents. The CEO reports to the board on policy matters and to the lead parent, if there is one, on operating items. He or she takes the initiative on new issues, steers proposals through the board, looks out for parent interests, and keeps board members informed between meetings. There should be a mechanism for removing the CEO for good reason at either parent's initiative.

The first CEO should have in-depth knowledge of the business, plus skills to build the new team and support links to the parents. To facilitate early understandings, this person should come from one of the parents. Outsiders lack political knowledge of and credibility with both parents.

In lead parent JVs, the CEO usually is appointed by the lead firm, with other posts being filled by the best candidate for each slot. When one parent appoints the CEO, it must select someone who can win both parents' confidence.

Other Key Positions

The most essential positions are often the hardest to fill. Designating these for either parent restricts the talent pool from which a venture can draw. Reserving positions for either parent beyond what is absolutely necessary—such as a critical technology transfer position—compromises the CEO's ability to build his or her own team. It also limits a venture's performance and inhibits integration.

Once a JV is under way, the CEO should fill all management slots except those designated for either parent. In such cases, the CEO, as leader of the management team, should have approval authority.

Always share your views with each other on all candidates for management positions. To reinforce parent relationships never fill a senior position with someone who is unacceptable to your partner.

Whenever a venture will be significantly differentiated from its parents, senior staff should be permanently transferred, with no right of return. Preventing return to the home company encourages people's commitments to the new course and fosters integration. Under this condition, pay and benefits must be integrated to ensure equal treatment and encourage teamwork.

J. INFORMATION FOR VENTURE CONTROL

Joint ventures are often asked to produce more information for their parents than similar wholly owned units. Typically, each parent needs distinct information for several purposes: to fit its management systems; match different fiscal periods; and satisfy tax, securities, and other regulatory requirements. Producing that data takes extra staff time, and management has to divert its attention regularly from the venture's business to review and approve two sets of documents.

To ease the reporting burden, consider what data your firm and your partner really need and avoid asking for the rest. Most firms tend to overreport on the inside by asking for information that might be needed, but is rarely used. Strong venture CEOs help ward off some parent requests by pointing out how double paperwork deflects time and effort from the main management tasks.

Another tactic some firms use to lower the reporting burden is to recast the numbers they get from a venture to fit their needs, rather than ask for separate reports. Yet a third way to curb the need for formal reporting is through frequent contacts between JV staff and relevant parent functions such as finance, human resources, quality, and legal. If one parent has operating control, the other should be able to limit its reporting requirements to what is needed to meet its statutory and budget needs.

Parents usually need the most information during the early months of a JV. At that time, much of the needed data are qualitative or to improve mutual comfort, as partners get to know each other and shape their venture. This information flows best in face-to-face interactions between board members and venture management. It is better to have frequent meetings than to ask for lengthy reports.

IV. BENEFITS OF ATTORNEYS AND CONTRACTS

■

Often impugned as agents of doom, lawyers can advance trusting relationships. If you have problems with attorneys, the profession is not the root cause. More likely it is their clients' expectations.

A. WORKING WITH ATTORNEYS

In many firms legal counsel is expected to protect the client, not help build outside relationships. In such cases, you can predict difficulties of the sort that happened on the way to a communications alliance where every issue became a confrontation.

In one of many such experiences, the attorneys needed three months to resolve a relatively minor issue about deferred payments. Another time they debated endlessly about rights in a tiny part of the market. "We were so frustrated by the lawyers, we kept asking each other why we couldn't get rid of them," said one manager. "Attorneys on both sides were building walls around each company. They made it impossible for us to be creative and flexible together."

During a break in one meeting, with counsel out of the room, I asked people from both firms if they knew who had instructed their lawyers to be this way. Both answered that their companies regarded the attorneys as defenders, not bridge builders.

Most of the issues in building an alliance are not legal, which means that management has the final word. Too often, however, management is silent.

Listen to the associate general counsel of a financial services firm: "After the managers agree on the concept, they go on to other things and leave it up to us to put the rest together. The attorney on the other side and I have to search for issues and resolve these to be sure it will all work. Sometimes the deal looks good at the top, but the devil is really in the details. We end up being lightening rods because we raise issues management did not address. They may have a common vision but did not want to deal with tough issues and turned these over to the attorneys. When we cannot resolve something because we don't know what they want, they call it a legal problem."

Lawyering does not have to be one-dimensional, nor should it be. In any healthy relationship you have to protect your separate interests while pursuing comfort and understanding at the same time.

"We have many successful alliances," says one corporate attorney. "If we know the other firm well, or if I develop a mutually confident relationship with another firm's counsel, I may raise possible issues early in the process but not even go to meetings. The best deals I have worked on are when the attorney on the other side and I see each other as partners facilitating a mutually beneficial business arrangement. We spot issues for management to address, make sure they understand the consequences, and look for legal questions that may need our attention."

"I don't want to hide my client behind a nonlegal risk with detailed contract clauses. If the business people understand the risk and are willing to take it," she continues, "in the great majority of instances where this has worked well we drafted flexible agreements which management wanted, which helped us avoid fighting over clauses later on. A battle would not be in the best interest of my firm or of most firms. We really want to find common ground up front."

These observations suggest some guidelines for managers and lawyers to be effective together. One, which is a senior management task, is to better align your firm's expectations for its attorneys with those for business management. Cooperation is always difficult and the results always suffer when people work at cross-purposes with one another.

A second principle is to recognize where the boundary should be. Business issues should be resolved by managers rather than by lawyers. That is not just because managers know more about the substance, but because resolving tough issues together is a shared skill that must develop as your alliance proceeds. Clearly, lawyers sometimes must take a lead role—as in setting limits on alliances between rivals and preparing formal agreements.

Another tenet is that, like any key contributors, attorneys involved in alliances should be good at facilitating processes and building relationships. They should know when not to push for clauses because these would only inhibit needed flexibility, and be able to sense whether understandings are clear.

B. WHAT CONTRACTS CAN DO FOR TRUST

If you are building trust, why bother with a contract? In fact, some companies don't—or they keep it simple. Canon and Hewlett-Packard have no formal agreement, for example, while Ford and ABB signed a few-page contract for the entire multihundred-million-dollar project.

In both cases people had worked together before these alliances began, and developed enough comfort to believe that traditional agreements would be superfluous. These are exceptions, not the rule. In other situations, contracts can be a source of comfort that the fundamentals have been nailed down. In a healthy relationship, a contract is a fallback just in case, not a constraint.

Whether you have a formal agreement or not, there is still a need for the same kinds of memos and plans every firm uses to help people communicate. For example, Canon and HP have discussed preparing a contract to be more transparently consistent with antitrust laws. But the complexities of their relationship have made writing a contract quite difficult. However, the firms share many documents that describe various aspects of their relationship.

If you expect to use a contract, include major issues of concern to either partner, such as each firm's obligations upon termination. Spell out basic assumptions to be sure you concur on the fundamentals. Keep details about implementation, monitoring, penalties, and control to a minimum. There is a difference between defining areas of understanding and concern and including all the options. Clause after clause of contingency planning limits your flexibility, implies an understanding will not be implemented fairly, and affects the tone of your relationship. You have to develop enough trust to be willing to leave some questions for later decisions.

Take SeaLand and Maersk, whose formal agreement is fewer than ten pages long. The contract outlines the alliance scope (relevant markets) and joint governance, notes that each partner will market to customers separately and independently, and refers to accompanying regional agreements. The agreement sealed the firms' basic commitments. They still had to plan the global network, which was a complex task. While the agreement also governs this activity, the document does not include all the details. Further, since network design is expected to be ongoing, whatever would have gone into an agreement would have had to be changed later. Consequently, joint planning of the firms' global vessel network depends on trust.

To be responsive to local government and business conditions, alliances that cut across national borders typically involve agreements tailored to each situation. For instance in Japan, Kodak and IBM entered a ten-year agreement that was separate from the one in Rochester. Still, the Rochester agreement was used as an input to craft the one in Japan.

C. SUGGESTED CONTENTS OF ALLIANCE AGREEMENTS

Alliance agreements should state specifically that both parties intend to have an alliance and define what that means. Note that any item in a contract—such as your business plan—could open the door to renegotiating the entire agreement if conditions change. Here are some useful features of agreements.

The Basic Arrangement
- Broad shared objectives
- The scope
- Important resource commitments by each firm
- Principles of how costs, revenues, earnings, risks will be shared

- Statement that firms are free to pursue other activities and alliances beyond the scope
- Activities to be coordinated or shared
- Each firm's separate responsibilities
- How you will avoid frequently encountered common problems[15]
- Liabilities, warranties, other obligations to third parties
- Any constraints due to applicable rules, laws
- Any conditions of exclusivity (see II.K.)
- Definitions of ownership of existing or future rights, know-how, other assets
- How governance will be exercised, including decisions reserved for either partner
- Criteria for important future decisions (e.g., how nonexclusivity will be decided)
- Provisions for termination

Also State

- That success will depend on continuing cooperation, which cannot be fully specified
- A desire to be guided by your mutual objectives, which will be periodically adjusted
- The centrality of trust in the relationship
- That you will adjust together to improve performance, respond to unexpected events
- How disputes will be resolved
- Continuity of key personnel for the longest possible time is needed to achieve highest performances
- Shared expectation that new people will accept their predecessors' commitments
- That, except as otherwise noted, decisions will be made by consensus
- For joint ventures, describe roles of and relationships between board and top executives

Termination Provisions

Termination may be planned or due to an unexpected event, and may be friendly or unfriendly. The provisions you develop should accommodate each possibility.[16] Because the trust conditions may no longer be met at the time of termination, this part of your understanding should be clear and tight. The provisions have to consider all the contingencies; this is typically the hardest part of an alliance document to draft.

There is an art to preparing termination agreements so that they reinforce trust without keeping either firm in an undesirable relationship. If termination is too easy, it might be tempting to pull out rather than work through a tough issue. On the other hand, a company may be forced to continue even though its interest has waned, lowering performance and sharpening conflict. Somewhere between these poles is the best place to be. The following summarizes key aspects of termination.

- Conditions for termination
  - Agreed alliance lifetime (e.g., product life, time to known external event)
  - Change in ownership or control
  - One firm's underperformance
  - Shift in either firm's priorities
  - Alliance does not meet partners' expectations
  - Change in government regulations
- Terms and consequences
  - Compensate remaining partner
  - "Leave whole" arrangement
  - Sale or allocation of alliance assets, liabilities
  - Protection of proprietary information, brands, other property
  - Restrictions on sale of assets to others
  - Care of customers, responsibilities to distributors and others after alliance ends

V. KEY IMPLEMENTATION TASKS

■

This material complements Chapter 7, which has more details on some of the topics below.

A. MONITORING PROGRESS

As in any endeavor, good measurement is essential for good management. Here are some practices that are useful with alliances.

When and Where to Monitor
- Include alliances in regular internal strategic and operating reviews.
- Monitor overall performance, each interface, and each participating unit.
- Conduct periodic joint reviews.

What to Measure: Results
- Use milestones based on your shared objectives.
- Benchmark your alliance against the market.
- Benchmark among participating units for multiunit alliances.
- Compare your performance with your partner's.

What to Measure: Contributing Factors
- Assess the persistence of a priority mutual need, as well as quality of relationships, effectiveness of joint leadership, and other trust conditions (see I.A., "Do You Meet the Conditions for Trust?").
- Evaluate joint teams, mutual creativity, conflict resolution, and other trust practices (see I.B., "Measuring Trust").
- Develop a scorecard of key processes that contribute to the results.

B. COMMUNICATING ALLIANCE
RESPONSIBILITIES

For clarity and to avoid later misunderstandings, identify and communicate the following to all participants.

Roles
- Board/steering committee
- Joint leaders at policy and operating levels
- Alliance teams
- Top executives in each firm
- Other key people, including those in legal, finance, human resources

Decisions and Decision Makers
- Policies regarding the alliance
- Day-to-day operations
- Changes in priorities or direction
- Issues that get escalated
- Known future events

In larger and more complex alliances, people may not know who to contact in the other firm. To facilitate coordination, prepare a formal list of who should link with whom. Cover at least the highest levels of the alliance, as well as joint projects that will involve many people. The same interfirm map can be used to outline the process for escalating and deciding tough issues.

C. ROLLOUT AT ALLIANCE LAUNCH

The launch meeting is chaired by the alliance co-leaders. Participants should include board or steering committee members, key operating staff, and others who will serve at interfaces and in support roles. This is an opportunity for people to ask questions and develop wider understandings. The agenda should include:

- Each firm's reasons for the alliance
- Alliance objectives and scope, and the rationale for major aspects of the plan

- Important milestones, including those that will need the attention of specific groups or individuals
- How progress will be measured
- How the alliance will be introduced to customers, key others
- The importance of trust, how to build trust, and how to avoid damage
- Early warning signs of trouble ahead
- Identification of who should connect with whom on particular matters
- How decisions will be made
- Key processes and communication patterns that deserve attention
- Questions or issues anyone has about the alliance or how it will work
- Roles of key occasional participants such as legal and finance
- Guidelines for expected conduct
- Processes for conflict resolution
- Shared expectations about how to ensure continuity will be managed when people change
- Pertinent aspects of the agreement, including benefit sharing
- How changes will be made to the initial plans or agreement

D. PLANNING INTERNAL EXPANSION

If you expect an alliance will grow across your firm's internal boundaries, build bridges before they are needed. At Ford, activities for the new Oakville plant were expected to evolve from engineering to construction to operations. To ensure smooth transitions, Ford's Vince Coletta sought early participation from those groups. He initially had sold the alliance concept to higher-level Ford executives. But he still had to convince those at the operating level of the merits.

"Ford's plant people had a great deal of pride of ownership in the traditional way of doing things," observed Paul Bechard, the ABB vice president. "We were proposing a radical change in layout. Oakville was particularly hard on them because they were already planning this and preparing bid packages before ABB was called in."

To win their allegiance, Coletta involved key plant managers in the joint engineering effort. Their participation made them more confident in the new approach, and their feedback effected changes in plant layout before construction. At the same time, Coletta persuaded plant staff that ABB would deliver on its promises. "This was a testing of the waters for us," Bechard recalls. "Vince was putting his faith in us, which further solidified his commitment to us in our eyes and reinforced our commitment to Ford."

As work progressed, Coletta and Ford's Larry Miller met with the auto maker's Oakville plant people and explained how the new approach was going to work. When construction neared completion, Ford involved its plant operating staff in the process. Working with the engineering construction team, they developed a joint launch plan as well as maintenance, operating, and safety procedures. The initial team building and early integration between the phases set a completion record for the industry.

E. SUGGESTED AGENDA FOR EXECUTIVE SUMMITS

Once an alliance is under way, annual meetings of CEOs or other senior executives help keep alignment at the top and signal joint leadership from the highest level. Orchestrate each meeting to ensure that people from both firms feel it was successful and that their future together is bright. Plans for such meetings should include:

- Review of recent results and progress against plans
- Resolution of outstanding issues, including relationships among key individuals
- Assessment of how governance is working
- Discussion of future plans, including each firm's ability to support them
- Agreement on how results of this meeting will be communicated to others

F. BE EVERY PARTNER'S BEST PARTNER

To remain attractive to your current partners, win new ones, and create the most value, your firm must remain their best choice. You can achieve that by:

- Benchmarking, emphasizing continuous improvement, and remaining at the frontiers of your business
- Managing each alliance to earn your partner's best effort
- Advancing your firm's ability to nurture trust

VI. TOOLS FOR SPECIFIC SITUATIONS

■

This material spotlights key aspects of alliances with various partners. The tools presented here are aimed specifically at alliances involving customers, rivals, different-sized firms, cost and profit centers, several units of two partner firms, or several partners.

A. GUIDELINES FOR CROSS-SELLING

The notion of cross-selling is simple: Convince customers that have decided to buy products from one business also to buy items from a partner. Even so, that does not always work. One common reason: a strategic mismatch.

For example, when Novell, a network software firm, bought WordPerfect, maker of a popular word processing product, Novell dropped the salespeople who came with the deal and handed the product to its network sales staff. Not being familiar with how to sell applications, they bumbled the job. Novell sold the unit to Corel, losing close to $1 billion in the process.[17]

In addition to being sure you have a good match, here are some guidelines for effective cross-selling in alliances.[18]

Begin with the Customer

Never justify cross-selling simply because you sell the same kinds of products or market to the same customers. If you believe that customers make intelligent choices about what they buy, cross-selling will succeed only when what is being sold best meets their needs. Either each product must be more attractive than available alternatives, or the benefits of buying a bundle of products must exceed those of buying individual products separately.

As an example of cross-selling based on individual product value, selling credit cards in a package of financial services will work only if customers believe they cannot get a better deal from others. To illustrate bundled selling: Buying the same make of computers helps ensure ease of service.

The distinctions between individual product and bundled selling are evident in how companies in different industries market their brands. In consumer goods, for instance, Procter & Gamble and Unilever allow each of their many brands to stand on its own. The brands benefit each other only through shared distribution networks.

Emphasize Consistency in Selling and Support

Delivering more value to each customer is not enough to be effective in cross-selling. Another requirement is that the selling context be compatible with what the sales process requires. One reason Sears, Roebuck failed to sell consumer financial services through its outlets was that the store environment was not the right place to sell such items.

Related considerations are that each sales force and support group involved must be able to handle the wider range of products with desired service levels, quality, cycle times, operations, and so forth. Recall from Chapter 3 how restaurant chains Arby's and ZuZu failed to recognize that their meals were cooked and served differently, which led to customer confusion, higher costs, and lower quality.

Build Smooth Organizational Alignment

Cross-selling works when everyone involved supports it. Getting all parties on board entails more than including appropriate incentives in compensation plans, however. Also needed is a collective awareness of sales opportunities and the ability to serve them seamlessly. That, in turn, depends on constant communications and ample face-to-face contact among sellers and product/market specialists and, as noted above, alignment on both sides of the interface. Achieving those behaviors can be particularly difficult in multibusiness unit or multisite alliances, or in those involving many products.

"The most important thing to understand about cross-selling," says Dick Kovacevich, president and CEO of Wells Fargo, "is that it's about execution. Implementation is tough. It requires doing literally hundreds of things well—and doing them consistently well—for all your customers."

B. IDENTIFYING HIDDEN RISKS IN LINKS WITH RIVALS

When you cooperate with a rival, the risk of damage is higher than with other partners. To judge risk and decide whether to proceed with an alliance, use your marketing and competitive research to answer the questions below. Based on the results of this analysis, determine if an alliance is still the best way to reach your objectives. Note that learning is often a hidden objective. In assessing learning potential, consider what each firm will observe, as well as each one's ability to put that know-how to use. Recall that VW learned Ford's cost management practices at Ford's expense in their Autolatina JV (see Chapter 11).

	Disclosed	Hidden
Their Objectives *Hidden*	Do *your* disclosed objectives advance the other firm's hidden ones?	What imbalances might occur if either firm's hidden objectives are met?
Disclosed	Is your disclosed shared objective important enough to support cooperation? What imbalances might occur if you meet your shared objectives?	Do the other firm's disclosed objectives advance *your* hidden ones?

Your Objectives

C. BUILDING TRUST BETWEEN SMALL AND LARGE FIRMS

Size differences often create problems in alliances. For instance, small firms allied with large customers often find that the relatively small volume—from the customer's perspective—does not warrant cross-functional teams. Instead, meetings are one-on-one between functions, as necessary. Fragmentation makes cross-functional understandings and trust harder to build and sustain. The remedy is for lead executives to invest more time in communicating internally and with each other. Ways to manage size differences are summarized below. For a discussion of benefit sharing in small firm–large firm alliances, see II.G., "Guidelines for Sharing Benefits, Costs, and Risks."

Concern	Remedy
Difficult to raise issues	Work on relationships; create an advisory board composed of several firms
Alliance is too small for team meetings	Leaders work harder at consensus building
Weak acceptance in larger firm	Delegate alliance to interface
Big firm uses bargaining power	Change style or alliance will suffer
Takeover	Standstill agreement
Entrepreneurial vs. bureaucracy	Confirm contrasts; designate champion in large firm to reduce red tape; lower expectations
Emotional vs. rational styles	Confirm differences, agree on norms
Small firm wants access to all of partner	Manage expectations
Small firm has limited resources	Set priorities that recognize the limits and allocate more costs to large firm
Small firm has problems	Big firm provides help
Small firm must protect cash flow	Include in objectives or provide financial help

D. COMPARING COST CENTERS AND PROFIT CENTERS AS PARTNERS

Contrasting performance expectations for separate groups cause different behaviors in alliances. The comparisons below indicate some of these differences.

Profit Centers	**Cost Centers**
Shorter time horizons	Longer time horizons
Sharper internal priorities	More flexibility to adjust priorities
Easier performance measurement	Easier to cross-subsidize between units
Must profit from change	Does not need profits from change

E. ALLIANCES INVOLVING SEVERAL UNITS FROM TWO FIRMS

To qualify as an alliance, a collection of units—profit centers, cost centers, and facilities—must produce more value together than they could in a commercial relationship among them. Such alliances create the most value when each link surpasses a transaction. To be included in an alliance, each of the participating units, must satisfy the same eight trust conditions, such as serving the same overall objective and needing each other to achieve it. Here are some additional guidelines, based on the trust conditions.

Corporate-Level Requirements for Best Performance

- Give leaders enough authority to make or get needed decisions in desired time frames.
- Constantly reinforce desired patterns of behavior for local levels.
- Change budgets and accounting systems as necessary and allocate benefits to win and keep corporate and local commitments.
- Include local participation in overall governance.

- Encourage and facilitate experience sharing across the alliance.
- Balance differentiation needed in local markets with the need for overall consistency.
- Emphasize conflict resolution at the local level.

Local or Individual Unit Requirements for Best Performance

- Seek a local role in partner choice.
- Ensure that the subordinate trust conditions (subobjectives, local mutual need, etc.) are met at each interface.
- Model local governance on overall alliance governance.
- Tie performance measures and incentives to local and overall success.

F. MANAGING MULTIPLE ALLIANCES BETWEEN TWO FIRMS

A growing trend involves pairs of firms having two or more kinds of relationships between them. To illustrate, Motorola and Hewlett-Packard compete in some markets. In others, they are respectively customer and supplier, as well as supplier and customer. In yet other markets, they share suppliers and customers. Several links between the two electronics firms are alliances. Similar patterns exist in the auto making, chemical, computer, pharmaceutical, and other sectors.

Having multiple relationships is a potential Pandora's box, creating many opportunities for confusion and conflict. To avoid such problems, let each relationship stand on its own merits. If you try to make one conditional on another, all become vulnerable to the weakest among them. The best way to achieve independence is to apply the trust conditions and practices rigorously to each link. Having a clear objectives hierarchy from top to bottom across your firm helps focus each link on the task at hand. Empowering every interface encourages that behavior.[19]

G. PRINCIPLES OF MULTIPARTNER ALLIANCES

Like all alliances, those of three or more partners are distinguished from transactions between the same firms by superior performance. To be a true alliance, performance should surpass a transaction for each interfirm link. A multipartner alliance is most effective if (1) adding another partner would not produce a net performance gain for the whole, and (2) removing any partner would detract from the performance of the whole.

In a multipartner alliance, member firms need one another to reach their shared objective. For example, in Global One (the joint venture of Sprint, Deutsche Telekom, and France Telecom) the firms could meet their objective of building a seamless worldwide network only by smoothly integrating their separate contributions.

Typically, multifirm alliances are created to meet demands associated with scale or complexity. Members' contributions may be similar (e.g., agreeing to purchase common items through a buying group) or dissimilar (e.g., joining different technologies for a new computer).[20]

Use the Trust Principles

The same conditions and practices discussed in the main text apply to multipartner arrangements—such as having clear objectives, assigning people who are team players, separating the alliance from conflict in each firm, and empowering the governance body. In selecting partners, best performance depends on meeting the trust condition of priority mutual need: Each firm gives the opportunity high importance and regards other contributors as best in their fields.

Satisfying the requirement for flexible organizations also helps. Had the partners that formed Global One heeded this guidance, the highly bureaucratic, intensely political, and locally focused behavior that weakened this alliance could have been foretold. At the time Global One was created, both Deutsche Telekom and France Telecom were government-owned monopolies. Though both would soon be privatized, their rigid cultures could not adapt to what the venture required.

Because there are more issues in multifirm alliances, each member needs more flexibility to resolve them. If that is not the case, expect to invest extra time in managing conflicts.

Objectives for multipartner alliances should be set by the customer, which helps align the partners to serve their intended market. When the customer does not participate in the alliance, whichever partner is closest to the market sets the direction. In alliances where individual partners serve separate markets, each must be able to do what its own market requires.

Globalstar, a worldwide satellite communications alliance, illustrates. Each regional partner has the authority to adapt to local markets, customer needs, and regulatory requirements. While this arrangement is far more challenging to manage than a traditional top-down business, it is the best way to serve heterogeneous markets.[21]

As with all alliances, exclusivity must be determined before launch, weighing each firm's interest against the collective interest (for more details, see II.K., "Alternatives for Exclusivity"). Buying groups, for example, stipulate a minimum volume for each member to ensure overall scale. Any uncertainty in the rules or their enforcement impairs an alliance. At Global One, both European partners separately pursued opportunities in Italy, Spain, and Denmark. Those actions conflicted with their commitments to their alliance and weakened it.

If you expect to have many members in an alliance, start small. Work with a few key players to develop early momentum—and to get results that will attract others.

Interfirm links in these alliances may be only with the lead partner (if there is one) or among various partners. Any link must be justified based on the value it contributes to the whole.

Establishing Leadership

By far the simplest leadership structure is for one company to be at the helm. Of course, that is standard practice in customer-led alliances involving several suppliers. More generally, the right choice for a single leader is whichever company is best positioned to help the alliance meet its objectives. That criterion can be divided into three parts: position and expertise in the alliance's market, technical know-how, and leadership traits. The lead firm must excel in the following areas, each related to the trust conditions:

- Selecting members
- Setting objectives
- Managing ongoing improvement
- Ensuring benefits for members that win their best efforts
- Orchestrating cooperation
- Setting an example of trust through its behavior

For instance Ball, one of the world's largest beverage can makers, is recognized as the lowest-cost producer in the industry. Due to its superior cost-management technology, Ball leads a worldwide alliance network involving twelve partners. The firms engage in joint developments and regularly benchmark with one another on labor productivity and materials use. Other activities include common purchasing and an alliance among the Asian partners that presents a common interface to Coke and Pepsi bottlers in the region.

After single firm leadership, the next best form is for two to lead. That was the case in the paint plant alliance of Ford and ABB, where Fluor Daniel, the construction partner, followed the others' lead. Multifirm leadership is by far the most difficult structure, due to the need for three-way comfort and understandings.

To illustrate, at the top of Global One "it was like a three-way tug of war," said one executive. Fragmentation there bred mistrust in the organization, stifled creativity, inhibited problem solving, made people hold back, and created constant losses.

Unlike the situation with two-company alliances, leading the multipartner variety requires a blend of power and persuasion. Without that, the leader is in the position of trying to broker a consensus, which is not much better than having several joint leaders. Performance in such cases tends to stay at lowest-common-denominator levels. This behavior may be acceptable for a standards group, but not for an alliance.

Besides having the trust characteristics outlined above, the leader of a multipartner alliance should have enough authority to drive needed change. However, there must be a balance. It's not constructive to pressure others in such a way that doing so weakens their commitment. These factors limit what leadership can do and illustrate why, as with all alliances, those involving several firms depend on whether all of them meet the trust conditions.

As Global One's difficulties worsened, for example, Sprint began assigning some of its strongest people to the alliance and gradually became recognized as the leader. In some ways its role was welcome. Its partners saw Sprint as aggressive and entrepreneurial, with shorter decision times. Both European firms knew they would have to emulate this behavior. Still, many decisions required a consensus at the top. Often, that could not be reached. Further, teamwork in Global One has gone well under Sprint's top executive there, but not under senior executives assigned by its partners. Sprint's frustrations and its continued pressure for change became irritants, causing resistance to cooperation.

VII. CREATING A CULTURE OF TRUST

■

This section summarizes actions that establish trust-building habits in a firm's culture. The material draws on Chapter 12 and earlier chapters. Alliances—whether internal or external—are facilitated when a firm's normal behavior reinforces the eight trust conditions and related practices. Such patterns must begin with top-level leaders.

ACTIVITIES THAT CONTRIBUTE TO A CULTURE OF TRUST

Trust Conditions	Recruiting, Training, Rewards	Management Behavior	Other Activities
Priority Mutual Need	Stress joint strategies in training	Highlight joint strategies	Expect each unit to stay at cutting edge in its field; use objectives hierarchy to keep all units aligned
	Use incentives and promotion criteria to encourage individual initiative and collective behavior	Apprise people of resources available in firm and its units	
		Inform staff of others' contributions in the past and instill a sense of gratitude toward them	Let each unit decide partner choice; go outside if best for unit
	Make cooperation results widely visible		
		Model teamwork for firm's collective benefit	Expect termination when mutual need is no longer a priority for units involved
Interpersonal Relationships	Emphasize relationship skills and leadership potential in recruiting	Model and coach people on how to improve interpersonal trust, including better mutual understanding, constructive problem solving	Create opportunities for frequent contact across units
			Actively discourage destructive rivalry

Continued

Trust Conditions	Recruiting, Training, Rewards	Management Behavior	Other Activities
Joint Leaders	Emphasize teamwork, interunit cooperation in training Emphasize relationship, networking, and leadership skills in evaluation and promotion criteria	Model teamwork for firm's collective benefit Coach teams on ways to improve their performance	
Mutual Objectives	Reward achieving firm-wide and local objectives	Demonstrate commitment to objectives	Use firm-wide objectives hierarchy reaching from top to operating units
Safeguards	Remind people what is to be protected, and how Punish offenders	Show respect for sensitive information	Plan any termination to provide the most benefits for the whole firm See also II.L., "Share Know-How Intelligently"
Commitment	In training, point out need for fair outcomes Performance evaluations recognize when a unit has made sacrifice for firm's overall benefit	Demonstrate fairness	Share benefits, costs, risks fairly (see II.G., "Guidelines for Sharing Benefits, Costs, Risks")
Adaptive Organization	Emphasize teamwork, constructive problem solving in training, performance evaluations	Make delegation normal practice Be competent at organizational change Keep vertical channels open	Unit management adjusts priorities to suit cooperation Continuous improvement is expected in all units
Continuity	In performance measures encourage relationship building and honoring predecessors' commitments	Coach people on honoring predecessors' contributions, commitments	Less turnover, more stability in employee population See also II.P., "Ways to Maintain Continuity"

APPENDIX: FOUNDATIONS OF
TRUSTED PARTNERS

■

This book was constructed from experience and draws on scholarly research. I have used each source to complement and validate the other. Starting with my definition of mutual trust, I then created the conceptual framework for *Trusted Partners,* building it on a set of eight conditions essential for trust. These are *priority mutual need, personal relationships, joint leaders, mutual objectives, safeguards, commitment, adaptable organizations,* and *continuity.*

These conditions, in turn, support a set of practices that will earn trust. The discussion below indicates the connection between the trust conditions and the research literature, and shows how the *trust practices* depend on the conditions. More detail on the research findings is in the notes to this appendix; to Chapters 1, 3, 7, 12; and to "Tools for Trust."

LINKS BETWEEN THE TRUST CONDITIONS AND THE RESEARCH LITERATURE

The following identifies some research roots of the trust conditions used in this book. Although scholarly research does not recognize *joint leaders* as a requirement for mutual trust, the condition may be implicit in the work.

Gulati and his colleagues describe the central role that mutual interest plays in defeating aberrant behavior between organizations. Their concept of mutual interest is akin to my notions of *priority mutual need* and *mutual objectives.*[1]

McAlister and Goleman separately present considerable evidence that cooperation depends critically on the quality of *personal relationships.* Goleman also describes why the emotional and intellectual components of such relationships are both important.[2]

On the basis of a literature synthesis, Das and Bing-Sheng conclude that trust is essential for alliances. In that regard, they propose several contributing factors. These include clear objectives, interfirm adaptation (anticipates my *adaptable organizations*), communications (related to to my personal relationships), and fairness in how benefits are shared (comparable to my *commitment*).[3]

As for my trust condition of *safeguards,* Inkpen observes that a partner's ability to protect information is a prerequisite for sharing know-how, which is the essence of cooperation. In my discussion of safeguards I include that concept, expanding it to cover termination provisions.[4]

In an analysis of vertical partnerships between manufacturers and dealers in the personal computer business, Mohr and Spekman find, as I do, that commitment, coordination within each organization (similar to my requirement for adaptable organizations), and communications quality (related to my personal relationships) correlate with success.[5]

Mayer and his colleagues (MD&S) describe three basic characteristics of trustworthiness from their review of the literature: ability, being the group of skills that enables one party to influence the other (I construe that as mutual need) within a specific domain; benevolence, being the extent to which one party is willing to do good for the other; and integrity, meaning one party's belief that the other adheres to an acceptable set of principles.[6]

In *Trusted Partners,* the condition of priority mutual need is comparable to and more specific than MD&S's concept of ability. My notion of a willingness to earn a partner's commitment is similar to and more specific than their description of benevolence. They use the term integrity to mean that both firms adhere to a set of mutually satisfactory guiding principles. My requirements for mutual objectives and for honest and candid personal relationships convey the same meaning, but are more specific.

In another useful work, Barclay and Smith describe trustworthiness as comprising four dimensions: character, role competence, judgment—the ability to act in a way that furthers parties' joint interests—and motives/intentions. Their term character implies an ability to build personal relationships. Their notion of role competence suggests mine of priority mutual need, while their concept of judgment suggests priority mutual need, mutual objectives, and adaptable organizations. MD&S's discussion of motives/intentions also implies the requirement for a mutual objective.[7]

As *Trusted Partners* observes, trust may suffer when people move on, making *continuity* a condition for trust. This observation is supported by Ring and Van de Ven.[8]

Various articles by academics and practitioners describe risk sharing as a requirement for trust. In *Trusted Partners,* risk sharing contributes to trust when it is a mutual objective and when risks are shared fairly, which encourages commitment.

The nearby table summarizes the links between this earlier research on trust and the eight trust conditions used in *Trusted Partners.*

RESEARCHERS

Trust Conditions	Gulati et al.	McAlister, Goleman	Das & Bing-Sheng	Inkpen	Mohr & Spekman	Mayer, Davis, & Schoorman	Barclay & Smith	Ring & Van de Ven
Priority Mutual Need	✔						✔	
Personal Relationships		✔	✔			✔	✔	
*Joint Leaders**								
Mutual Objectives	✔		✔				✔	
Safeguards				✔	✔			
Commitment						✔		
Adaptable Organizations			✔			✔	✔	
Continuity								✔

* The academic literature seems not to have anticipated joint leadership as a condition for mutual trust.

CONNECTIONS BETWEEN THE CONDITIONS AND PRACTICES FOR TRUST

The practices needed to earn mutual trust can be effective only when the trust conditions are met. Each practice depends on one or more of the conditions, as summarized in the table. Take, for example, the practice of sharing sensitive information. It requires a priority mutual need to justify doing so, relationships to disclose tacit knowledge as well as understandings about people and politics, objectives to focus the effort, safeguards to ensure that what is shared will be protected, and commitment to encourage everyone's best effort.

TRUST CONDITIONS

Trust Practices	Mutual Need	Relation-ships	Joint Leaders	Objec-tives	Safe-guards	Commit-ment	Organi-zations	Contin-uity
Right People	✔	✔	✔	✔	✔	✔	✔	✔
Interfirm Teams	✔	✔	✔	✔	✔	✔	✔	✔
Alliance Ethics		✔	✔	✔		✔		
Share Information	✔	✔		✔	✔	✔		
Joint Creativity	✔	✔	✔	✔		✔	✔	✔
Conflict Resolution	✔	✔	✔	✔		✔	✔	✔
Clear Scope	✔	✔	✔	✔	✔	✔	✔	✔
Internal Alignment	✔	✔	✔	✔		✔	✔	✔
Realistic Plans		✔	✔	✔		✔	✔	✔
Right Structure					✔	✔		
Effective Governance	✔	✔	✔	✔		✔	✔	✔

Trust Practices	Mutual Need	Relation-ships	Joint Leaders	Objec-tives	Safe-guards	Commit-ment	Organi-zations	Contin-uity
Performance Measures		✔	✔	✔				
Everyone on Board	✔	✔	✔	✔			✔	
Meetings Special	✔	✔	✔	✔	✔			
Anticipate Issues	✔	✔	✔	✔	✔			
Don't Try to Win	✔	✔				✔		
Communi-cate Widely	✔	✔	✔	✔	✔	✔	✔	✔
Keep It Balanced		✔				✔		
Review the Future	✔	✔		✔			✔	
Celebrate Success		✔				✔		

NOTES

■

Preface

1. For excellent discussions of the prisoner's dilemma and the nature of cooperation, see Matt Ridley, *The Origins of Virtue,* Viking, 1997; and Robert Axelrod, *The Evolution of Cooperation,* Basic Books, 1984.

2. For a recent history of Napoleon, see Alistair Horne, *How Far from Austerlitz?* St. Martin's Press, 1997.

3. Jordan D. Lewis, *The Connected Corporation,* Free Press, 1995.

Chapter 1. Build Trust

1. In July 1999, CSX Corporation, SeaLand's parent, agreed to sell the container shipping unit to Maersk. The move allowed CSX to focus on its troubled railroad operations. Daniel Machalaba, "CSX Agrees to Sell Lines of SeaLand to Danish Maersk," *Wall Street Journal,* July 23, 1999, p. B7.

2. For a more detailed comparison of transactions and alliances, see Jeffrey S. Harrison and Caron H. St. John, "Managing and Partnering with External Stakeholders," *Academy of Management Executive,* Vol. 10, No. 2 (1996), p. 46. A useful review of basic work on the nature of cooperation is provided by Ken G. Smith, Stephen J. Carroll, and Susan J. Ashford, "Intra- and Interorganizational Cooperation: Toward a Research Agenda," *Academy of Management Journal,* Vol. 38, No. 1 (1995), p. 7.

That trust leads to superior results is evident in the cases described in this book. As another example, a study of an auto parts maker and 429 of its retailers found that trust led to higher sales of 11 percent or more, as well as to more stable relationships. Nirmalya Kumar, "The Power of Trust in Manufacturer-Retailer Relationships," *Harvard Business Review,* November–December 1996, p. 92ff.

3. Arguably, the most important interfirm links are between companies and their customers. Performance here has been far below expectations. In a sampling of its members, all of whom are top sales executives in medium to large firms, the Strategic Account Management Association found that 10 percent rated the quality of their partnerships with customers as *very good,* while 27 percent said they were *good* and 53 percent stated

they were *poor*. The survey included 125 participants, with a response rate of 100 percent. Ginger Conton, Lisa Napolitano, and Mike Pusateri, *Unlocking Profits*, Strategic Account Management Association, 150 N. Wacker Drive, Suite 2222, Chicago, IL 60606, 1997, p. 19.

Based on a sample of nearly 2,000 alliances, researchers concluded that such links play a key role in virtually all industries. Further, alliances have grown in number by some 30 percent annually for the past decade. By 2004, they will account for more than 40 percent of the value of nearly one quarter of all firms. Still, 61 percent of all alliances have been disappointments or failures. Charles Kalmbach Jr. and Charles Rousell, "Dispelling the Myths of Alliances," *Outlook* magazine, special edition, October 1999, published by Andersen Consulting.

4. Sources for KLM-Northwest: interviews with current and past employees, plus Carl Quintanilla and Susan Carey, "Successful Northwest, KLM Partnership Hits the Skids," *Wall Street Journal*, November 2, 1995, p. B4; Shawn Tully, "Northwest and KLM: The Alliance from Hell," *Fortune*, June 24, 1996, pp. 44–50; Gordon Cramb, "KLM Seeks to Mend Relations with Northwest," *Financial Times*, July 2, 1996, p. 20; Barbara Smit, "KLM Shares Take Off on Sale Talk," *Financial Times*, July 4, 1997, p. 22. The two companies have since come to an agreement. "KLM, Northwest to Sign Agreement for Long-Term Cooperation," *Chicago Tribune*, September 23, 1997, p.C3.

5. Recent scholarly research has made great strides in advancing our understanding of trust. A useful source is the special issue of the *Academy of Management Review*, July 1998, devoted to trust in and between organizations. In one article, Rousseau et al. describe trust as a psychological state composed of the experiences of individuals, pairs of individuals, and firms. The definition of mutual trust in *Trusted Partners* builds on that concept. Denise M. Rousseau, Sim B. Sitkin, Ronald S. Burt, and Colin Camerer, "Not So Different After All: A Cross-Discipline View of Trust," p. 393. A second article, by Sheppard and Sherman, observes that trust may be one-or two-way (what they term dependence and interdependence). Mutual trust defined in *Trusted Partners* fits the second category. Blair H. Sheppard and Dana M. Sherman, "The Grammars of Trust: A Model and General Implications," p. 422.

One-way trust can lead to false expectations. In an examination of the links between a major manufacturer of auto replacement parts and 429 retailers, Kumar found that many of the 218 retailers that distrusted the manufacturer were actively developing alternative suppliers, while the manufacturer, which assumed that trust was mutual, was not exploring alternatives to those retailers. Nirmalya Kumar, "The Power of Trust in Manufacturer-Retailer Relationships," *Harvard Business Review*, November–December 1996, p. 92.

As a general definition, Lewicki et al. present trust as "confident positive expectations regarding another's conduct." The authors also cite evidence that trustworthiness cannot be accounted for by a single variable. In the context of *Trusted Partners,* this means, for example, that being able to count on a partner to be guided by your shared objectives does not imply that you can trust it to maintain continuity when people move on. Roy J. Lewicki, Daniel J. McAllister, and Robert J. Bies, "Trust and Distrust: New Relationships and Realities," *Academy of Management Review,* Vol. 23, No. 3 (July 1998), p. 438.

6. Nypro Inc., based in Clinton, Mass., had $275 million net worldwide sales in 1997 with a 26 percent pretax return on equity. The firm's primary business is plastic injection molding. It has twenty-four plants worldwide, including fifteen joint ventures that contribute about 20 percent of the firm's total revenue. Major customers include Allied Signal, Duracell, GE, Gillette, Hewlett-Packard, Johnson & Johnson, Matsushita, Motorola, Sandoz, 3M, Sony, and Toyota. According to Gordon Lankton, Nypro's president, those of the ten injection-molding ventures that have had time to get up to speed perform at least as well as the company's overall P&L.

7. Gulati et al. point out that the presence of mutual interest makes the prisoner's dilemma, a concept from game theory, irrelevant to alliances based on trust. In the prisoner's dilemma, each partner fears the other will gain an advantage by acting opportunistically in its own self-interest, and contrary to its partner's interest. That attitude leads to both partners choosing not to cooperate, thus reducing the value they receive. In alliances, having a priority mutual need and a joint objective makes both partners' interests coincident. See Ranjay Gulati, Tarun Khanna, and Nitin Nohria, "Unilateral Commitments and the Importance of Process in Alliances," *Sloan Management Review,* Spring 1994, p. 61.

8. Joint leadership in alliances is distinct from the more demanding variety often used in mergers, where two executives serve as co-CEOs. In alliances, each leader has his own turf. By contrast, when two individuals run a company together, their actions cannot as easily be separated. Doing the job well is like two people trying to wear the same hat at the same time.

9. Bill Vlasic, "Can Chrysler Keep It Up?" *Business Week,* November 25, 1996, pp. 108–120.

10. Trust is also needed to share knowledge between and within orga-

nizations. See Andrew C. Inkpen, "Creating Knowledge Through Collaboration," *California Management Review,* Fall 1996, p. 1.

11. Paul Eng and Susan Chandler, "Prodigy: A Five-Year-Old Underachiever," *Business Week,* October 30, 1995, p. 150; Bart Ziegler, "How Do Joint Ventures Go Wrong? Ask Kaleida," *Wall Street Journal,* November 22, 1995, p. B1; David J. Lynch, "How Prodigy Fell from Envy to Near-Ruin," *USA Today,* May 30, 1996, p. B1.

12. Ample evidence from psychology and sociology indicates that, when negotiation for cooperation is treated as a step-by-step iterative process of building formal and informal (interpersonal) understandings, more desirable outcomes result. See Peter Smith Ring and Andrew H. Van de Ven, "Developmental Processes of Cooperative Interorganizational Relationships," *Academy of Management Review,* Vol. 19, No. 1 (1994), p. 90; also E. J. Zajac and C. Olsen, "From Transaction Costs to Transactional Value Analysis: Implications for the Study of Interorganizational Studies," *Journal of Management Studies,* Vol. 30 (1993), p. 130.

Kim and Mauborgne add that people are most likely to trust and share their ideas when they feel recognized for their intellectual and emotional worth, through what the authors call "fair process"—continuously engaging them in the process, explaining the logic of the actions being taken, and setting clear expectations. See W. Chan Kim and Renée Mauborgne, "Fair Process: Managing in the Knowledge Economy," *Harvard Business Review,* July–August 1997, p. 65.

Chapter 2. Pick Team Players

1. Bendoff quote from Jerry Useem, "Company Goes Crazy Over Partnerships, Gets Committed," *Inc.,* June 1997, p. 24.

2. David Bank, "Microsoft's CEO Summit Draws on Person-to-Person Networking," *Wall Street Journal,* May 19, 1999, p. B4.

3. Having a permanent alliance staff can help business units find prospective partners and build alliances, so long as (1) staffers are accountable to the groups that will benefit from the alliance, and (2) teams are built, led, and populated by people from those groups. When central staff takes a larger role it blurs accountability for alliance results, weakens joint leadership, gets in the way of relationships, and runs the risk of introducing another agenda.

4. Thompson et al. show how achieving stretch targets depends on leaders who can align their organizations to support and accommodate re-

quired changes. See Kenneth R. Thompson, Wayne A. Hochwarter, and Nicholas J. Mathys, "Stretch Targets: What Makes Them Effective?" *Academy of Management Executive*, Vol. 11, No. 3 (1997), p. 48. See also John P. Kotter, *Leading Change*, Harvard Business School Press, 1996.

5. For a detailed discussion of team building and the work of teams, see Jon R. Katzenbach and Douglas K. Smith, *The Wisdom of Teams*, Harvard Business School Press, 1993.

6. Goleman presents substantial data showing that teamwork depends crucially on interpersonal relationships. Daniel Goleman, *Working with Emotional Intelligence*, Bantam Books, 1998.

7. That a company will benefit from taking the initiative to be helpful may seem unreasonable. However, this conclusion reflects the prisoner's dilemma model, wherein the parties' interests are not aligned. Given a priority mutual need and clear shared objectives, partner firms have the same interest within the scope of their alliance. In this case, unilateral efforts to help have merit if the other party sees the effort as contributing to their shared objective.

Still, unilateral actions are limited by the need to keep each party committed. Should a firm take initiatives for which it is not eventually rewarded—either by reciprocal initiatives or by greater benefits—such initiatives will end. Recognition of such initiatives is variously termed creating psychological credit or adding to an emotional bank account.

Chapter 3. Define a Single Purpose

1. The Global One description is from interviews with executives. Global One results are from Jennifer L. Schenker and James Pressley, "European Telecom Venture with Sprint Hasn't Become the Bully Some Feared," *Wall Street Journal*, December 23, 1997, p. A11; "Global One Chief Resigns After Losses," *New York Times*, February 14, 1998, p. D2; Alan Cane, "Global One Break-Even to Be Delayed," *Financial Times*, October 9, 1998, p. 19.

2. Allana Sullivan, "BP-Mobil Downstream Merger Serves as Industry Model," *Wall Street Journal*, August 1, 1997, p. B4.

3. Jeffery A. Tannenbaum, "Mexican-Food Joint Venture Gives Arby's Indigestion," *Wall Street Journal*, August 12, 1997, p. B1.

4. Successful manufacturer-dealer partnerships rely more than unsuccessful ones on using constructive problem solving, avoiding destructive

practices such speaking harshly, refraining from turning to outside arbitrators, and discussing tough issues. Jakki Mohr and Robert Spekman, "Characteristics of Partnership Success: Partnership Attributes, Communication Behavior, and Conflict Resolution Techniques," *Strategic Management Journal,* Vol. 15 (1994), p. 135.

5. Serapio and Cascio describe how the absence of a termination agreement can cause serious problems. Though their scope is international alliances, their logic applies to domestic ones as well. See Manuel G. Serapio, Jr., and Wayne F. Cascio, "End Games in International Alliances," *Academy of Management Executive,* Vol. 10, No. 1 (1996), p. 62.

6. Elizabeth Jensen and John Lippman, "ABC and Brillstein Discuss Ending Production Venture," *Wall Street Journal,* June 28, 1996, p. B2.

Chapter 4. Align Your Organizations

1. From interviews with former executives, plus David J. Lynch, "How Prodigy Fell from Envy to Near-Ruin," *USA Today,* May 30, 1996, p. B1.

2. Michael Skapinker, "Flights in Formation," *Financial Times,* January 10–11, 1998, p. 6.

3. Sources for USAir–British Airways: interviews with USAir staff, plus Peter Behr and Anthony Faiola, "USAir Sues to Break Up with British Airways," *Washington Post,* July 30, 1996, p. C1. USAirways 1998 Annual Report, pp. 39–40. USAir filed suit in July 1996; BA filed counterclaims in February 1998. As of June 1999, the suit was ongoing.

4. Estimates of the annual growth rate of domestic and cross-border alliances range from 25 percent to 50 percent. The lower number comes from Joel Bleeke and David Ernst, "Is Your Strategic Alliance Really a Sale?" *Harvard Business Review,* January-February 1995, p. 97. The higher number is reported by the Association of Strategic Alliance Professionals, P.O. Box 812-027, Wellesley Hills, MA 02482.

5. Bart Ziegler, "How Do Joint Ventures Go Wrong? Ask Kaleida," *Wall Street Journal,* November 22, 1995, p. B1.

6. Though the joint venture, named Autolatina, was profitable, it could have done far better without the constant and intense internal friction it endured. Autolatina benefited largely from cost savings created by closing Ford and VW plants and by making cheap models that, in Ford's case, were almost three decades old.

Data on internal problems and their consequences from interviews with Ford and VW people in Argentina and Brazil. Data on sources of cost saving from Keith Bradsher, "Ford and VW: One Thrives, the Other Doesn't," *New York Times*, May 16, 1997, p. C1.

Chapter 5. Orchestrate Many Units

1. For more detail on the interface of multiunit customer-supplier alliances, see Jordan D. Lewis, *The Connected Corporation*, Free Press, 1995, Chapter 11, "Leveraging the Corporation."

2. Service levels for other regions were not benchmarked. However, in Japan, for example, along with significant cost savings the alliance achieved 100 percent availability for all on-line systems and met or exceeded every response time objective.

Chapter 6. Reinforce Trust with Structure

1. "Farmland Industries and Ernst & Young Form Joint Venture," *Wall Street Journal*, April 9, 1997, p. B10.

2. Nypro's consensus culture is one that managers in many other firms would find enviable. Even Nypro's fully owned plants are run by inside boards of directors, an idea stemming from its early joint ventures. There are no group vice presidents, only boards of Nypro employees from other plants. Each board chooses its own chairman, and the plant general manager reports to the board. The arrangement not only facilitates rapid cross-company learning and impressive productivity growth, but contributes to Nypro's consistent and exceptionally high return on equity.

3. British Airways saw the investment in USAir as cement for a long-term relationship. See Christopher Lorenz, "A Meeting of the Minds," *Financial Times*, October 25, 1993, p. 15. For more on minority investments, see Jordan D. Lewis, *Partnerships for Profit*, Free Press, 1990.

4. Global One description from interviews with executives. Data about its CEOs from "Global One Chief Resigns After Losses," *New York Times*, February 14, 1998, p. D2.

5. Laws or regulations in some countries require management participation on joint venture boards. This can be awkward when a board needs to review sensitive issues regarding management or partner relations. In such cases, to have candid conversations and avoid discomfort these matters are usually discussed and agreed upon informally before regular meetings.

6. Based on interviews, plus Bart Ziegler, "How Do Joint Ventures Go Wrong? Ask Kaleida," *Wall Street Journal,* November 22, 1995, p. B1.

Chapter 7. Take Nothing for Granted

1. Richard Waters and Alan Cane, "BT and MCI at Odds over When Losses Were Revealed," *Financial Times,* July 18, 1997, p. 1; "Culture Clashes," *Financial Times,* July 19–20, 1997, p. 4; Mike Mills, "The Journey of MCI's Local Hero," *Washington Post,* July 28, 1997, p. F12.

2. Gulati et al. note that because each partner is subject to changes in its unique environment, alliances are vulnerable to forces on both firms, so are more likely than either firm to change over time. That makes it important to actively manage alliances. Ranjay Gulati, Tarun Khanna, and Nitin Nohria, "Unilateral Commitments and the Importance of Process in Alliances," *Sloan Management Review,* Spring 1994, p. 61.

3. Being specific about roles is more important in relationships between groups, where accustomed internal frameworks don't exist. See J. J. Gabarro, "The Development of Working Relationships," in J. W. Lorsch (Ed.), *The Handbook of Organizational Behavior,* Prentice-Hall, 1987, p. 172.

4. Hamel et al. describe alliances as learning races, wherein whichever partner learns the fastest can leave an alliance, having gained what it sought. As Chapter 7 in *Trusted Partners* notes, that outcome may be defeated if each partner emphasizes continuous improvement in those are as that make it attractive to the other. Gary Hamel, Yves Doz, and C. K. Prahalad, "Collaborate with Your Competitors and Win," *Harvard Business Review,* January-February 1989, p. 133.

Chapter 8. Repair Broken Trust

1. Gordon Cramb, "KLM and Northwest Settle Row and Signal New Links," *Financial Times,* July 31, 1997, p. 23; Susan Carey and Shailagh Murray, "Northwest, KLM Agree to Improve Frayed Alliance," *Wall Street Journal,* July 31, 1997, p. C18; John Harwood, "Ex-Airline Tycoon Takes Off for Governorship of California in a Fog of Political Inexperience," *Wall Street Journal,* August 6, 1997, p. 16.

Chapter 9. How to Trust Difficult Customers

1. Most sales executives who responded to a survey on the quality of their firms' partnerships with customers rated these as poor. See Ginger Conton, Lisa Napolitano, and Mike Pusateri, *Unlocking Profits,* Strategic Account Management Association, 150 N. Wacker Drive, Suite 2222, Chicago, IL 60606, 1997, p. 19.

Chapter 10. How to Sell Alliances to Customers

1. The changes in roles and authority needed to build a more effective purchasing function are detailed in Jordan D. Lewis, *The Connected Corporation*, Free Press, 1995. This text also describes how alliances with its suppliers have helped Chrysler become the lowest-cost auto producer in the United States, and possibly in the world.

2. Exxon Chemical Europe first reduced the number of carriers, then formed alliances with those that stayed.

3. For more on backups and ways to avoid overdependence, see the discussion of focused competition in *The Connected Corporation*.

4. Results to a survey conducted by the Strategic Account Management Association, at its 34th Annual Conference, 1998. See Chapter 1 notes for more detail.

5. One half of surveyed account managers report that their firms either do not use formal customer evaluations, or use them less than once a year. See Ginger Conton, Lisa Napolitano, and Mike Pusateri, *Unlocking Profits*, Strategic Account Management Association, 150 N. Wacker Drive, Suite 2222, Chicago, IL 60606, 1997, p. 19.

Chapter 11. How to Trust a Rival

1. John Gapper, "FT and WSJ in Russian Venture," *Financial Times*, April 8, 1999, p. 20.

2. Visa and American Express data are from Neil Buckley, "AmexCo and Visa Join Smartcard Group," *Financial Times*, July 30, 1998, p. 18; Dresser and Ingersoll data are from Jonathan Welsh, "Two Rivals Strike Oil with Joint Venture," *Wall Street Journal*, August 5, 1996, p. B4; other examples are from interviews.

3. Keith Bradsher, "Ford and VW: One Thrives, the Other Doesn't," *New York Times*, May 16, 1997, p. C1.

4. William M. Carley, "GE-Pratt Venture, Like Others Before It, Faces Hurdles," *Wall Street Journal*, May 10, 1996, p. B4.

5. Bradsher, "Ford and VW: One Thrives, the Other Doesn't."

Chapter 12. How to Build Trust Between Internal Groups

1. Liedtka notes that internal collaboration calls for a shift in attitudes and organizational behaviors that cause people to want to cooperate. She

explains why this is more effective than mandating cooperation, identifies trust as a central ingredient, and underscores the need for committed leadership, a culture steeped in honesty, and complementary processes for measurement and reward. See Jeanne M. Liedtka, "Collaborating Across Lines of Business for Competitive Advantage," *Academy of Management Executive,* Vol. 10, No. 2 (1996), p. 20.

2. It is often claimed that an organized work force can inhibit cooperation. However, in this case, employees of the six plants involved were represented by a labor union. That fact had no bearing on interdivisional cooperation at Butler.

3. Originally developed for the parent's commodity chemical business, treasury's policies are more attuned to that than to specialty products. One such policy requires that credit for any sale be based on the customer's net worth. The practice works well for industrial customers but fails for PrimeCrops' customers, who are distributors and typically have low fixed assets. That is not a problem in developed economies, where they go to the credit markets to finance their purchases. But such markets have not yet matured in Brazil.

4. That the leaders in this case sought less participation than might be expected in North American settings is consistent with the Latin American culture, which typically emphasizes more leading from the top. Of course, the pattern in any firm depends on its own culture and on how much that varies from local norms. As the Latin economies integrate into the global economy, local business cultures are evolving toward more participative behavior.

5. J.P. Morgan ranked first on *Euromoney*'s 1998 capital-raising poll, and ranked number one in its industry in *Fortune*'s "The World's Most Admired Companies" survey. See *Euromoney,* September 1998, p. 225; Jeremy Kahn, *Fortune,* October 26, 1998, p. 206.

6. Walt Disney uses another tactic to surface internal opportunities. The firm has "synergy managers" whose job is to find ways their divisions can add value to others. One result is that, before a film is released, shorter versions appear in Disney theme parks, and the film is promoted on Disney's TV network, ABC. Whenever appropriate, a film will be joined by promotional tie-ins such as dolls, toys, and T-shirts. However, a bad business does not improve just because it is included in a larger picture. Thus, despite Disney's programming, the ABC network has not done well. See "Size Does Matter," *The Economist,* May 23, 1998, p. 57.

7. The description of Motorola's problems and their causes is from interviews with current and former executives. The consequences are described in Roger O. Crockett and Peter Elstrom, "How Motorola Lost Its Way," *Business Week,* May 4, 1998, p. 140.

8. Bradley quote is from Jeremy Kahn, "What Makes a Company Great?" *Fortune,* October 26, 1998, p. 218.

9. Accountability for risks is assigned to individuals, because teams would be inclined to take too much risk if no one was accountable.

10. Description of rewards at Morgan from interviews, plus Saul Hansell, "Is J.P. Morgan Living Up to Its Namesake?" *New York Times,* August 10, 1997, p. 1; and Jeremy Kahn, "What Makes a Company Great?" *Fortune,* October 26, 1998, p. 218. Comments about Rod Peacock from Laura M. Holson, "J.P. Morgan's Role in Changing Oil Industry," *New York Times,* December 2, 1998, p. C5.

11. For more on the cultures of successful companies, see James C. Collins and Jerry I. Porras, *Built to Last,* HarperBusiness, 1994. For a description of HP's and J.P. Morgan's values see, respectively, www.hp.com/abouthp/hpway, and www.jpmorgan.com/corpinfo/history/overview.

Chapter 13. How to Build Trust in Mergers and Acquisitions

1. For details, see "Tools for Trust," II.B., "Choosing Among Transactions, Organic Growth, Acquisitions, and Alliances," and accompanying notes.

2. Following any rationalization, ongoing superior performance (compared with what each firm could do separately) comes from access to each other's resources. An example of resource access: when a purchased firm's products reach a larger market through the buyer's stronger sales, marketing, and distribution. Even then, an alliance of product developers and marketers will produce better results than a transaction between them.

3. Claudia H. Deutsch, "The Deal Is Done, the Work Begins," *New York Times,* April 11, 1999, p. D1.

4. Based on discussions in the industry, plus Marcia Baringa, "Science on the Auction Block," *Science,* February 23, 1990, p. 906.

5. Deutsch, "The Deal Is Done, the Work Begins."

6. "Why Too Many Mergers Miss the Mark," *The Economist,* January 4, 1997, p. 61.

7. Carol Hymowitz, "How New Chief Forged One Company from Two While Boosting Profit," *Wall Street Journal,* February 2, 1999, p. B1; and Tracy Corrigan, "Emergency Treatment Pays Off for P&U," *Financial Times,* April 8, 1999, p. 25.

8. Daimler and Chrysler data from interviews, plus: Edmund L. Andrews and Laura M. Holson, "Daimler-Benz Will Acquire Chrysler in $36 Billion Deal," *New York Times,* May 7, 1998, p. 1; Alex Taylor III, "Gentlemen, Start Your Engines," *Fortune,* June 8, 1998, p. 138; Gregory White, "Chrysler, Daimler Leaders Already Have a Plan," *International Herald Tribune,* September 18, 1998, p. 3; Alex Taylor III, "The Germans Take Charge," *Fortune,* January 11, 1999, p. 92; Haig Simonian, "All Eyes on the Mega-Merger Integrator," *Financial Times,* February 3, 1999, p. 12; Anne Swardson, "Taking a Jeep Round the Benz," *Washington Post,* February 5, 1999, p. E1.

9. Robert Frank and Steve Liesman, "While BP Prepares New U.S. Acquisition, Amoco Counts Scars," *Wall Street Journal,* March 31, 1999, p. 1.

10. Information on Daimler-Benz businesses comes from the company's 1997 annual report, plus other company documents.

11. Keith Bradsher, "Management by Two Cultures May Be a Growing Source of Strain for DaimlerChrysler," *New York Times,* March 24, 1999, p. C2; Daniel McGinn and Stefan Theil, "Hands on the Wheel," *Newsweek,* April 12, 1999, p. 49; and Warren Brown, "Shrugging Off American Defections," *Washington Post,* April 1, 1999, p. E1. Schrempp quote is from Brown.

Tools for Trust: A Guide for Practitioners

1. Airline data are from a study by the Boston Consulting Group cited in *The Economist,* April 5, 1997, p. 62.

2. Richard Waters and Louise Keyhoe, "Eastman Kodak and Intel Form Partnership," *Financial Times,* May 1, 1998, p. 27.

3. *Fortune's* Shawn Tully points out that many CEOs seem to believe that issuing shares to make an acquisition is less expensive than paying cash, particularly if the deal adds, or soon will add, to the buyer's earnings per share—a practice known as accretion. To appreciate the fallacy here,

Tully asks us to suppose that a company with stock selling at thirty times earnings buys another with the same profits but a multiple of only ten. In that case, it might seem that the acquirer can pay a 50 percent premium and still come out ahead. In effect, the deal doubles the buyer's earnings while increasing its shares outstanding by only half.

However, Tully notes that the reasoning is bogus. Regardless of whether you pay in stock or in cash, what matters is the premium paid and the chances of earning it back. If only accretion mattered, Microsoft, with a multiple, say, of fifty, would be attracted to absorb a low-multiple electric utility. It is not, because there are no synergies between the firms. The only thing that would happen is that the market would lower the multiple of the newly combined firm. Shawn Tully, "Premium Priced," *Fortune*, January 11, 1999, p. 99.

4. Research on the performance of mergers and acquisitions is extensive. For a comprehensive analysis and review of the topic, see Mark L. Sirower, *The Synergy Trap*, Free Press, 1997. Sirower concludes that, on average, acquisitions reduce the value of the acquiring firm. He also finds that immediate stock market reactions (i.e., whether the acquirer's stock price rises or declines) indicate long-term performance. See p. 167 for details. Other dimensions of the topic, from classic literature on M&A, are cited below.

Biased Advisers. One cause of underperformance seems to be that investment banks doing the most M&A business are motivated to complete the deals, whether or not they add or destroy value for the acquirer. More specifically, a larger percentage of the fees of top-tier investment banks is tied to completion than are fees at lower-ranking banks. And the higher the completion fee paid by an acquirer in a tender offer, the worse its stock generally performed over the next twelve months. P. Raghavendra Rau, "Investment Bank Market Share, Contingent Fee Payments, and the Performance of Acquiring Firms," *Journal of Financial Economics* (forthcoming). See also Robert McGough, "Top Deal Makers Aren't Best Matchmakers," *Wall Street Journal*, June 3, 1999, p. C1.

Motivation. Executives who make winning bids appear to be more concerned with expanding their firm than with benefiting shareholders. Evidence for this comes from takeover patterns, which occur in waves that are coincident with bullish stock markets. Given the frequency of financial failures in M&A, it seems that, when times are good, corporate executives have more money to spend (or can raise it more easily), and have less reason to believe stockholders will call them to account for what they do with it. Andrew Shleifer and Robert W. Vishney, "The Takeover Wave of the 1980s," *Science*, August 17, 1990, p. 745.

Distractions and Sustainability. Acquisitions make buyers vulnerable to competitive attacks, because they get distracted by the challenge of integration. Further, a purchase will give the buyer a sustainable advantage only if it creates a position that others cannot easily duplicate. Sirower points out that within days after Quaker bought Snapple, a fruit beverage firm, Coca-Cola expanded its competing Fruitopia line and matched Snapple's ad budget, causing Quaker to lose money on Snapple. See Mark L. Sirower, "What Acquiring Minds Need to Know," *Wall Street Journal*, February 22, 1999, p. A18.

Financial Performance. In a survey of the economic literature, Mueller reports that mergers and acquisitions do not generally increase profits, and that acquiring firms generally earn returns substantially below a market portfolio of comparable firms over the post-deal period. Dennis C. Mueller, "Mergers," in *The New Palgrave Dictionary of Finance*, Vol. 2, Stockton Press, 1992, pp. 700–707.

In M&A deals done by a balanced sample of 116 companies over an eleven-year period, McKinsey found that just 23 percent earned their cost of capital. Research by McKinsey & Company, reported in *Fortune*, November 25, 1996, p. 78.

Business Week and Mercer Management Consulting found, in a joint study, that of 150 deals valued at $500 million or more done in the 1990s, about half destroyed shareholder wealth, judged by stock performance in relation to industry indices. Another third contributed only marginally to stockholder wealth. Further, of the nation's five hundred largest firms, those that made no acquisitions larger than $5 million outperformed their industry indices more often than active acquires. Philip L. Zweig et al., "The Case Against Mergers," *Business Week*, October 30, 1995, p. 22.

A study by Lehman Brothers similarly finds no evidence that large-scale mergers and acquisitions lead to performances that exceed the results of firms in their peer groups. See Edwina Neal, Joe Rooney, and Ian Scott, "Global Strategy Q1 1999," Lehman Brothers, February 17, 1999.

Firms acquired in conglomerate mergers and those acquired in horizontal mergers were both found to experience substantial losses in market shares relative to control group companies following the mergers. Dennis C. Mueller, "Mergers and Market Share," *The Review of Economics and Statistics*, Vol. LXVII, No. 2 (May 1985), p. 259.

Mergers generate abnormal gains for stockholders of acquired firms. The competitive nature of the bidding marketplace and the buyer's apparent optimism make any gain to its shareholders small at best. The post-merger profitability of acquisitive companies has been either less successful, or not significantly more successful, than the experience of otherwise comparable nonacquisitive companies. Allen Michel and Israel Shaked, "Evaluating Merger Performance," *California Management Review*, Spring 1985, p. 109.

Acquisitive firms generally achieve more rapid sales and asset growth than similar nonacquisitive firms. But this results from adding the parts, not from any change in the merged components' basic growth rates. Sayan Chatterjee, "Types of Synergy and Economic Value: The Impact of Acquisitions on Merging and Rival Firms," *Strategic Management Journal,* Vol. 7 (1986), p. 119.

Based on a survey of 776 industrial firms, Hitt and his colleagues found that firms having aggressive acquisitions strategies emphasize financial controls, deemphasize strategic controls, produce less internal innovation, and spend less on R&D than firms that rely on organic growth. Michael A. Hitt, Robert E. Hoskisson, and Douglas D. Moesel, "The Market for Corporate Control and Firm Innovation," *Academy of Management Journal,* Vol. 39, No. 5 (1996), p. 1084.

Health of Target Company. More successful acquisition strategies involve the purchase of highly profitable companies. Paying lower prices for low-profit firms in the hopes of turning them around involves high risks that are not adequately compensated for in the lower prices. John B. Kusewitt, "An Exploratory Study of Strategic Acquisition Factors Relating to Performance," *Strategic Management Journal,* April–June 1985, p. 151.

Specific Sectors. Of the hospitals that acquired physician practices between 1989 and 1994—a major thrust in health care at the time—only 17 percent made a positive return on their investments. Robert Tomsho, "Bonus Babies: 'Free Agent' Doctors Are Selling Practices, Signing Job Contracts, " *Wall Street Journal,* March 12, 1996, p. A1.

Empirical evidence from bank mergers and acquisitions shows clearly that, on average, there is no statistically significant gain in value or performance from the activity. Further, most American bank mergers have been done in the name of cost cutting. Yet merged banks have generally cut costs more slowly than their non-deal-making peers. See Steven J. Pilloff and Anthony M. Santomero, "The Value Effects of Bank Mergers and Acquisitions," Working Paper Series, Wharton Financial Institutions Center, The Wharton School, University of Pennsylvania, October 29, 1996.

5. "Ride Along, Little Tanker," *The Economist,* August 2, 1997, p. 19.

6. Janet Guyon, "The Sole Competitor," *Fortune,* January 12, 1998, p. 102.

7. These ideas were confirmed by a study of eight hundred auto dealers in the United States and the Netherlands. Nirmalya Kumar, "The Power of Trust in Manufacturer-Retailer Relationships," *Harvard Business Review,* November–December 1996, p. 92ff.

8. Some of this material draws from Daniel Goleman, *Working with Emotional Intelligence,* Bantam Books, 1998, and Daniel J. McAllister, "Affect- and Cognition-Based Trust as Foundations for Interpersonal Cooperation in Organizations," *Academy of Management Journal,* Vol. 38, No.1 (February 1995), p. 24. Both authors point out that interpersonal cooperation depends on intellectual and emotional confidence.

9. Not having such limits may compromise future relationships. For example, as a reward for helping Astra win U.S. regulatory approval for the Swedish firm's drugs, Merck won perpetual rights of first refusal for the U.S. market to all new Astra products. This created a barrier for potential Astra partners, which did not like the prospect of products they shared with Astra being available to Merck. See "Merck, Astra Near Restructuring of Unit," *Wall Street Journal,* June 5, 1998, p. B6.

10. "Who Dares, in China, Can Still Win," *The Economist,* June 7, 1997, p. 62.

11. Some observers claim that because equity structures involve a shared asset—some writers term this "holding a hostage"—such structures offer partners more control than the nonequity variety. To be sure, an equity arrangement makes shared assets more transparent to both partners. But in some JVs, significant assets remain within the parent firms and out of view to others.

Gulati notes that, all else being equal, equity alliances take more time to negotiate and organize than nonequity alliances (direct cooperation). He then shows, through empirical research on more than two thousand alliances, that repeated alliances between the same partners tend to evolve from equity to nonequity structures. He posits that this shift demonstrates growing trust. An entirely separate reason might be that experience with the higher administrative costs and longer cycle times of equity structures leads partners to use direct cooperation for future comparable activities. Ranjay Gulati, "Does Familiarity Breed Trust? The Implications of Repeated Ties for Contractual Choice in Alliances," *Academy of Management Journal,* Vol. 38, No. 1 (1995), p. 85.

12. For more, see Jordan D. Lewis, *Partnerships for Profit,* Free Press, 1990, Chapter 8.

13. You took a step in the right direction if you first considered the firms' separate objectives. In fact, these objectives are too vague in the description to determine the best structure. For instance, if the service offering to be marketed by each partner will be substantially distinct in

each market, then the most effective structure may not be a JV. Instead, the firms might be better off setting an interface protocol to ensure connectivity, cross-licensing their technologies and developing them separately. This approach is also likely to best support their cycle time objectives.

By contrast, if the firms' objectives call for one consistent technology across their regions, a joint development program might be best. But again, this does not require a joint venture. The two companies involved in this case chose a JV for reasons that were never clear to me. The JV failed, partly because the firms were never clear about their objectives.

14. Some of this discussion draws on Jordan D. Lewis, *Partnerships for Profit*, Free Press, 1990, Chapters 9, 10, 11, and 12.

15. As an example of a common problem, in some countries local firms often use joint ventures with foreign partners to make undisclosed loan guarantees to wholly owned units. A precaution in this case would be to give the foreign partner control over, or at least more access to, relevant financial data.

16. Some of these ideas are from Manuel G. Serapio, Jr. and Wayne F. Cascio, "End Games in International Alliances," *Academy of Management Executive*, Vol. 10, No. 1 (1996), p. 62.

17. Rosanna Tamburi and Don Clark, "Corel to Acquire Novell's Word-Perfect for $124 Million in Cash and Stock," *Wall Street Journal*, February 1, 1996, p. B5.

18. Some of these ideas draw from John Authers, "Cross-Selling's Elusive Charms," *Financial Times*, November 16, 1998, p. 17. The Kovacevich quote is from John Authers, "The Cross-Selling King," *Financial Times*, November 30, 1998, p. 11.

19. For a more detailed discussion of these points, see Jordan D. Lewis, *The Connected Corporation*, Free Press, 1995, Chapter 13.

20. For more on multifirm alliances involving complementary technologies, see Benjamin Gomez-Casseres, "Group Versus Group: How Alliance Networks Compete," *Harvard Business Review*, July–August 1994, p. 62.

21. James Surowiecki, "The Last Satellite Startup Lifts Off. Will It Too Explode?" *Fortune*, October 25, 1999. p. 237.

Appendix: Foundations of *Trusted Partners*

1. Ranjay Gulati, Tarun Khanna, and Nitin Nohria, "Unilateral Commitments and the Importance of Process in Alliances," *Sloan Management Review,* Spring 1994, p. 61.

2. See, e.g., Daniel J. McAlister, "Affect- and Cognition-Based Trust as Foundations for Interpersonal Relationships," *Academy of Management Journal,* Vol. 38, No. 1 (February 1995), p. 24; and Daniel Goleman, *Working with Emotional Intelligence,* Bantam Books, 1998.

3. T. K. Das and Bing-Sheng Teng, "Between Trust and Control: Developing Confidence in Partner Cooperation in Alliances," *Academy of Management Review,* Vol. 23, No. 3 (July 1998), p. 491.

4. Andrew C. Inkpen, "Learning and Knowledge Acquisition Through International Strategic Alliances," *Academy of Management Executive,* Vol. 12, No. 4 (1998), p. 69.

5. Jakki Mohr and Robert Spekman, "Characteristics of Partnership Success: Partnership Attributes, Communication Behavior, and Conflict Resolution Techniques," *Strategic Management Journal,* Vol. 15 (1994), p. 135.

6. Roger Mayer, James Davis, and F. David Schoorman, "An Integrative Model of Organizational Trust," *Academy of Management Review,* Vol. 20, No. 3 (1995), pp. 709–734.

7. Donald W. Barclay and J. Brock Smith, "The Effects of Organizational Differences and Trust on the Effectiveness of Selling Partner Relationships," *Journal of Marketing,* Vol. 61, No. 1 (1997), pp. 3–21.

8. Peter Smith Ring and Andrew H. Van de Ven, "Developmental Processes of Cooperative Interorganizational Relationships," *Academy of Management Review,* Vol. 19, No. 1 (1994), p. 90.

INDEX

■

ABOUT THE AUTHOR

■

Jordan D. Lewis, an international consultant, author, and lecturer, advises many of the world's leading firms on the art of alliances. Working with both partners, Lewis typically gets involved early on to help the firms reach their highest potential together. He is also called on to get troubled alliances on a healthier track.

Lewis's work has been featured in *The Wall Street Journal*, *The Economist*, *The Financial Times*, and *The Japan Times*, among other publications. His op-ed pieces on alliances have appeared in *The Wall Street Journal* and *The New York Times*. Besides being profiled on CNN, National Public Radio, and Reuters Television, Lewis has addressed major audiences for *Business Week*, *The Economist*, *Fortune*, Keidanren (Tokyo), and annual meetings of the World Economic Forum. He was named a fellow of the Forum in 1993, 1994, 1996, and 1998.

Lewis's earlier books include *The Connected Corporation* (Free Press, 1995) and *Partnerships for Profit* (Free Press, 1990). Together, they have been published in twelve languages.

Lewis, who holds a Ph.D. in thermonuclear physics from the University of Michigan, has taught at Michigan and at the University of Pennsylvania's Wharton School. He also teaches the top management course on alliances at Management Centre Europe and has been a guest lecturer at Columbia University's Graduate School of Business. Based in Washington, D.C., he can be reached at jordan@jordanlewis.com.